# FOUR FACES OF THE LAW

Few have shaped the field of law, both as practitioner and writer, as Michael Beloff KC. This expertly curated collection tracks this impact through his writings and lectures.

In a work divided into four interrelated parts – Advocacy, Judges, History and Sport – each is singly illuminated by the author's own experience and insight reflected in the accompanying illustrations.

# Four Faces of the Law

Michael Beloff KC

•HART•
OXFORD • LONDON • NEW YORK • NEW DELHI • SYDNEY

HART PUBLISHING

Bloomsbury Publishing Plc

Kemp House, Chawley Park, Cumnor Hill, Oxford, OX2 9PH, UK

1385 Broadway, New York, NY 10018, USA

Bloomsbury Publishing Ireland Limited, 29 Earlsfort Terrace, Dublin 2, D02 AY28, Ireland

HART PUBLISHING, the Hart/Stag logo, BLOOMSBURY and the Diana logo are trademarks of Bloomsbury Publishing Plc

First published in Great Britain 2026

1



A catalogue record for this book is available from the British Library.

A catalogue record for this book is available from the Library of Congress.

ISBN: HB: 978-1-50998-674-3
ePDF: 978-1-50998-676-7
ePub: 978-1-50998-675-0

Typeset by Compuscript Ltd, Shannon
Printed and bound in Great Britain by TJ Books, Padstow, Cornwall

For product safety related questions contact productsafety@bloomsbury.com

To find out more about our authors and books visit www.hartpublishing.co.uk. Here you will find extracts, author information, details of forthcoming events and the option to sign up for our newsletters.

*I dedicate this book to my three grandsons, Max, Luke and Jack.*

# *Foreword*

In early 1980, I had the very good fortune to become Michael Beloff's pupil at 2 Hare Court in the Temple (now Blackstone Chambers). His father, Professor Max Beloff, told me, 'You will have fun'. I certainly did. I was introduced to a brave new world of judicial review, human rights and sports law, in which Michael would inform and amuse himself and others. He is one of the few barristers I have watched who could get away with defying the basic principle of advocacy that you should leave jokes to the judge. He could force a smile, occasionally a chuckle, out of austere judges who sat in our appellate courts or even those in Luxembourg and Strasbourg who were listening to him via the interpreter.

Michael would appear in at least one court every day, with conferences before and after (and sometimes also at lunchtime). In the evening, I would go home to bed, exhausted. Michael would begin work on his column as legal correspondent for *The Observer* on a battered typewriter which Lord Halsbury would have thrown out as well past its best at the beginning of the twentieth century. Or he would run a half marathon. Or give a lecture.

In the years that followed, Michael has supplemented his career as a highly successful barrister and much respected arbitrator by continuing to moonlight as an author and lecturer. The chapters which follow demonstrate his knowledge, wit and wisdom on the topics which interest him most and on which he has great expertise: advocacy, judges, history and sports.

I was present at some of the legal events he describes, as his junior or opponent. Though not when he visited 'Spearmint Rhino' – a 'gentlemen's club' – for professional purposes (see Chapter 5). Like many in the legal community, I heard and admired some of the lectures when delivered and I read to my advantage many of these essays on their original publication. They merit a return visit.

Michael's advocacy taught me that there is always another side to a case, a different perspective, or at least points of interest and importance to be made. The chapters which follow confirm the depth of learning, the breadth of interest and the sheer originality of his thinking. Michael says that his aim "is to entertain as much as to educate". An aim which this book fulfils.

Lord Pannick KC<br>
*Blackstone Chambers*<br>
*Temple*<br>
*21 December 2025*

# *Acknowledgements*

THERE WAS A display of dark and light blue amity shown by the Oxford University Press for waiving copyright in the four obituaries that I wrote for the *Oxford Dictionary of National Biography*,[1] and the Cambridge University Press for waiving copyright in 'Law and the Judiciary in Blair's Britain',[2] which I contributed to Anthony Seldon's volume of essays entitled *Blair's Britain.*

No lesser display of amity, in this instance Irish, was shown by the *Irish Jurist* in waiving copyright in my John M Kelly Memorial Lecture[3] and the *Northern Ireland Legal Quarterly* in waiving copyright in my MacDermott Lecture.[4]

The University of Buckingham Press waived copyright in my articles published in *The Denning Law Journal*[5] and the Honourable Society of Gray's Inn waived copyright in my articles published in *Graya.*[6]

Mr Justice Soole, claiming a knowledge of copyright law no greater than my own – it could hardly be smaller – waived any copyright the *Inner Temple Yearbook* might have in my Reader's Lecture.[7]

I thank all the above for their kind co-operation.

I have granted myself copyright in a lecture originally published in a UK journal which I edit (I have assumed that it carried over when it was reprinted in a German publication[8]) and in a lecture given to an association of which I was President.[9]

I have optimistically assumed that silence to my outstanding request for copyright waiver should be construed as implied consent.

I thank Mihaela Reade and Lucy Tylecote Thierl for ensuring that my draft text, barely more legible in electronic form than it would have been if handwritten, was, at least in form, fit to present to my editor Sinead Moloney, whom I thank for her expert guidance and exemplary patience. I also thank my copy editor Vicki Hillyard, and my daughter Natasha for her careful proof reading.

[1] HISTORY ch 12.
[2] HISTORY ch 11.
[3] Delivered in Dublin; JUDGES ch 6.
[4] Delivered in Belfast; ADVOCACY ch 4.
[5] ADVOCACY ch 2; JUDGES ch 8.
[6] HISTORY chs 9–10.
[7] SPORT ch 16.
[8] SPORT ch 15.
[9] SPORT ch 14.

# *Contents*

*Foreword* .......... *vii*
*Acknowledgements.* .......... *ix*

1. Introduction .......... 1

PART I
ADVOCACY

2. 'A View from the Bar': Sir David Williams Lecture 2010 .......... 7
3. 'Advocacy as Art': Margaret Howard Memorial Lecture .......... 26
4. 'Virtuous Voices – The Advocate's Contribution to the Rule of Law': MacDermott Lecture 2014 .......... 47
5. 'Looking at the Locus' .......... 66

PART II
JUDGES

6. 'Towards a Supreme Court? The British Experience': John M Kelly Memorial Lecture .......... 73
7. 'Neither Cloistered nor Virtuous? Judges and their Independence in the New Millennium': The Atkin Lecture 1999 .......... 90
8. 'Paying Judges: Why, Who, Whom, How Much?': Neill Lecture 2006 .......... 105

PART III
HISTORY

9. 'Sisters in Law: The Irresistible Rise of Women in Wigs': Barnard's Inn Reading at Gresham College 2009 .......... 127
10. 'FE Smith … Lessons from a Legal Life': Birkenhead Lecture 2009 .......... 143
11. 'Law and the Judiciary' in Blair's Britain .......... 158

12. Oxford Dictionary of National Biography ........ 176
12.1. George Alfred Carman ........ 176
12.2. Gordon Slynn, Baron Slynn of Hadley ........ 179
12.3. Donald James Nicholls, Baron Nicholls of Birkenhead ........ 182
12.4. Sir John Grant McKenzie Laws ........ 187

## PART IV
## SPORT

13. 'Pitch, Pool, Rink ... Court? Judicial Review in the World of Sport' ........ 193

14. 'The Specificity of Sport: Rhetoric or Reality?': Edward Grayson Memorial Lecture 2012 ........ 204

15. 'Is there a *Lex Sportiva*?': Lecture at Max Planck Institute, Hamburg 2012 ........ 221

16. Sport Ethics and the Law: Reader's Lecture, Inner Temple 2023 ........ 235

Postscript ........ 240

*Index* ........ *241*

# 1

# *Introduction*

IN OR ABOUT a date, whither my memory and records runneth not, I proposed to Richard Hart, founder of the eponymous publishers, that the firm might publish a selection of my articles on legal topics. He agreed in principle but, as always, the devil was in the detail. We had irreconcilable views of which articles were fit to print – at any rate by Hart. But Richard did suggest that I might instead write a memoir and so, after an interlude, with, in theory at any rate, my professional life coming more or less peacefully to its close, I wrote and Hart published *MJBQC: A Life Within and Without the Law*. The acronym in the title was made obsolete within a bare six months by the death of Queen Elizabeth II, which, I hasten to add, was the least of the consequences of that significant moment in the nation's history.

Generally autobiographies, or indeed biographies, usually come after, not before, publication of the subject's earlier writings. This collection bucks the trend; it is a prequel masquerading as a sequel, though both character (mine) and context (its) have infused it with a *soupçon* of personal reminiscence. Buoyed by the reception of my memoir, with feedback and (happily) sales, from jurisdictions from across the globe – including a solitary one behind the Iron Curtain, which did not violate the UK sanctions regime, but resulted in its impounding by the Russian authorities for undisclosed reasons, and required a second sending via Estonia; and another single sale in the People's Republic of China where the (first) 1999 edition of my book *Sports Law* translated into Mandarin still circulates among aspirant Chinese sports lawyers – the publishers, now nestling under Bloomsbury's wings, revisited the idea of this collection which has, at any rate, grown in size, as well as differing in content, since given the thumbs down by the firm's online begetter.

But the constraints of space, if nothing else, require winnowing of all the chaff and even some wheat. There was, if not *un embarras de richesses*, certainly *un embarras de quelque chose*.

I have not even shortlisted several lectures on matters educational, which fall squarely within my life 'without the law', using the preposition in what the *Oxford English Dictionary* describes as its archaic but, more encouragingly, literary sense, ie to mean 'outside'. This may have been a prudent cull, given that a chapter in my first book, *A Short Walk on the Campus*, co-authored with Jonathan Aitken (later, in a rollercoaster career, pressman, politician, perjurer and priest) describing our Oxford Union debating tour of the USA east of the Mississippi in 1963 contained a chapter, 'Not so Much an Education More a

Way of Life', which was less than even superficial, though, to make the case for the defence, my next – and solo-authored– book, *The Plateglass Universities*, at least commanded enough attention to be favoured with its last review in 2024 which, if my maths hasn't entirely deserted me, was 68 years after publication.

I have removed any pieces which had co-authors and by definition an input, albeit unquantifiable, from others for which I could not reasonably claim credit, as well as mere contributions to some encyclopaedia such as *Mrs Beeton's Book of Household Management* (which could, in a spirit of charity, be described as one of my early works) or the *Oxford Companion to Law* and miscellaneous pieces from lesser known journals such as *The Sikh Courier*, *Legal Antiquities*, and the *San Diego Law Journal* whose UK Legal Correspondent I briefly became for reasons, if any, long forgotten.

I have by contrast put a premium on named lectures often set up in honour of this or that individual which my late father, Lord Beloff, always said it was a privilege to be invited to deliver: so, it may have been, albeit a privilege without concomitant fee. But I had succumbed to the invitation on no less than 10 occasions so even that selection, if imported in whole, would have overtopped the publisher's plimsoll line for length. On two occasions, however (Tom Sargant (2005) Alexander (2009)) while retaining the title, the organisers had substituted a debate or dialogue for the lecture, so there was in reality, if not in fiction, nothing to publish. I could have chosen another marker, 'Festschrifts', again a form of solicitation to *pro bono* authorship, but to avoid any discrimination in prioritising the honorands, omitted all five.

Elsewise, I had to fit the unculled into my preferred quartet of legal subjects linked, if remotely, by my title 'Four Faces of the Law': Advocacy, Judges, History and Sport.

The first reflected my interest in the means whereby I had practised my profession for a half century; the second my perception of the key elements underpinning the practice of judging into which I personally had chosen to dip a toe rather than take a plunge; the third as, initially a history and only afterwards a law graduate, my fascination with the influence of particular individuals on the development of the law; the fourth, to explain, if not to justify, the *soubriquet* familiarly applied to me as 'The Godfather of Sports Law', I could hardly ignore. I lack the courage to look back at, still less to offer for reprint, my quarterly editorials for the *International Sports Law Review* which number more than a century. Time's winged chariot tends to bring subjects for such ephemera round on a repetitive basis. It is often said that there are only seven basic plots for fiction. I would estimate no larger number of themes exist for sports law.

I discarded the large number of pieces devoted to judicial review, which constituted, until I shifted my focus to sports law, the bulk of my practice, because the subject developed so rapidly over recent decades that my reflections, fresh though they may have been when written, had a built-in obsolescence. One on prisoners' rights, delivered at a Moscow seminar in 1996 I have only in Russian (the interpreters', not mine). My lecture 'Life, Death and the Law'

(2004) is already beyond repair or recycling, so rapid have been the changes since wrought by maturing medical science.

The Peter Taylor lecture at the Royal Grammar School, Newcastle upon Tyne had to go because a substantial part of it was later replicated in the David Williams lecture, which I ringfenced because it was seductively said by my host to be the most important law lecture in the Cambridge University calendar, in the same position as that occupied by the Oxford equivalent, the Neill Law Lecture. Be that as it may, I lacked the boldness of Sir Stephen Sedley who made the identical lecture satisfy both invitations.

For a choice from my 24 essays written for the *Oxford Dictionary of National Biography* I had two criteria: the intrinsic interest of the lives so summarised; and the maximisation of the readership who would, like I, have known the subjects personally and, as in obituary equivalent of a balloon debate, threw the others overboard.

To adapt the podcasters' favourite cliché, what rests is the rest.[1]

I wondered whether I should edit out passages in one lecture, where I paraphrased, but not plagiarised, passages from another, but such exercise would inevitably disturb such equilibrium as the later one may have possessed, and I console myself with the thought that consistency is a virtue and that, if something is worth saying once, it is usually worth saying twice – if no more.

I also wondered if I should, if not top, at least tail some of the pieces to update them and refer to developments after they were first published as illustrated by the following random examples, Women's upward mobility in the law has gained maybe unexpected velocity culminating in the first Lady Chief Justice, if not yet challenging in gender terms the putative title of the first female head of civil justice – will it remain Master of the Rolls? Threats to judicial independence have increased since members of the Court of Appeal who reached a decision which delayed Brexit (for reasons of law, not politics), could be excoriated as 'enemies of the people'; indeed individual judges at lower levels of the hierarchy have been the victims of actual threats for a variety of less headline-hitting reasons The gap between the earnings of the grandees of the Bar in particular and the senior judiciary has expanded to the extent that fewer and fewer of the best and brightest are willing to go down the one-way street which is the consequence of a change of profession from arguing to deciding cases. Advocacy itself in modern times involves more writing and less speaking, albeit its object is always to persuade.

But my purpose has never been merely to describe, but to analyse and evaluate; and my aim is as much to entertain as to educate. In a chapter in my memoir

[1] The lectures were necessarily delivered without footnotes which only appeared if and when they were printed. But for anyone, if anyone, who wanted to check the source of some observation, I have given the reference to the journal in which they enjoyed a public written afterlife. I have, to avoid imbalance, excised footnotes from all pieces, even those which first appeared in script, not speech. So this is mercifully the only numbered footnote in the book.

I posed the question 'Change or Decay?' and, in answering it in broad-brush terms – a lot of the former, only a little of the latter – noted that the essential structure of our legal system and the values it protects are permanent. The kind of readership that I optimistically seek to attract will be sufficiently live to, and familiar with, the dynamic of the law not to be misled by the fact that the contents of this collection reflect always the time and occasionally even the place which gave them birth. In the vernacular of Gen Z, whatever that is, they are what they are. So be it.

# Part I

# Advocacy

# 2

# 'A View from the Bar' Sir David Williams Lecture 2010*

THE SENSE OF privilege that I feel in being invited to deliver this lecture is tempered by my sadness that the distinguished lawyer, in whose honour it was founded, is no longer with us.

David was my friend, and mentor to me for many years. We first met in the 1960s when he was a Law Fellow at Keble, Oxford – a part of his career which was mysteriously airbrushed from the Memorial Service which took place earlier this year in Great St Mary's Church. He became an academic tenant in the chambers at 4/5 Gray's Inn Square of which I was then joint head. He acted, as he put it, as my 'junior' when I chaired the Judicial Subcommittee of the Senior Salaries Review Body: We were clearly suspected in tandem of apparent, if not actual, bias towards the payees, since at the conclusion of our term no lawyers appointed were to replace us. He was one of my referees when I became President of the smaller – I choose the adjective with care – of the two Oxbridge Trinities. It was characteristic of David, whose modesty was preeminent among his many memorable qualities, that in asking me to be the tenth lecturer in this series, he told me only *after* I had accepted, that he was in all likelihood destined not to be among the audience. Alas, his prophecy was fulfilled. I miss him greatly.

My predecessors as lecturer have all been lawyers of the highest repute – the last four being Chief Justices of major democracies. Indeed, for me to follow in the immediate footsteps of the Chief Justice of the United States of America, albeit a stripling some years younger than I, risks giving a new meaning to the word '*bathos*'. But incapable of matching these generals in delivering *ex cathedra* statements from the mountain peaks of the law, I, a mere foot soldier, have decided to pitch my perspective from its plains.

I have been for more than four decades a member of the Bar of England and Wales so crossing what my researches for this lecture identify as a chronological plimsoll line. In the Bodleian Law Library, I came across *two* memoirs entitled '*Forty Years at the Bar*' one by Edward Abinger, the other by James Balfour-Bowen, only to find, a few shelves on, a volume entitled '72 *years at the Bar*' by Ernest Bowen-Rowlands – a quantum leap of forensic longevity, equivalent in terms of record breaking to Usain Bolt's exploits as a sprinter. Abinger's

* (2011) 23 *The Denning Law Journal* 1.

plea in mitigation for his autobiography rested on the coincidence that, as he wrote, he had 'nearly attained the three score years and ten usually allotted to men' coupled with the urgings of his many friends. I could only avail myself of half of that not altogether convincing excuse. And it is *not* my purpose, in mimicry of these worthies, merely to indulge in titivated courtroom reminiscence nor to give an *apologia pro vita mea*, although my lecture will be in part a credo. At the end of that classic sixties film *Alfie*, the hero played by Michael Caine, turns towards the camera, and asks 'What's it all about?'. It is that question, that as a veteran jobbing attorney, I shall seek to answer.

But let me start my voyage in that now iconic decade.

I was called to the Bar by Grays Inn in November 1967. In order to qualify, aspirant barristers, who did not need to be graduates, could study law in their own time from nutshell notes, scripted by Gibson and Weldon. My practical training consisted of watching my pupil-master, to whom I was apprenticed for the next year, and learning from his trials and his errors in equal measure. For this facility I had to pay him the princely sum of £50.

In those days barristers still conventionally wore cutaway black jackets and striped trousers; and a handful continued to affect bowler hats. There were few females in the profession – in the year of my Call approximately 7% of new barristers. Objections were still voiced, devoid of any sense of shame, to women being admitted to chambers on the basis that they would inevitably soon depart to pursue their proper and predestined role of child-bearing and rearing.

Ethnic minority counsel were still rarer. While the Inns of Court played host to a significant proportion of overseas students from new Commonwealth and old Empire, those same students were expected to return to their own country and exploit the title of barrister-at-law to immediate advantage, accelerating to positions such as Attorney General or even Chief Justice with a velocity which their English equivalents could only emulate in their dreams.

Chambers were generally small – my own set, 2 Hare Court, had when I arrived, 12 members and no QCs. Chambers' names were then their addresses too. Membership was for life. Departure from the set to which one had been admitted as a tenant, indeed as a pupil, on the solitary say-so of the Head of Chambers, himself selected on the principle of Buggin's turn, was as rare, and as disagreeable, as divorce.

Chambers' administration rested exclusively on the clerks, who arranged one's diary, negotiated one's fees, and took 10% of them – the so-called shilling in the guinea.

Control of the profession still rested substantially with the Inns: the Bar Council being more a representative than a regulatory body and its Chairman, in Bagehotian terms, more dignified than efficient.

Solicitors were a segregated, separate and unequal branch of the legal profession. The relationship between barrister and solicitor was a vertical, not a horizontal one, even though solicitors were the single source of barristers' instructions. On that basis solicitors came to seek advice only in the barristers' chambers. It was a breach of the bar's professional etiquette to fraternise with them or otherwise to advertise a barrister's own expertise (such as it was), however discreetly. The all but omnipotent clerks acted as the barristers' agents to the outside world, and could make, but also break, careers.

Solicitors enjoyed no rights of audience in the higher courts of law, where silks still appeared with juniors, who were paid 2/3rds of their leader's fee. Judicial appointments were made entirely from the ranks of Bar. The Lord Chancellor by means of the usual – but archaic – processes of consultation himself determined who should become a Queen's Counsel or a Judge. It was clear that some who aspired to such status had a black mark against them; but who had put it there was obscure; and there was no formal means by which it could be exposed, still less eradicated. It was assumed that most barristers *did* aspire to the High Court Bench. If invited to accept such an appointment, a QC was expected to accept it; and one Judge, Harry Fisher, who swiftly abandoned the office, first in favour of City and then of University life, after brief exposure – I parody – to the monotony of personal injury litigation in Sunderland, punctuated by the occasional affray in Darlington, was regarded as having done that which a gentleman should not do.

In Court the tradition of oral advocacy and oral evidence was unchecked: precedents relied on would not infrequently be recited in full. Judges conventionally declined to read *any* papers before coming into court in case it prejudiced their otherwise open minds. They acted as referees, determining who won or lost, penalising breach of rules, but otherwise uninvolved. Cases would be frequently adjourned for '*Counsel's Convenience*' or sometimes because the Judge had '*a public duty to perform*' – occasionally a euphemistic synonym for an invitation to a Royal garden party. Barristers uniquely among the profession, were immune from suits for negligence, although *also* they could not sue for their fees. The only established form of dispute resolution, alternative to litigation, after the demise long since of the duel, was arbitration.

The technology to support such litigation was immature. Typewriters were at best electric, not electronic: the fax machine had but recently arrived on the scene; the word-processor was unheard of. Blackberries were still fruit. Copying files was a laborious process. Conferences took place face-to-face. Research was done in libraries. Judges recorded evidence and argument in manuscript.

Under the legal aid system inaugurated in 1949, in broad terms anyone who satisfied a means and a merits tests could walk through the door of any solicitor who was entitled, regardless of expertise, to take with Counsel's assistance, a case through from start to finish at public expense.

England was truly an offshore island in the legal world. Although QCs could still travel to exotic regions of the old Empire – Singapore, Malaysia, Hong Kong, the Caribbean islands, newly independent African states – to appear in full fig and with white wig in courtrooms cooled only by revolving fans, the domestic common law was uninfluenced by the law of the Common Market, or by the European Convention on Human Rights. The writings of academics were only cited in court after their authors were dead, but not, by venerable tradition, before.

Fast forward the clock to 2010, four and a half decades later. How different is the picture!

Barristers are still called to the bar by the Inns of Court – institutions of medieval origin but with considerable staying power, but the Bar is now a wholly graduate profession. Pupillage is still a necessary part of the aspirant barrister's education; but it is preceded even for those, who with law degrees, are spared the monotony of the Graduate Diploma in Law, by a year's specific training by the Bar Professional Training Course in such matters as advocacy, negotiation, client relations and other matters which previously the fledging barrister had been expected to acquire by a mysterious osmotic process.

Pupils no longer pay for the privilege of pupillage, now itself a structured training programme; on the contrary the major sets of chambers fall over themselves to offer substantial scholarships of up to £50,000 per annum to attract the best and brightest of their generation. OLPAS, the Mark 2 model of PACH – the pupil's application clearing house, itself based on UCAS, restricts the window for applications to a specified time of the year – in common with professional football transfers – to prevent unseemly competition.

The barristers' formal attire of yesteryear gathers mothballs in the attic. Dark suits are still obligatory – although the concept of darkness appears somewhat flexible. Women, who now constitute 58% of those admitted to the profession, usually wear the trousers.

Minority ethnic counsel are on the rise, constituting almost 24% of pupils in 2007.

Chambers are larger. In Birmingham two sets have more than 100 tenants. *My* old set, now numbers 75, of whom almost half are QCs. It has been rechristened Blackstone in the modern style, where no significant figure in English legal history from Bracton and Erskine, to Denning and Wilberforce has *not* been pillaged to add borrowed lustre to a chamber's name – not to speak of Matrix, professional home of Cherie Booth, which has looked to Hollywood rather than history or the House of Lords for inspiration in its title.

Tenants, and pupils, are chosen by a rigorous process conforming to modern best practice, informed by anti-discrimination legislation and the Human Rights Act. And not only is it now conventional for upwardly mobile barristers to move to different sets, but transfers are even solicited, again just as they are between football clubs.

The clerks, a durable race, have been supplemented by Practice Managers or even by Chief Executives – all now salaried. The clerk's 10% has gone with the wind, once it was appreciated that its survival would guarantee the recipient an income far in excess of that enjoyed by the highest earning barrister.

The Bar itself has been affected by waves of legislative regulation: the Courts and Legal Services Act 1990, the Access to Justice Act 1999, the Legal Services Act 2007. In order to react to but also to anticipate further control, the Bar

Council has become an executive engine, spawning committees, position papers and guidelines on every subject from international relations to maternity leave; the Chairmanship is a full-time post.

The balance of power between the professions has shifted. Barristers will dispense advice in *solicitor's* offices. Solicitors are no longer prohibited guests; but encouraged to attend chambers' parties, where they are wooed with champagne and canapés – some would say excessively. Movement within the Bar is paralleled by movement from one profession to another. Between the Bar and solicitors is no longer a Rubicon but a rivulet.

There is a wealth of legal directories in which lawyers' specialities can be recorded. It is nonetheless irritating to be flattered by some publisher as a leading expert in a particular field, but then invited to pay several hundred pounds so that this remarkable piece of intelligence can be broadcast to the wider world. These weighty volumes proliferate with their own ranking lists, treated by barristers with reverence or contempt depending on how they are personally assessed – in the same way as politicians variously treat opinion polls. There are the lawyers' equivalent of the Oscar and BAFTA ceremonies held in the ballrooms of leading London hotels in which titles such as 'Construction and Technology Junior' of the year are handed out by celebrity compères.

Solicitors, subject only to fulfilment of certain criteria in terms of experience and training, have rights of audience in the highest courts, where QCs now often appear without the buttress of a Junior. As a quid pro quo the Bar has promoted direct access, cutting out the solicitor middleman. This has not, despite dire predictions, brought a halt to the expansion of the independent Bar. When I was called there were 2,300 barristers in independent practice: now there are over 12,000. In the law's house there are many mansions. There will always be scope for the buccaneer as well as the backroom boy.

Solicitors can aspire too to the highest judicial posts: QCs as well as Judges are chosen by Commissions with a strong lay component.

But the Bench itself is no longer the inevitable culmination of a successful career at the Bar. The charms of college or boardroom, a preference for advocacy over adjudication and the growing gulf between the income of a fashionable silk and even the Lord Chief Justice has ensured that by no means all who could be on the High Court Bench are, or, increasingly, will be.

Modern technology has transformed the operation of the law. Video conferencing has become common. Courts can accommodate simultaneous displays of evidence on screen. Submissions are handed up and judgments handed down on disk. Research is increasingly done through the electronic database and the worldwide web. Professor Richard Susskind has termed the lawyers of the future 'legal information engineers'.

In Court, influenced by civilian and transatlantic example, written now accompanies oral advocacy. Skeleton arguments and witness statements have to be provided. Judges are expected to read them in advance, and *some* indeed do. They have become case managers controlling the timing and pace of litigation, conscious of the need to meet targets and to cut costs. Barristers can be sued for negligence; and even exposed to wasted costs orders. They are obliged to carry insurance but can enter into contracts to provide legal services to their professional clients. Adjudication has been part privatised, with mediation and other forms of ADR supplementing more conventional arbitration.

There is a Community Legal Service and a Criminal Defence Service – a system of state defenders – to complement the Crown Prosecution Service. Old style conventional legal aid for civil work has swept away – it no longer exists for personal injury claims or most damages actions – and the Legal Services Commission enters into franchised contracts with vetted practitioners to provide services. Conditional fees are now allowed to support privately funded litigation.

It is closing time in the Gardens of the East. Malaysia has ceased to be an area where English silks can appear: Singapore almost so and even in Hong Kong the Bar Council operates a justifiable protectionist policy. Strasbourg and Luxembourg have provided new fora to replace the old.

In civilian terms doctrine as well as jurisprudence can be relied on in litigation: and *living* academics can collect the number of their citations in judgments as well as in the footnotes in prestigious journals. Comparative law has infiltrated forensic argument. As Tom Bingham presciently noted 'There is a world out there'.

But has the transformation of the context transformed the content? Are the values and the virtues of the Bar what they were? Can they, and should they, survive this tsunami of reform, whether imposed from without or generated from within?

Tom Bingham, amplifying his much quoted Williams Lecture on the rule of law into a slim volume, wrote in his chapter on a Fair Trial:

> scarcely less important than an independent judiciary is an independent legal profession, fearless in its representation of those who cannot represent themselves, however unpopular or distasteful their case may be.

In that single sentence are identified links elements crucial to the Bar's ethos: availability, fearlessness and independence – but the greatest of these is independence.

It is the availability as much as the quality of representation which is the guarantee provided by the Bar. Under the so-called 'cab rank rule' any barrister not otherwise engaged or conflicted out and competent in the relevant area of law must appear for any client willing and able to pay an appropriate fee, even if he disapproves of the clients' character or cause. It was said to be, in one analysis of legal ethics, 'to barristers what the Hippocratic oath is to doctors'.

In *Arthur Hall v Simons* the Law Lords variously described it 'a valuable professional rule' or 'ethic' a 'long and honourable tradition' as 'a fundamental and essential part of a liberal legal system' and

> 'a public duty which advocates perform without regard to such private considerations such as general gain or personal inconvenience'.

In the same case various rationales were supplied. The rule ensures that no one is left without representation, even the most

> 'unpopular and anti-social.'
>
> 'It protects barristers against being criticised for giving their services to a client with a bad reputation.'
>
> 'It negates the identification of the advocate with the cause of his client and therefore assists to provide him with protection against governmental or popular victimisation.'

Some have elsewhere pitched its justification high. Erskine defended his own defence of Thomas Paine, author of the *Rights of Man*, with the words:

> 'From the moment that any advocate can be permitted to say that he will or will not stand between the Crown and the subject from that moment the liberties of England are at an end.'

Some have pitched it low. Geoffrey Robertson QC wrote:

> 'it reduces the amount of excrement through the letter box.'

Yet the virtues of the cab rank rule are not always recognised outside the profession.

The abolitionist Granville Sharp, the prime mover in *Somerset's case* when Lord Mansfield famously determined that slavery was unlawful in England, criticised Dunning, Counsel for the slave owner, who had represented a slave in an earlier case for his forensic *volte face*, recording his disapproval of:

> 'an abominable and insufferable practice in lawyers, to undertake cases diametrically opposed to their own declared opinions of law and common justice.'

And when I appeared within the Committee of Privileges in a vain effort to postpone the ejection of the hereditary peers from the House of Lords, Margaret Jay, then Leader of the House, came up to me in the Moses Room shortly before the hearing and expressed her surprise at my appearance, as she phrased it, 'on *that* side'. But when some years later in an article in *The Spectator* I suggested that *retired* members of the University who lived in Oxford had no more obvious right to vote on the University affairs than hereditary peers to participate in the deliberations of the Upper House, Lord Trefgarne, one of my sometime clients, wrote a letter complaining that my views seemed inconsistent with my representation of the hereditary interests in the earlier litigation.

Others have suggested that the rule is more mantra than mandate. Lord Steyn in *Arthur Hall v Simons* said:

> Its impact on the administration of justice is not great. In real life a barrister has a clerk whose enthusiasm for unwanted brief may not be great, and he is free to raise the fee within limits.

Yet the menace, if any, comes less from avarice than from ideology. In setting up chambers in Lambeth as a barristers' co-operative where profit was not the prime mover, Lord Gifford, hereditary peer and *soi-disant* Passionate Advocate said:

> we let it be known that we would not want to prosecute cases for police, nor would we act for landlords against tenants or for employers against employees.

Threatened with disciplinary proceedings by the Bar Council, he ingeniously defended that stance on the basis that his Chambers had indicated a preference, not imposed a prohibition. But even in sets which house the alternative Bar or those of avowedly left of centre persuasion, there is no reason to believe or evidence to support that their members could, or indeed would purge from themselves what the current Chairman has called 'the DNA of the Bar'.

As a barrister cannot disdain neither can he prejudge his clients' case, Dr Johnson said:

> A lawyer has no business with the justice or injustice of the cause which he undertakes, unless his client asks his opinion, and then he is bound to give it honestly. The justice or injustice of the cause is to be decided by the judge.

So, does the barrister, then, in accepting a brief, become monocular, or may he have a broader vision?

Henry Brougham, to justify his controversial defence of Queen Caroline, proclaimed:

> An advocate, by the sacred duty which he owes his client, knows in the discharge of that office but one person in the client and none other, ... he must go on reckless of the consequences, even if his fate it should unhappily be, to involve his country in confusion for his client's protection.

By contrast Lord Macmillan, a Law lord, commented extra-curially:

> In the discharge of his office the advocate has a duty to his client, a duty to his opponent, a duty to the Court, a duty to the State, and a duty to himself. To maintain a perfect poise amidst these various and sometimes conflicting claims is no easy feat.

Amongst that quintet of perceived obligations, only a pair may command general agreement – the duty to the Court and the duty to the client, the former wrongly omitted from Brougham's catalogue of one. As is recorded in the Gospel according to St Matthew, no man may serve two masters; but a barrister *must*. He owes, as Lord Hoffmann put it, 'a divided loyalty' for the duty to the client is subordinate to advocate's principal duty. Lord Denning gave a classic enunciation of the duty's pith and purpose. He said of the barrister:

> He has a duty to the court which is paramount. It is a mistake to suppose that he is the mouthpiece of his client to say what he wants: or his tool to do what he directs. He is none of these things. He owes allegiance to a higher cause. It is the cause of truth and justice.

The practical effects of this duty now enshrined in statute are many, and illuminated by a wealth of judicial dicta.

An advocate may not deceive or knowingly mislead the court nor allow the judge to take what he knows to be a bad point in his client's favour. He must bring to the attention of the court all relevant decisions and legislative provisions of which he is aware, even those that are adverse to his argument.

He must conduct the proceedings economically and 'not waste time on irrelevancies even if the client thinks they are important', and notwithstanding, as the Chief Justice of Australia Anthony Mason graphically put it, that

> the client may wish to chase every rabbit down every burrow.

Still less may he 'take false points however much his client may insist he should do so'. He must help the court to further the overriding objective of the Civil Procedure Rules. He must not set his name to a plea which 'he does not consider to be properly arguable'.

He must not unjustly make a charge of fraud, without evidence to support it. He must see that his client discloses relevant documents, even those that may be fatal to his case.

These principles apply to barristers in criminal as well as in civil proceedings. Prosecuting counsel play an important public role in promotion of an open and fair criminal justice system, so the Bar Council prescribes:

> Prosecuting counsel should not attempt to obtain a conviction by all means at his command

– although Mervyn Griffith-Jones QC qualified this by warning Middle Temple Students in 1973

> don't act as second defending counsel as some young men seem to think they should do in order to be fair.

When, twelve years earlier, prosecuting Penguin Books, the publishers of *Lady Chatterley's Lover*, as Crown Counsel he lost the jury's sympathy in his opening speech by asking them whether it was a book that a jury man would like his wife or servants – I stress the plural – to read, he was presumably *not* anticipating his own later advice.

While the *defence* lawyer's role in criminal proceedings is essentially partisan, he is still required to place the interests of justice first.

If his client confesses his guilt prior to trial, he is limited to testing the strength of the prosecution case. He must not 'set up an affirmative case inconsistent with that confession nor call evidence in support of an alibi or otherwise which he knows to be untrue'.

Subject to that proviso, as again the Bar Council prescribes:

> It is the duty of counsel when defending an accused on a criminal charge to present to the court, fearlessly and without regard to his personal interests.

Counsel may be partially consoled, by the obiter dictum of Lord Justice James in *R v McFadden*:

> Forensic techniques may vary from time to time but it is still *possible* to point to success at the Bar based upon a reputation for courage in standing up to the judge when occasion demands.

It is, however, worth pausing for a moment to reflect upon the significance of this unusual constraint, and to imagine its impact if it were transposed, *mutatis mutandis*, as we were once permitted, but no longer, to say in submissions to the Court, to other arenas. We are a mere fortnight away from a general election in which politicians appealed to the verdict of the people, who gave what might reasonably be described as a reserved judgement, indeed a split decision. During the campaign – and I make no partisan point – there was a wealth of examples, in the language of old-fashioned pleading too numerous to specify, of *suppressio veri* – economy with the truth – if not of *suggestio falsi*. Imagine for a moment how the democratic process would be transformed and improved if politicians were under a duty *not* to deform statistics, or to *make* full and frank disclosure, of material, say, relating to the national debt. Imagine for a moment if cricketers walked, footballers refrained from diving, rugby players from committing that contradiction in terms the professional foul or team managers in any game from berating match officials, how that too would purify the culture of sport. That barristers operate in this unusual way is not a testament, of course, to their inherent morality; they are cut from the same crooked timber of humanity as all of us. But as with the cab rank rule, the duty to the court, the second pillar of the Bar's wisdom, is something rare and precious, to be preserved and protected.

In my view the duty to the Court, deeply embedded in the English common law tradition, no more acts as an *undesirable* restraint on the barrister's freedom of action than do the Queensberry rules on professional pugilists. Indeed, as the same Chief Justice of Australia said, it fortifies him in the exercise of an independent discretion or judgment in the conduct and management of a case.

How far then should the barrister *himself* fortify the structures of independence? Should a barrister be a cause lawyer or a case lawyer? Autobiographies with titles such as *Memoirs of a Radical Lawyer* or even *The Passionate Advocate* (more intriguing perhaps than even *72 Years at the Bar*), are accounts of the careers of advocates who, without violating the cab rank rule, wear on their sleeve not only on their hearts, but their minds. Why *do I* prefer an alternative style in which the barrister's views are as private as his vote, even accepting the price to be paid in erosion of civic commitment and even of moral sensibility?

There are two reasons: one is actuality, one is appearance.

The function of the advocate is to give advice and then to conduct a case with detachment, his only passion being for success on behalf of his client.

Ideological or emotional involvement in an outcome seems to me to risk infection of analysis and presentation. I am very conscious that when I am on the side of the case I prefer, I have to guard against an excess of the adrenalin – not an exogenous prohibited substance – essential to the most effective advocacy. In 1976 I appeared in an unsuccessful effort to preserve St Marylebone Grammar school, the last of its kind in London, Lord Denning in one of his most elegiac passages was able to indicate how he would have wished to decide the case: 'Many will grieve,' he said 'when that which was great is passed away. But so it must be.' I grieved too, but necessarily in silence.

More recently I fear that my dislike of the Strasbourg-inspired rule that the United Kingdom cannot deport individuals, proven to be a threat to its own national security, to their country of origin because of concerns about risk of the treatment they would there receive, may, despite my best endeavours, have percolated into my submissions before the House of Lords as a sub-text if not in the text itself. Lord Hope felt constrained to address full-frontally the argument:

> surely the sooner they are got rid of the better. On their own heads be it if their extremist views expose them to the risk of ill-treatment when they got home

and administered what Touchstone called the 'reproof valiant':

> That, however, is not the way the rule of law works. The lesson of history is that, by depriving people of its protection, because of their beliefs and behaviour, however obnoxious, leads to the disintegration of society.

Clients, be they prisoners, parents or public authorities, may welcome the barrister's sympathy as well as his skill, but they are best served if they enjoy, without any sacrifice of courtesy on the barrister's part, only the latter. The case he advances is after all his client's, not his own: that is why the advocate formally abstains from any expression of belief, and deploys the neutral concept of submission. But how he advances it must be the product of his own best dispassionate judgment. Alastair Campbell in his diaries records of Jonathan Sumption QC, briefed in the Hutton Enquiry:

> It was absolutely clear that he was not taking something out (sc: of the diaries) just because the Prime Minister would do.

and concluded,

> What I admired about Sumption most was that he didn't seem to care what the press or public were thinking about this. He was totally focussed on the judge.

In circumstances of far less gravity I once had myself to tell my instructing solicitor that my client could promote his case with Max Clifford or with Michael Beloff, but not with both. After, in *Wednesbury* terms, taking all material considerations into account, the barrister must, as Frank Sinatra would have recommended, do it *his* way.

It is, of course, difficult for emotions to become engaged in a question of construction of an arcane provision of the Hague Visby rules, or even of the obscure outer boundaries of the volatile law of negligence. And although those who practise in the fields of criminal may from time to time develop a strong belief in a client's innocence as those who practise in the field of family law may empathise with a client in custody disputes, the issues in those cases do not easily fit into some *ideological* template.

It is the development of *public* law and its supplanting of private law as the most important element in appellate adjudication, and the concurrent migration of political issues from the legislature to the courts which expose the advocate more readily to the temptations of partisanship and more importantly to the perception of it.

In his foreword to a leading commentary on human rights practice, Lord Phillips, previous holder of the triple crown of Master of the Rolls, Lord Chief Justice and Senior Law Lord, and who has now – to mix the sporting metaphor – achieved the grand slam by becoming first President of the Supreme Court – reminisced:

> … when I practised at the Bar, the staple diet of the House of Lords consisted of civil law and tax appeals … Judicial Review was in its infancy …. How things have changed. Baroness Hale and we her colleagues devote the majority of our energies to public law. The Human Rights Act 1998 bears significant responsibility for this change.

In this new environment I am particularly uncomfortable with the too ready association of the barrister with his clients' case.

In the highly sensitive and increasingly complex field of immigration law in which, in my far off days as a junior, I used regularly to practise, I noted the significant attachment of clients to lawyers of their own ethnic background, not always to the advantage of their claim, sometimes because their chosen champion had inadequate command of the language in which the Court had to be addressed. I am uncomfortable too with the converse position when women advocates are instructed to defend men on trial for rape – not on account of their forensic abilities but on the crude calculation that juries will be beguiled into thinking that no woman would defend someone who had committed an act of violence against members of their own sex.

I do *not* believe that barristers of known left wing sympathies are necessarily best placed to defend striking Trade Unionists or those of publicised Europhobic tendencies to represent UKIP. A barrister who can appear at *different* times for the BNP and the Socialist Workers League is not the forensic equivalent of the Vicar of Bray, but an adherent to the true professional faith. It is dangerous to adopt a mind-set that virtue can only repose on the claimants' side (or vice-versa). For it is not only the advocates for claimants but those for respondents too who are responsible for assisting in the construction or clarification of the law. Barristers, after all, do not make law, they supply from *either* side of the Court, the materials from which the judges can fulfil their own distinctive role.

In an essay entitled 'Early Days' Lord Justice Sedley reminisces about his triumphs and disasters as a novice barrister, present at the creation of modern judicial review. It is an exhilarating and entertaining account of his role in seminal cases involving gypsies, low income tenants, immigrants and prisoners. In some of those I was myself involved; in the self-same case about control units, the product of a philosophy which was tough on crime, if not necessarily on its cause, being led by Stephen at first instance, and leading him in the Court of Appeal, the result of an idiosyncratic silk selection by the then Lord Chancellor, Lord Hailsham. But it never occurred to me that I was, or could be thought to be, bent on advancing some radical political agenda. I was simply doing my daily job. Lesser advocates than Stephen can, if they always appear on the same side of the argument, cause confusion in the minds of those who try the case between the client and his advocate to the detriment of the former. It is surely axiomatic that a barrister's arguments, whether mediated through advice or advocacy, will be given greater weight and respect if he is recognised by any test to be truly independent.

The recent case of *McFarlane v Relate Avon Limited* provides a much publicised example of what I have in mind. A psycho-sexual therapist failed in his claim for religious discrimination against his employers who had refused to exempt him from providing his services to same-sex couples. He was supported by Lord Carey, the former Archbishop of Canterbury, who in a witness statement invited the Lord Chief Justice to establish a Panel of Judges designated to hear cases involving religious rights. The Appellants' advocate has a unique expertise in such cases, but as his website and record shows, is a legal crusader for evangelical religious values. A Counsel not only more detached but seen to be more detached from the principle contended for, ie, of allowing religious belief to qualify from the rigidities of anti-discrimination law, might have adopted a more nuanced approach, which eschewed the gratuitous and doomed plea for a specialist non-secular court, trenchantly dismissed by Lord Justice Laws as 'deeply inimical to the public interest'. Those who cannot appreciate that there may be two sides to a question are not best placed to argue in favour of one.

Criminal law is not immune to this problem. Members of the Crown Prosecution Service, originally created so as to separate the functions of police and prosecutor, have started to colonise frontline advocacy, with the consequent risk that as employees of a public authority they will become 'prosecution minded and seen to be so'.

The era is long since gone when it was possible to combine at one and the same time a full-time practice at the Bar with an active political career. But F.E. Smith, a paradigm example of someone, who, a century ago, was able to do both, understood well the matters at stake.

When criticised by his fellow conservatives for representing the liberal Herbert Samuel in the Marconi trial he wrote to The Times:

> Political issues constantly present themselves for decision in the Law Courts. In the overwhelming majority of cases juries have done their duty indifferently between

> the parties, treating their own views upon politics as immaterial. How long do you think this stage of things will endure if every conservative case is to be presented by Conservative advocates and resisted by Liberal advocates.

The Law Officers face peculiar challenges. The then Attorney General was reported to the Bar Council for investigation that his advice to the Government on the legality of war in Iraq, misjudged the distinction between his legal and political roles. That body, in receipt of opinions by both Sir David and myself (provided in isolation from each other) rejected jurisdiction, leaving Lord Goldsmith to the no doubt tenderer mercies of the Chilcot Inquiry. It seems to me inevitable that the role of the AttorneyGeneral will have to be de-constructed, like that of the Lord Chancellor, and for analogous, if not identical, reasons of disentangling roles seen to be in tension. Wearing two hats is less difficult than wearing three, but a single item of headgear is more becoming.

There are institutional as well as ideological pressures on the independence of the Bar. Sir Gavin Lightman in a much discussed lecture, 'The Civil Justice System and Legal Profession – the challenges ahead', somewhat like a former cabinet minister, freed from the burdens of collective responsibility, rediscovered the path of true principle for the profession he had left a decade before. He excoriated 'the metamorphosis of the legal professions into legal business' and the consequent impact on the internal organisation of the Bar.

> 'The dominant philosophy today amongst many chambers', he wrote, 'is to place the highest premium on keeping all available work for clients 'in house'. Indeed, chambers have increasingly in all but name and law become partnerships between the members committed to the pursuant of the best interest of members. Chambers have for practical purposes a corporate existence. Chambers increasingly publish legal works as a chambers exercise to publicise the chambers and attract the work to the chambers. Chambers have put into effect 'rules' (enforced by chief executives and barristers' clerks) that, when counsel has been instructed from amongst the members of the chambers, if that counsel requires a leader or junior, that leader or junior will be selected from the available pool in that chambers (mopping up local employment) rather than on the basis of talent or price (the relevant considerations for the client) from the available pool of the Bar as a whole.'

There is, if not a ring, at least a tinkle of truth in what he says. For what is certain is that the perception of the Bar from outside has altered.

A decade ago, an issue arose whether a barrister who had been appointed an arbitrator by one party to the arbitration should be removed by the Court on the ground that another barrister from the same chambers had been instructed in the arbitration that gave rise to justifiable doubts about the arbitrator's impartiality.

Rix J in rejecting the application emphasised the uniqueness of the Bar's organisation and the fact that it provided a structural protection both for the interests of the client and for the interests of justice:

> It is the essence of practice at the bar, as that barristers are all self-employed. This is not a mere matter of form. On the contrary, practising barristers are prohibited by

> the rules of their profession from entering partnerships or accepting employment precisely in order to maintain the position where they can appear against or in front of one another. If it were otherwise, public access to the bar would be severely limited: each time a member of a set of chambers accepted instructions, he would debar any other member of those chambers, although independently practising self-employed barristers, from accepting instructions from any other party with a different interest in the dispute; nor would he be able to appear before a Recorder, Deputy Judge or arbitrator in the same proceedings. This would be a severe limitation on the administration of justice in this country.

Several years later an ICSID Tribunal, considering the converse situation that is, whether a QC could any longer act as counsel in a case where a member of the Tribunal was from the same set, decided that what Rix J had seen as a matter of substance was or would be seen as a matter of form. Accepting that *de jure* barristers in a set of chambers were independent of each other, the Tribunal ruled that they would be seen *de facto* as having a collective connotation.

These warning flags are fluttering elsewhere. The Court of Arbitration for Sport, whose adjectival law is substantially Swiss, regard, in the words of its Secretary-General, the notion of a member of a set of Chambers acting as arbitrator when a party is represented by a member of the same set as 'problematic', although I have never in all my time at the Bar expected, still less, received favours from judges whom I know well.

The problem will be exacerbated if barristers exploit the permission newly given to work in partnerships, or in both a self-employed and employed capacity at the same time (though not in the same case!), or to become managers in and hold shares in legal disciplinary practices (LDPs), the more so if they participate in the alternative business structures (ABS) contemplated by the same legislation which would allow them to work alongside both other legal professionals and non-lawyers – a development optimistically described by Lord Falconer as the legal system's Tesco. The influence of outside ownership, the promotion of profit over professional standards, and the commodification of legal issues, all threats inherent in these putative entities may yet cause us to mourn the eclipse of at one and the same time – to embroider the analogy – the neighbourhood corner shop and Harrods.

Similar concerns are generated by the serious commercial pressures on substantial sections of the Bar. Within what the Chairman of the Bar has recently called 'an increasingly broad church', there are in fact many Bars. Those who depend upon public funds, in particular in the areas of criminal and family law, suffer, if not death, at least damage by a thousand cuts. Freeze has been followed by fall. Judicial review of the latest pre-election Government decision was briefly on the agenda.

The outgoing Minister for Justice retorted by identifying, with less than complete accuracy, the top legal aid earners for 2008–2009 as if the income of the few was characteristic of the income of the many. The hourly earnings of the majority were, in a counter-attack, described by the Chairman of the Criminal

Bar Association as less than those of a garage mechanic. This led predictably to an amusing, if unedifying correspondence in the letter column of The Times as to which provided a more valuable social service.

The real victims, of course, will be the most vulnerable members of society – who are not, I hasten to add, the barristers themselves – to whom the barristers, distracted by a wish, in no way dishonourable, to receive a reasonable income for demanding work will increasingly be inhibited in their ability to provide proper representation, and may be even compelled to avail themselves of the exit route permitted by the cab rank rule itself.

The palliative of conditional fee agreements, shifting the burden of financing of many types of litigation from state to persons, natural or legal, and now available in all except criminal and specified family proceedings, confers on barristers, as Sir Gavin Lightman pointed out:

> a financial interest in the outcome of litigation in which they are engaged which is calculated to create unacceptable conflicts of interest and duty and creates unacceptable pressures to win.

In this uncertain financial climate, Baroness Deech, the Chairman of the BSB has said:

> We have to negotiate a path between the Scylla of fusion and the Charybdis of attrition of the bar.

In identifying the perils on that path I have sought tonight to make a summary case for the survival of a professional, independent in mind, spirit *and* appearance, and a member of a profession itself independent though not unaccountable; capable when called upon, of defending individual rights against the power of an ever burgeoning state and its sundry satrapies, but equally of representing the state when it seeks to enforce the public interest against those who act in a way inimical to it. In a surface sense everything has changed. In a subterranean one nothing has – or should. The environment in which the Bar operates at any one time may be ephemeral: but its values must be eternal.

In his book *The End of Lawyers?*, Richard Susskind, a proselytiser for information technology explains, albeit in a footnote:

> I reiterate the *question mark* in the title is intended to confirm that this book is an inquiry into whether lawyers have a future rather than a prediction of their demise.

And, equally mercifully, while prophesying that:

> lawyers who are unwilling to change their working practices and extend their range of services, will, in the coming decade, struggle to survive,

adds,

> dispute avoidance and online dispute resolution will chip away at some of this domain, but I do not see these as eliminating advocacy entirely.

So, I end by considering the moral issue created by the art of advocacy itself.

A recent consultation paper by a trio of legal regulators described advocacy as 'a fundamental pillar of the Justice system', as certainly it is, viewed from a national perspective. Lord Hoffmann noted that

> the substantial orality of the English system of trial and appellate procedure means that the judges rely heavily upon the advocates appearing before them for a fair presentation of the facts and adequate instruction in the law …
>
> The Court procedures of Europe and the United States, for example, lack the predominantly oral character of litigation in the United Kingdom.

It is regarded as axiomatic that the services of a professional advocate are beneficial: whether of Cicero, the hero of Robert Harris's projected trilogy, of William Murray, later Lord Mansfield, of whom Alexander Pope hymned:

> Graced as thou art with all the power of words,
>
> so known, so honoured in the House of Lords

– a couplet which would have required modification had the Supreme Court been established 300 years ago – and which was parodied by the actor Colley Cibber, a victim of Murray's eloquence, in a style worthy of William McGonagall:

> persuasion tips his tongue whene'er he talks.
>
> And he has chambers in the Kings Bench walks.

of Clarence Darrow who, in the Scopes trial, proved a more doughty destroyer of creationism than even Richard Dawkins, and was memorably played by Spencer Tracy in the film *Inherit The Wind*, or of modern giants such as Sir Sydney Kentridge or the late George Carman. There is much nice learning on whether and when natural justice requires that barristers use be permitted or required.

Indeed, the principle of equality of arms, inherent in the right to a fair hearing guaranteed by Article 6 of the European Convention on Human Rights, requires that everyone who is a party to proceedings must have a reasonable opportunity of presenting his case to the Court under conditions which do not place him at a substantial disadvantage vis à vis his opponent. But equality of arms does not mandate parity of representation. It has been held that a fair trial does not necessarily entail representation by a QC merely because the Crown is represented by one.

> 'The importance' said Lord Woolf 'is to have an advocate, whether he be a barrister or solicitor, who can ensure that a defendant's defence is properly and adequately placed before the Court'.

Up to a point, Lord Woolf … for there are but two possibilities. Either the relative quality of representation has no impact on the outcome or it does. The first possibility is at odds with everyday experience in the Courts. In another context Mr Justice Megarry wisely said:

> As everybody who has had anything to do with the law well knows, the path of the law is strewn with examples of open and shut cases which, somehow, were not.

Claims in civil cases should not reach the stage of requiring adjudication by judge or arbitrator unless there was at least *some* scope for more than one outcome. Prosecutions would, at any rate should, not be brought or pleas of not guilty entered unless there is a measure of uncertainty, however small, about the verdict. It is precisely to alter the odds that particular advocates are selected. A senior silk at the top of his game is worth as much to a legal, as a Rooney, a Ronaldo or a Messi is to a football team. Let me call two witnesses from north and south of the Equator.

First again, Sir Gavin Lightman who said:

> A party's performance at the trial very much turns on the investment made by the respective parties in the litigation: at all stages in the litigation money talks loud and clear. The human right to equality of arms has little, if any, meaning or practical effect in this context and the judge, however fair-minded and interventionist, has limited scope to redress the balance. A litigant purchases the quality of justice he can afford. The quality of solicitors and counsel varies as does the quality of wine from 'unfit to drink' to vintage. Vintage tends to be very expensive beyond the means of the ordinary litigant. Most must be satisfied with 'plonk'. A failure of advice at the first stage is calculated to cause irreversible harm. The prospects of success of a case very much turn on the quality or lack of quality of preparation for trial. Cases are won and lost by reason of the quality of representation at the trial: hence the extravagant fees paid to litigation lawyers. Tell it not in Gath but the scales of justice favour those who can afford to buy it.

Second, if more succinctly, Michael Kirby, the peripatetic former Antipodean High Court Judge who wrote:

> In an adversarial system such as exists in the UK and Australia, the party that argues most persuasively will often win the day.

It is not always the case that he who pays wins: but it is certainly the case that whereas all barristers are equal, some are more equal than others. Geoffrey Robertson QC entitled his interim autobiography 'The Justice Game'. Contests between unevenly matched contestants may be acceptable in a game, but not when justice is the intended trophy.

It would be little consolation to the clients of Jerry Guerinot, twenty of whose clients have been sentenced to death in Texas, that Vanessa D. Gilmore, the Federal Judge in Houston, in turning down an appeal by a British woman, Linda Carty, convicted of murder which was grounded on Guerinot's incompetence in handling of her case said without conscious irony 'The Constitution does not require perfection in trial representation.'

There may be a hollow in the crown of the adversarial system but how it is to be filled, in the real, as distinct from the ideal world, I confess do not know.

But let me not conclude on so dispiriting a note!

In *Metcalf v Mardell* Lord Hobhouse said:

> The judicial system exists to administer justice and it is integral to such a system that it provides within a society a means by which rights, obligations and liabilities can be recognised and given effect to in accordance with the law and disputes, justifies (and efficiently) resolved. The role of the independent advocate is central to achieving this outcome.

So, in a lecture which is inevitably decked out in borrowed plumes, I hope I may be forgiven for plagiarising myself with a tail feather:

> They also serve who only stand and speak.

# 3

# 'Advocacy as Art'

# Margaret Howard Memorial Lecture*

PIRANDELLO WROTE OF *Six Characters in Search of an Author*. I find myself with one phrase in search of a subject. So, I shall postpone momentarily the effort to associate text with title, and express my gratitude to Gillian Howard for switching – it may be experimentally – the venue for this annual lecture from University College London, to Oxford, and, in particular, to Trinity. I noticed that *The Times* in one of its now fashionable league tables, recently ranked Oxford law in second place just behind Oxford's earliest imitator – the percentage was well within a margin of error – with University College London in fifth place. I hope I shall not, by reason of this single lecture, reverse those two standings. But while I shrink from such profound pessimism, I should equally make it clear that my lecture is certainly not an over-optimistic piece of autobiography. I have from time to time dreamt about making the perfect submission, but I have never during my 33 years in practice at the Bar of England and Wales come close to doing so. In *R v Horsham Justices ex parte Farquharson* Shaw LJ said that a submission of mine was 'with all respect to Mr Beloff's forensic prowess talking in the air'.

In *The Raphael* Donaldson LJ said, 'Finally Mr Beloff put forward a new submission. Initially I thought that I was being obtuse in not understanding it, but I was relieved to find that My Lords appeared to suffer from a similar disability.' This was not all. After identifying the content of the submission, the learned judge continued, 'Mr Beloff frankly admitted that this was an argument of last resort. Not only is it an argument of last resort, it is also plainly wrong …'.

In *Saunders v Richmond Upon Thames LBC*, a sex discrimination case, I was accused of making 'numerous submissions, mainly many of a trifling nature'. Since one of those submissions was that there was prima facie evidence that the respondent golf club only ever intended to appoint a man as its resident professional, in that the reply to my female client's application started with the words 'Dear Sir', I still think the criticism a trifle unfair.

It is, of course, a rule of thumb that the more you are praised by the judge, the more certain it is that you have lost the case. Congratulations are rarely

* Trinity College, Oxford (2000).

accorded by the court to advocates who have had the satisfaction of a judgment in their clients' favour. Absence of congratulations does not, alas, mean that you have won!

But my moment of maximum humiliation came when I was perusing an academic work and I noticed that the author had written about the matter of *R v Secretary of State for Employment ex p EOC*, 'It may well be that the case was one of the worst argued by government counsel in history'. I was Leading Counsel in that case for the government: and my concern was only partly cured where the writer admitted to me that he had intended to say that the case was the most difficult government counsel had ever had to argue, not that it was the least well argued. Academics, no less than practising lawyers, must remember that precise language is the tool of their trade.

My experiences have been manifold. In an early case when, barely out of pupillage, I unwisely allowed my client to speak for himself in his defence. His speech appeared to me to be an incoherent plea to some inchoate spirit of justice rather than to a principle of law firmly located in the pages of *Archbold: Criminal Pleading, Evidence and Practice*. After consulting hastily among themselves, the Bench ordered my client to be detained under a provision of the Mental Health Act. I went to bid farewell to him in the cells underneath the court. 'Does this mean I'm mad?', he asked me pitifully. 'Only,' I replied, in an answer of whose tact I remain proud, 'in the eyes of the Tower Bridge Magistrates.'

Later years took me to more august tribunals and more exotic litigation. I have languished in a sports arbitration up to midnight (after an 8.00am start), before a panel consisting of a Finn, a German and a Francophone Senegalese who followed the proceedings – in so far as he did at all – only with the aid of an interpreter, who saw herself as an advocate *manquée*. The issue was how a world champion sprinter, in order to deceive the dope testers, might have hidden an uncontaminated urine sample in an intimate part of her anatomy. But I have also appeared at more civilised hours before the Privileges Committee of the House of Lords to argue an arcane point about the medieval writ of summons in a vain effort to trip up the Government's legislation to abolish the hereditary peerage. In an age of increasing specialisation, I doubt that many other contemporary barristers can claim as much – or as little.

So, in a variety of fora and an equal variety of cases I have had the opportunity to study a variety of styles of advocacy, and in such leisure moments as a barrister is ever permitted either by his clerk or his conscience to enjoy, to consider whether advocacy is art, science, a mixture of the two, or something *sui generis* – a Latin phrase now, of course, banned from the courts of law.

There is surprisingly little written by advocates about advocacy, and materials are scanty. A historian of courtroom oratory has written:

> Our early lawyers were not eminent for their eloquence, and … there was little to encourage the graces of address … The most impressive utterances of the Bar were entombed in those prosaic records the Year Books and Reports.

The stately sequence of volumes constituting the State Trials provide a source and some famous advocates were honoured with compilations of their courtroom contributions. But there is no recording of the great speeches of the past in court, nor has it yet been decided to invite television cameras into the courts of law as they have been invited into the High Court of Parliament. The tapes used nowadays to produce transcripts of the shorthand writers may be a hidden archive, but no one has yet, to my knowledge, sought to publish them as compact discs. And so dependent is advocacy on mood, tone and gesture that it cannot be appreciated by a mere reading of the transcript of legal proceedings. Its power inevitably vanishes into the air.

Biographies (auto- and otherwise) of judges and advocates (more common in the past than now) tend to be chronological rather than the analytical, and any comment to be hagiographical, not least because the authors were so often descendants of the deceased or their clerks. To these Sancho Panzas, Don Quixote was indeed a hero! The astringent approach of a Lytton Strachey was never applied. The sycophantic tone is more characteristically displayed in the following lines from a memorial ode to the Great Advocate:

> No judge will hear him now: beneath his flail.
> No witness now shall writhe – no felon quail,
> No jury by his eloquence be swayed.
> The Roman head on Saxon shoulders set,
> The silver hair; the tall heroic frame
> Are seen no more ...

Older autobiographies tend too often towards the banal, in the Victorian and Edwardian eras full of ponderous wit, self-regarding anecdotes, florid tributes to eminent contemporaries, and stern be-whiskered portraiture.

One's heart despairs when one comes in a recollection of *Forty Years at the Bar* (which seems – to judge from the several memoirs with that title to have been regarded as a period entitling, even obliging, the barrister to reminisce) to Chapter XXVI headed 'Sewage Disposal' with its alluring opening 'Sewage does not at first sight seem to be a matter for popular exposition'.

Lord Hewart LCJ may not hugely have enhanced the sum total of human knowledge when he got back to basics and opined, 'The speaker by the use of a comparatively simple oral mechanism, produces a succession of sounds.'

Nor indeed did Lord Alverstone, both Master of the Rolls and afterwards Lord Chief Justice, and so the last judge before Lords Bingham and Woolf to become a legal transvestite, tell aspirant counsel much that was novel when he wrote:

> As I am upon the subject of early hours, I desire to give it as my distinct opinion that the most important work of a barrister – namely the acquisition of the facts with a view to ascertaining how far they will stand the test of examination – is better done in the early hours than at night.

Sir Patrick Hastings made the Delphic oracle appear a model of lucidity when he reflected 'No-one has ever yet known what are the qualities which must be possessed by any advocate if he is to reach the highest rank'. And Lord Birkenhead wrote an essay on oratory in which he referred the divine Phryne, accused of impropriety, who unveiled her bosom, and was at once set free by the impressionable judge, and asked (maybe rhetorically) whether she was eloquent. Lord Birkenhead was nothing if not politically incorrect.

More modern works tend to be accounts of what the author did, rather than how he or she did it. Helena Kennedy QC wrote in a chapter entitled 'Playing Portia' an account of problems of women in law which she herself, it should be noted, has wholly successfully surmounted.

Geoffrey Robinson QC – like Kenneth Branagh, the actor-director, suffering from a slight touch of premature autobiography – was cynical rather than educational when he wrote 'The stars of the Bar ... know that justice is a game: they play it with other people's money and lives, but never, if it can be avoided, risk their own.'

Nor do the classic works of instruction advance the matter much further. *Harris's Hints on Advocacy*, which went through no less than 18 editions from 1887 to 1943, when it became, apparently, another casualty of war, concluded 'Common sense is the foundation of good advocacy'.

Yet the adversarial tradition, the hallmark of the English legal system, breeds the need for advocates. In an inquisitorial system the lawyers are mere spear carriers: the judge dominates the stage. In an adversarial system the judge should be far more dependent on the advocate. Justice must not only be seen to be done, but be heard to be done as well.

In *Ridehalgh v Horsefield* Bingham MR said:

> Our legal system developed over many centuries, rests on the principle that the interests of justice are on the whole best served if parties in dispute, each represented by solicitors and counsel, take cases incapable of compromise to court for decision by an independent and neutral judge before whom their relationship is essentially antagonistic: each is determined to win, and prepares and presents his case so as to achieve a favourable result. By the clash of competing evidence and argument, it is believed, the judge is best enabled to decide that happened, to formulate the relevant principles of law and to apply those principles to the facts of the case before him as he has found them.

And this dependence means that advocates must, as far as possible, excel. In *Abse v Smith* where it was held – as it would not be now – that a judge both could and should refuse a solicitor to appear in open court to read a statement in settlement of a libel action approved by all parties, Donaldson MR said:

> The conduct of litigation in terms of presenting the contentions of the parties in a concise and logical form, deploying and testing the evidence and examining the relevant law demands professional skills of a high order.

This critical role of the advocates is recognised in constitutional principle. In *Maltez v Lewis* Neuberger J held that 'The level playing field' envisaged by the

Civil Procedure Rules did not affect the 'fundamental right of every citizen that he or she should be represented by the legal advisers of their choice'.

Nothing is more illogical or ill-founded than the notion that since advocates speak, and all but the dumb can speak, anyone can be an effective advocate. The lay presenter usually bears as much relationship to the top-rank barrister as a bathroom tenor does to Pavarotti. The contemporary debate over the limitation of public funding for litigation, is, after all, properly founded on the assumption that the unrepresented is at a disadvantage compared with the represented litigant. Although Thomas More's *Utopia* contains no advocates at all, Sir Patrick Hastings was right to describe most litigants in person as 'floundering through a mass of evidence, quite unable to express the simplest point in such a way that anyone can understand it', notable exceptions being provided in the law reports by those outstanding platform orators, Tony Benn and Arthur Scargill, who received judicial *encomia* for their court performances.

Despite this, the little interest shown by commentators in advocacy is mirrored by the lesser consideration given to advocates. With a few unnamed exceptions, the most celebrated contemporary advocates tend to be those who are famous for journalism, political correctness, or sometimes just for being famous. The golden age of advocacy, the age of Rufus Isaacs, FE Smith, Edward Clarke, Edward Carson, and afterwards Marshall Hall, Norman Birkett and Patrick Hastings – names that appear with unfailing regularity in lists of forensic superstars – is said to have gone with the wind.

Golden ages are always past: it is not in their nature to be anything else. But there are a variety of reasons that the public eye no longer focuses on the barristers of today as it did on the barristers of yesteryear. First, the major advocates all combined their legal with political careers. Of the magnificent seven, that I have named, every one had a parliamentary career, though with varying degrees of distinction, reminding one that the concept of 'horses for courses' is one whose validity is not confined to the racetrack. The barrister-politician, flourishing in the early part of the last century, of whom Sir Edward Leithen, a familiar figure in the novels of John Buchan, represents the template, has all but disappeared. Political parties nowadays have the greatest difficulty in finding persons of adequate stature to fill the post of law officers: hence the almost unnoticed constitutional novelty of the present administration in placing first the Solicitor General and then the Attorney General in the House of Lords. Gone are the days when a back-bench silk like Sir Robert Morton in Terence Rattigan's *The Winslow Boy* could pursue his client's cause in a twin track strategy in the Commons and in the courts.

Secondly, capital punishment has been abolished. When an advocate's skills were all that stood between a man and his maker – or, less sentimentally, the rope – their importance could hardly be exaggerated.

Thirdly, in the modern world, fantasy provides more entertainment than reality. Court reports, still the *à la carte* dish of so much journalism, were the *table d'hôte* of broadsheets as well as tabloids in an era which knew nothing of cable, the video recorder or the Internet, indeed in the Victorian era were a substitute for the music halls. Maybe televised trials would change all that – although the TV channels in the USA dedicated to court broadcasting merely remind me at any rate that the lows of trials are more characteristic than the highs.

That the advocate does make a difference cannot be disputed. How much difference is another matter. Lord Maugham said:

> There is only a small percentage of cases in which he can secure a triumph for his client, and added pessimistically and then perhaps more often because of the mistakes of his opponent than by reason of his own adroitness, eloquence and skill.

Sir Patrick Hastings actually put a figure on it, estimating that '90% of cases win themselves'. Such empirical research has been carried out, in particular, the Chicago Project provides some confirmation of these stabs in the dark. It was, however, mercifully decided by the Court of Appeal in March this year that it is no breach of professional obligation for a barrister when giving advice to the legal aid board not to assess the chance of success of particular points in a claim in percentage terms.

While we shield our gaze from the delicate issue as to how the perceptible difference in the advocate's skills impacts upon the notion of equality of arms, we know well that the function of advocates is to persuade and know too the price the client pays (not to speak of the fee) if the advocate fails.

Read what Lord Devlin said of Sir Reginald Manningham-Buller, the then Attorney General who conducted the prosecution of Dr John Bodkin Adams (the Harold Shipman of the 1950s):

> His disagreeableness was so pervasive, his persistence so interminable, the observations he made so far-fetched, his objectives apparently so insignificant that sooner or later you would be tempted to ask yourself whether the game was worth the candle: if you asked yourself, you were finished.

Trevor Grove, an experienced journalist pressed into jury service, who made a virtue of necessity by writing a book about it, summarised the hostility provoked by a barrister whose oratory 'seemed to be addressed over the heads of us rude mechanicals in the jury box to some invisible audience of impressionable law students'. It appears incidentally that Mr Grove was not the only one upset by counsel's tactics. It emerges later in the book that the defendant dispensed with his services – an embarrassing experience for any advocate!

At the other end of the scale of merit, advocacy has affinities with various branches of art. Although in anthologies of law judges provide more material than advocates – the dicta of a Mansfield or a Denning crowd out the speeches of a Scarlett or a Russell – Lord Birkett, himself a prime example of the rule that the great advocates do not always make great judges, rightly said:

> Many of our advocates have been orators of the first rank. When Erskine made his first speech before Mansfield and won the rapturous praise of Lord Campbell, and when John Somers 'broke the back of the oppressor' in defence of the Seven Bishops and won the acclaim of Macaulay, they enriched the annals of the law, but at the same time they made a lasting contribution to literature.

Yet there is a crucial difference. Judgments do not depend for their impact on their delivery, but on their content only. Advocates' speeches depend upon both. You can *read*, you cannot *hear*, verbatim reports of trials. Transcripts are one-dimensional; they lack atmosphere; above all they lack voice.

Advocacy does not engage the attention of a solitary muse. It has often been likened to acting as well as to literature. In his *The Seven Lamps of Advocacy* Judge Edward Parry wrote:

> The great advocate is like the great actor; he fills the stage for his span of life, succeeds, gains the applause, makes his last bow and the curtain falls. Nothing is so illusory as the art of acting less it be the sister art of advocacy.

But if there is some affinity of attitude, the differences are again more obvious than the similarities. An actor fashions a part, and plays it many times on the stage, and in films capable of endless showing. An advocate plays his role but once; in truth it is the most transient of activities. It is captured only in immaterial part by the record, in which the advocate appears more as author than actor – he writes the lines as well as playing them – and barely at all in the summaries of the law reports. 'X replied' may be a brutal *précis* of a brilliant epilogue. Advocacy is often impromptu; and frequently interrupted. It is conditioned by the circumstances of the case. To assess its impact, one has to rely on the judgmental faculties of those who witnessed trenchant cross-examination or great speeches.

The peroration of Robert H Jackson, an Assistant Justice of the United States Supreme Court and Chief Counsel of the American team at the Nuremberg Trials is justly celebrated:

> It is against such a background that these defendants now ask this Tribunal to say that they are not guilty of planning, executing, or conspiring to commit this long list of crimes and wrongs. They stand before the record of this trial as bloodstained Gloucester stood by the body of his slain King. He begged of the widow, as they beg of you: 'Say I slew them not.' And the Queen replied, 'Then say they were not slain. But dead they are.' If you were to say of these men that they are not guilty, it would be as true to say there has been no war, there are no slain, there has been no crime.

Our appreciation of this spare but subtle crescendo is enhanced by the observations of Lord Shawcross QC, co-counsel in the American parlance, who wrote of it:

> None of the arts of the actor was on view. This was no dramatic declamation, but uttered calmly in the words of dignity and authority, the demand of a lawyer and statesman that law and justice should in the end prevail.

But if there are no exact analogies, advocacy has this in common with many breaches of art. Styles change. 'Savagery', according to one commentator, was the most notable quality of Tudor and Stuart advocates. The *State Trials* series first published in 1719 disclose a transition to a more florid, but less intemperate mode of address. But not until 1836, when statute accorded to all accused persons the full right of representation by counsel did the nineteenth century witness the rise of the hectoring prosecutors and histrionic defence counsel, which were its legacy. As (the now Professor) Cornish, the scholar of the jury trial, has written, 'The style of advocacy practised in English courts in the early years of the present century has left behind it a legendary aura of high drama'; and it was certainly the allocation of the decision-making function to juries which stimulated the more rhetorical advocacy of which Sir Edward Marshall Hall KC provided the paradigm example. In the trial of Edward Lawrence, a brewer charged with murder of a barmaid with whom he had had an adulterous affair, he for the first time performed the dramatic exhibition which came to be known as 'Hall's scales of justice act':

> It may appear that the scales of justice are first weighed on one side in favour of the prisoner, and then on the other against the prisoner. As counsel on either side puts the evidence in these two scales I can call to my fancy a great statute of justice holding those two scales with equally honest hands. As the jury watch the scales, they think for a moment that one scale, and then that the other, has fallen and then again that they are so level that they cannot make up their minds which was lower or higher. Then in the one scale, in the prisoner's scale, unseen by human eye, is placed that overbalancing weight, the weight of the presumption of innocence. When the balance is so struck that you cannot tell which pan is nearest the ground, then it is your duty to remember the invisible weight of that invisible substance – the right of every man to demand the acceptance of his innocence until he is proved guilty … I will leave it in your hands. Try this case upon the evidence, and upon the evidence with the help of God.

Mark Anthony said on the Capitol, 'If you have tears, prepare to shed them now.' Marshall Hall went one better. He cried himself.

But the pure jury advocate was like a one-club golf player. Marshall Hall fell short of true greatness because of his inability to adapt himself to his tribunal. He struggled in the appellate court. 'You must take this point', he would whisper loudly to his junior. 'There's some law in it.'

A more conversational style became fashionable by the turn of the last century in consequence of higher standards of etiquette, the increasing dignity of the Bench, the better education of juries. And nowadays with the virtual elimination of juries from civil litigation in England – with even such redoubts as defamation falling to be disposed of by judge alone, as in the Aitken and Irving cases – and the increasing worldliness of jurors in criminal courts, it has shifted decisively from cavalier to roundhead. 'Jury advocate', a term which used to be neutral, carries today a critical innuendo.

The impact of the rise of women in the profession has been profound. *Le style, c'est l'homme*: but also *le style, c'est la femme*. It was only as a result of the Sex Disqualification Removal Act 1919 that the first women were called to the Bar. Some men were sceptical of their chances of success. In a lecture in Cambridge in 1924, His Honour Judge Edward Parry made it clear that he considered that the key virtues of barristers were unevenly distributed between the sexes: 'Honesty and courage women have: but industry crushes them: wit they admire but do not possess. Eloquence they neglect: judgment they lack: fellowship is alien to them.'

And Henry Dickson KC wrote only a decade later:

> As to whether women are likely to make a real success in the profession in the future, it is rather too early to judge. I have had some experience of their work in the Central Criminal Court of late years: but I prefer to withhold my judgment on such a very delicate question at the present time.

Women, who now make up 50 per cent of the Bar have, you may feel, decisively and positively answered this delicate question.

Styles vary not only from century to century, and from gender to gender, but from country to country. My experience of American advocacy is culled from international arbitration, from watching televised trials, such as those of OJ Simpson and Louise Woodward, and from childhood exposure to the fictional and therefore unsurpassed advocacy of Perry Mason and his always dogged but always outgunned opponent, Hamilton Burger. I observe that in general what for the English advocate is hyperbole is understatement for the American attorneys – and for two main reasons. First (certainly) jury trials have remained in the USA a primary vehicle of dispute resolution in the civil (as well as in the criminal fields). Secondly, (speculatively) the guarantee of freedom of expression in the first amendment is seen as something whose existence invites maximum exploitation.

Some say that advocacy is capable of being taught. Its general techniques were considered by the Greeks even before Aristotle wrote his *Rhetoric*. Later the Romans, Cicero and then Quintilian, considered it specifically in the Court context.

In medieval England, the Bar provided the blueprint for a communal oral tradition of education based on lectures, moots and taking notes in court. From the beginning of the seventeenth century at least, the performance of learning exercises during the three years after call was a minimum requirement. While the practice of mooting was neglected after the Restoration – and in the eighteenth century ceased to play any part in legal training – it was revived in Gray's Inn in 1875 by His Honour Judge JA Russell QC, a Bencher. Holdsworth described legal education in the eighteenth century as 'a very melancholy topic'. In the nineteenth century, the Inns of Court sought to standardise their education: in 1852 the Council of Legal Education was created. Since 1988 the Bar Vocational Course has placed a double weight on advocacy compared to the other skills taught on the course. Neither Bar nor the Law Society impose any further training requirement relating to advocacy following the acquisition of the right to appear in any particular court.

Textbooks on advocacy proliferate – Page, Munkman, Napley, DuCann. Keith Evans has authored three books in a single decade – *The Golden Rules of Advocacy*, *Advocacy in Court*, *The Language of Advocacy* – a prime example of that old precept: 'say what you're going to say: say it: and say what you've said'. The authors naturally justify their existence by insisting that advocacy skills *can* be transmitted. Napley declined to entitle his book *The Art of Advocacy* since it conjured to his mind a natural gift rather than an acquired skill. Munkman was less certain: 'Advocacy is not a science like law, but an art, and, therefore to a great extent, it is a highly individual attainment …', but recovered himself to say:

> These rules of technique can be explained as learnt. They are like the principles of perspective and the use of colours in painting, or scales and arpeggios in music, and the making of incisions and the insertion of stitches in surgery.

Judge Michael Hyam sagely wrote 'even Mozart had to learn the technique of composition'.

But in *Rondel v Worsley* Salmon LJ said, 'Advocacy is not an exact science. It is an art. Whether a question should or should not be asked what witnesses should be called. What points should be taken, and how they should be taken, are all matters about which able and experienced counsel may differ.' And his was not a solitary doubt. Sir Peter Bristow wrote, 'You cannot find the advocacy skills in the books. You have to learn them from your betters and think them through for yourself as you go along.'

Such sceptics would paraphrase George Bernard Shaw in the context of education – 'Those who can do; those who can't teach' – with the proposition, in the context of the law, 'Those who can practise; those who can't instruct'.

I admit to an old-fashioned view that tuition in advocacy may be essential to achieve minimum standards, but will be incapable by itself of guiding the tutee to the higher rungs of achievement. In making the same essential point, AG Bowker, clerk to both Marshall Hall and Norman Birkett, drew the analogy between football players and advocates. I would myself prefer a metaphor from athletics: you can acquire stamina, but you are born with speed. The laudable BVC identifies advocacy, with a modicum of bathos, as a sub-species of 'inter-personal skills' – itself a sub-category of case-work skills and written skills, and highlights among the course's virtues: 'Advocacy … may be appraised by videoed performances of practical training', which provides 'a risk free environment that encourages you to develop and hold your skills in a realistic setting.' Risk-free it may be: realistic it is not! Even the most natural advocate, even the best taught, will not prosper without constant practice in the courts of law themselves. Sir Edward Coke was right to articulate a *via media* (or third way) which recognises the values of both forms of enhancement of the inborn skills, when he said 'causes which concern the life or inheritance or goods or fortunes of his subject are not to be decided by natural reason, but by the artificial reason and judgment of law, which law is an art which requires long study *and* experience before that a man can attain to the cognizance of it'.

So some people are born advocates; some achieve advocacy – but I would not advise the instinctively reticent to have advocacy thrust upon them!

And after all, the debate as to what makes a great advocate is endless. Judge Edward Parry's Seven Lamps, which he listed in his diatribe against women, were supplemented by Sir Patrick Hastings, who said of an opponent: 'He has four of the five attributes of a great advocate – presence, manner, intellect and voice – but lacks the most important, courage'; the four being more ingredients not writ of in Judge Parry's philosophy.

Lord Denning said more prosaically:

> Dress neatly, not slovenly. Be well groomed. Your voice must be pleasing, not harsh or dissonant. Pitch it so that all can hear without strain. Pronounce your consonants. Do not slur your words. Speak not too fast nor yet too slow. All these things are commonplace, but they are so often forgotten.

Physical presence, such as enjoyed by FE Smith or Marshall Hall or Edward Carson, may be God-given; neatness is not.

And both Lord Denning and Lord Atkin – a dynamic judicial duo indeed – were at one in stressing the importance of language: a voice may be God-given: vocabulary is not.

But the more old-fashioned tricks of the trade may be lost on modern juries, and would never appeal to the modern judge. Marshall Hall would make a grand entrance always *after* the opening of the case preceded by his clerk carrying his cushion and other odds and ends which he arranged. When his opponent started to make submissions, he picked up what appeared to be a scent spray and squirted it three or four times up his nostrils.

Sir Henry Curtis-Bennett, known as Harry, the epitome of the fashionable silk of the next decade, learned from the master. His entry into the courtroom with his clerk Hollis in attendance carrying his book, papers and coloured pencils, as well as his favourite lozenges, was described by his biographer as a piece of pure theatre. He gave a phrase (now obsolete) to the patois of the Bar, 'doing a Curtis'. The modern equivalent might be 'doing a Carman', that is to say, producing videos, letters, receipts and the like helpfully unearthed only at a critical moment in the trial, the product, however, more of luck than of showmanship.

Nor in these democratic days is there much utility in Sir Peter Bristow's advice, 'You need to study your tribunal's backgrounds and interests: in our chambers we kept a drawer full of old school and club and regimental ties. Should you, for example, deploy service, club or old school tie?'

The pre-eminent quality for the modern barrister (as for advocates down the ages) is simplicity. In the first century AD, Quintilian observed that lawyers should concern themselves only with the essential points: 'we must not always burden the judge with all the arguments we have discovered since by so doing we shall at once bore him and render him less inclined to believe us'.

Too elaborate an argument is always dangerous. Nothing fails in advocacy like excess.

Sorting the wheat from the chaff, identifying what is relevant, that is the key.

Adaptability is another vital quality. A quite different style is appropriate for different tribunals. What works before the Appellate Committee of the House of Lords at Westminster will not do so before a disciplinary tribunal of the Football Association at White Hart Lane. In the European Court of Justice at Luxembourg and the European Court of Human Rights at Strasbourg the English advocate endures the added terror of simultaneous translation. He must provide the interpreters with a text in advance, and a text in which the sentences are short. No sterner test of the advocate is presented than trying in Strasbourg to make – in translation – a smile flit across the flint-like face of the Icelandic judge.

Remember always that the object of the exercise is not to show how clever the advocate is, but how clever the judge is.

Yet these rules of thumb cannot capture that elusive X factor. One can only conclude:

> The successful advocate, of any generation, is the one who has the power, by persuasion to move the mind or the heart of the judge or jury. Many techniques may be available. It may be by cool logic or by legal rigorous analysis of the legal material. It may be by naked appeal to the emotions.

Great advocates still have their distinctive styles, if you like, their signature tunes. I can tell a phrase from Carman as easily as a melody from *Carmen*. A submission by Pannick is quite distinct from a submission by Pollock. The badges of excellence are not uniform.

And I do not believe that today's advocates cannot bend the bows of their predecessors. Those who so think are those who believe that all change is for the worse and that all difference is deterioration.

But I am concerned that advocacy as an art is nowadays under threat; and it is to the threats to it that I shall now turn. For much law reform, however benign in object, may carry with it insidious and unanticipated consequences.

The first enemy of advocacy is the contemporary pressure for brevity.

Historically, the pace of litigation was dictated by the Bar (in the same way as cases used to be fixed, as nowadays they rarely are, to suit counsel's convenience). This did not, I readily accept, always lead to the best use of court time. Within living memory, it was the function of junior counsel in a libel case in the High Court to open the pleadings to the jury. Nor was the position better at more elevated levels. As Sir Jack Jacob has observed until quite recently:

> The whole appeal was expounded and unfolded before the judges through the oral presentation of their respective cases by counsel on both sides, with no limit on the length of time each took to do so.

The pendulum now has swung decisively the other way. At the turn of the last decade, Lord Templeman excoriated the verbosity of counsel in a number of characteristically trenchant dicta uttered in a trilogy of cases.

The flavour of his observations is to be found in this passage from *Banque Keyser Ullmann*:

> The present practice is to allow every litigant unlimited time and unlimited scope so that the litigant and his advisers are able to conduct their case in all respects in the way which seems best to them. The results not infrequently are torrents of words, written

> and oral, which are oppressive and which the judge must examine in an attempt to eliminate everything which is not relevant, helpful and persuasive.

Nowadays the House of Lords conventionally demand time estimates from counsel refined to the nearest fraction of an hour. I am not aware of any advocate who has had the temerity to articulate his private thoughts on this instruction – 'with interruptions or without?'.

Lower courts follow the fashion.

The Commercial Court Guide, first produced in 1986, says that the judges 'will positively discourage oral procedures which are wasteful of time and costs without compensating advantage'. In 1986 the same court introduced time limits for interlocutory observations. In 1995 a civil litigation case management Practice Direction stated that the paramount importance of reducing the cost and delay of civil proceedings required the courts (and in particular first instance judges) to assert greater control than had hitherto been customary to identify crucial issues, to see that they are tried 'as expeditious and inexpensively as possible' and (critically) to limit 'the length of oral submissions and the time allowed for the examination and cross-examination of witnesses'. Among the key features of the new regime incarnated in the Civil Procedure Rules 1998 is the control of oral advocacy.

Though I plead guilty to being involved in a case in the House of Lords in which nine days were spent debating the construction of the phrase 'ordinarily resident', whose constituent words, their Lordships ultimately concluded, should be given their ordinary and natural meaning, I am not opposed in principle to brevity. As Leggatt LJ aptly observed, 'Increase in the intensity of oral argument may reasonably be expected to increase its quality.'

And while legal soap operas' most obvious lack of correspondence with forensic reality lies in their concentration of the timescales inherent in ordinary litigation, yet as an aficionado of that long-running Hollywood saga *LA Law*, I am impressed by the fact that in every episode the advocates' closing submissions to the jury managed to penetrate to the pith of the case in a clutch of short, sharp sentences, leaving one to wonder whether indeed there was any more to say.

But brevity should be a means to an end. My concern is that brevity may soon be seen, under these relentless pressures, as an end in itself. It may be the soul of wit, but it is not necessarily the heart of persuasion.

At the same time there has been a gradual substitution of written for oral advocacy. Although judges continually suggested that the one was to be complementary of the other, the reality has proved different.

The history is illuminating. The Working Party under Lord Scarman, set up in 1978 to report to Lord Denning on ways and means of relieving the pressure on the Court of Appeal, recommended a series of institutional and procedural changes, but expressly rejected the idea of 'curtailing or abridging the right to an oral hearing'. One of the novelties, the introduction of a so-called 'perfected notice of appeal', concealed within itself the germ of more fundamental reforms, the 'skeleton outline of ... respective arguments annotated by reference to the documents and authorities'. This was described by Donaldson MR on 4 October 1982 as 'another possibility', but it ripened into a mandatory practice direction by 12 April 1983, only mitigated by a statement that it 'in no way usurped any part of the function of oral argument in Court'. Just earlier the House of Lords in *MV Yorke Motors v Edwards*, exhorting use of more succinct printed cases, stated that the practice of the House – more honoured on occasion in the breach than the observance – to read in advance the printed case was *not* to bring about the submission of written briefs as used in the United States or 'to reduce the importance of the role played by oral argument in the decision making process'. Francis Mann, the very epitome of the scholar-solicitor, and a comparatist *sans pareil*, wrote ominously that 'it is possible to see in the developments, which have been described, the thin end of the wedge which will eventually lead to the American style brief and the practical elimination of the oral argument'.

It was a sea-change:

> From its creation in 1875 until 1955, the remarkable feature of the procedures of the Court of Appeal was that the judges came to hear the appeal entirely fresh knowing nothing about the case or the questions arising from their decision. There was no speaking notice of appeal until the latter date.

I recollect in an early case on equal pay in the Employment Appeal Tribunal where I was led by Anthony Lester, and opposed by Anthony Grabiner, in which a mere offer of written argument was rejected even in that avowedly modernising forum. By 1986 the Commercial Court mandated written submissions in advance. In 1989, by Practice Direction, skeleton arguments were for the first time made compulsory in the Court of Appeal. They had been voluntary for half a decade before that. In his introduction Lord Donaldson MR asserted that 'I cannot emphasise too strongly that the English Court of Appeal remains firmly wedded to its long established tradition of oral argument in open court'. The Crown Office List Practice Direction of 1994 is firmly prescriptive as to form.

In my experience, English courts have as yet adapted ill to the introduction of skeleton arguments; intended to curtail length and to diminish costs, they have on numerous occasions increased both. To be effective they demand discipline from both judge and advocate – mastery by the judge of the material alluded to in the skeleton argument in advance; acceptance by the advocate that the judge's task has been duly performed and that he may proceed to put forward submissions, not merely information.

As an advocate, I am well aware of the extent to which some of those judges who have read the skeleton argument come to depend upon it, sometimes saying, a little testily, 'Where is that in your skeleton?' as if one's mental processes both had and should have become entirely frozen the moment the skeleton was constructed.

As a judge, I am equally well aware of the advantage that someone who produces a timely, neatly presented and comprehensive skeleton has over someone whose skeleton lacks any of those essential qualities, especially where an unreserved judgment is required. In *R v IAT ex p Murugandarajah*, no less a person than the then Master of the Rolls said of my skeleton:

> I wanted to pay tribute to Mr Beloff's skeleton argument which is, if I may say so, probably the best skeleton argument I have seen for two reasons. First it goes one to two foolscap sheets of paper and contains in one-line summarises the whole scope of the argument. Secondly, he has uniquely borne in mind the fact that judges, at the end of the argument have to give a judgment and on the first page of his skeleton argument he has provided the whole of the necessary note in order that I might give this judgment in so far as it relates to non-contentious matters. If others would follow his example – and I will spare his blushes and not publish the terms of his skeleton argument – we would be faced with a very much easier task and might even be able to give ex tempore judgments.

Again, needless to say, consistent with the rule which earlier expounded, I lost the case, but the quotation serves to prove my current point.

The shift from the oral to the written is driven not by considerations of justice, but of economy – the motive force of so much contemporary law reform – or, at any rate, not of justice in the particular sense of the best disposition of the case before the court, but of justice in the general sense of oiling the wheels of the legal system overall.

And the development of sophisticated computer technology can only accelerate the move to a position when the judiciary becomes readership and not audience.

In *Morris v Bank of American National Trust* Morritt LJ said:

> There is no reason why the judge should not be provided with material in electronic form, such as pleadings, skeleton arguments and statements of issues, supported by hypertext (or other) links enabling him to move rapidly from what the claimant says about a matter to what a defendant says about a matter, or enabling him to take up a cross-reference to an earlier part of a document (or to another document) instantaneously. There is also no reason why more efforts should not be made to enable the judge to move rapidly by electronic means, in due course, from a skeleton argument to the case law or statutory material cited in the skeleton argument.'

Machine takes over from man in the brave new world of computerised justice!

All those changes reflect the new emphasis on judicial control. Judges have ceased to be referees: they have become players. The balance of power has shifted in favour of the judge and away from the advocate, as illustrated, in another way, now trickling up from the Court of Appeal to House of Lords, by the use of judicial assistants to supply the court with material (comparative or academic) which it used to be the responsibility of the advocate (if anyone) to provide.

Francis Mann may have put it too high when he posed the stark-termed options between a system where the judge comes into court with an open mind (the traditional English system) or where he comes in with a mind shaped by preconceptions generated by the reading of the papers (or I would now add), a steer from his assistant, but my experience suggests that he was right to predict:

> It is the oral argument which is bound to lose its force where it is no longer a dialogue in the traditional sense, but an attempt to dislodge or fortify an existing impression, however provisional it may be said to be. The danger is that in course of time we reach the position prevailing on the continent where it is a very great exception that the 'oral argument' (which hardly ever occurs) succeeds in changing judicial views formed as a result of pre-reading.

I am painfully aware about how the dialogue with the Bench in fact forces new thinking not hinted at the skeleton itself. So my concern is not only with the cramping of the advocate's style, but with the deterioration of the judge's decision.

Advocates face new pressures too from other developments. For the first time from 1 October 1991 counsel were exposed to liability for costs incurred by a party 'as a result of any improper, unreasonable or negligent act or omission'.

The dangers to counsel saddled with obstreperous or obtuse clients are obvious. Bingham MR said in *Ridehalgh v Horsefield*:

> Legal representatives will, of course, whether barristers or solicitors, advise clients of the perceived weakness of their case and of the risk of failure. But clients are free to reject that advice and insist that cases be litigated, whereas in *R. v. Horsham DC ex p. Wenman* Brooke J, said 'Counsel must also remember professional duty not to set his name to a plea which he does not consider to be 'properly arguable'. The tension between these two dicta may be soluble in theory by identifying the second as a qualification of the first but counsel will have to navigate between the Scylla of abandoning his client and the Charybdis of putting his own purse at risk. We have moved some way from the confidence of Lord Brougham's exposition of his defence of Queen Caroline.
>
> An advocate by the sacred duty of his connection with his client knows in the discharge of their office, but one person in the world and no-one other. To save that client by all expedient means – to protect that client at all hazards and costs to all others – and among others to himself – is the highest and most unquestioned of his duties.

Lord Brougham's concept of the cost to himself that an advocate might run embraced loss of friendship or favour, not vulnerability to pay for the litigation itself. The threat of wasted costs orders may not only make counsel overly defensive but, in some circumstances, overly aggressive. Aldous J has observed that there is a danger that applications for wasted costs orders can be used at an interlocutory stage to harass the other side's advocate and so diminish his objectivity by making him more obdurate in his client's defence.

The dilemma faced by counsel who wish to be loyal to para 203 of the Code of Conduct, which provides that a practising barrister 'must promote and protect fearlessly and by all proper and lawful means his lay client's best interests and do so without regard to his own interests or to any consequences to himself or to any other person' are most vividly exposed in *Vernon v Bosley (No 2)*. In that case, a claim for post-traumatic stress disorder in a personal injury action, counsel did not reveal to court unhelpful psychiatric reports from family proceedings involving the plaintiff, which came into being after the hearing of the action but before judgment. There was a three-way split on the Bench as to what was the proper course. Evans LJ thought no disclosure was necessary at all, Stuart Smith LJ that counsel should have advised the client to make disclosure or withdraw from the case, Thorpe LJ that counsel should have disclosed the reports himself. The compass was scarcely steady. Thorpe LJ said (revealingly):

> In general terms the balance between the advocate's duty to the client and the advocate's duty to the court must reflect evolutionary change within the civil justice system. If evolutionary shifts are necessary to match civil justice reforms they should in my judgment be towards strengthening the duty to the Court.

If that be right, we are one step further down the path in which advocates are transformed from pugilists, even if operating under the Bar's own Queensbury rules, to cogs in a bureaucratic litigation machine.

But counsel are not only now liable in some circumstances for costs; they may soon be liable for damages too. The Courts and Legal Services Act 1990, s 6 enshrined the immunity of barristers from suits in negligence in respect of the carriage of a case in court and the pre-trial work connected with it, confirmed in *Rondel v Worsley* and reiterated *Saif Ali v Sydney Miller & Co (a firm)*. But this immunity is now under review in the House of Lords.

The perceptions of public policy which informed the earlier judgments (not least that unsuccessful clients would use negligence suits as a means of reopening the decision, which went against them), may have changed. It is cogently argued that a reform of the law would be designed to deter not combative, but incompetent counsel. But if the old principle is abandoned, there will be one more stimulus to defensive advocacy.

Lord Reid, more than 30 years ago, observed, although with all a lawyer's characteristic mountain of qualification, 'I do not think it at all improbable that the possibility of being sued for negligence would at least subconsciously lend some advocates to undue prolixity'. So counsel will be trapped between judges who want him to shut up and clients who want him to go on.

It is not only the means by which litigation is conducted, but litigation itself which is under threat. The 1980s saw the transplant of this transatlantic device of alternative dispute resolution to England, which could in theory make litigation as obsolete a way of settling differences as duelling. Certainly so astute an observer of the legal scene as Joshua Rozenberg has been prompted to ask seriously, 'what chance is there that alternative dispute resolution should supplant the Courts?'

The Commercial Court in 1993 issued a practice statement which said: 'While emphasising the primary role of the commercial court as a forum for deciding commercial cases, the Judges of the Court wish to encourage parties to consider the use of ADR.' The Civil Procedure Rules 1998 places further emphasis on mediation, conciliation and other forms of ADR. Now billable hours are billable hours whether the lawyer is involved in ADR or in trials. But the courtroom is the habitat for the specialist advocate. And in the same way as destruction of the rainforest robs the planet of a variety of species, so the pure advocate becomes endangered to the extent that his environment is confined.

And what will be the character and capacity of the advocates who roam like the Asian tiger in an ever more restricted terrain? Under the Courts and Legal Services Act 1990, suitable qualified solicitors were enabled to acquire rights of audience in the High Court. Next, the Access to Justice Act 1999 removed the two main constraints on the Lord Chancellor's powers to exceed such rights, the advice of the Advisory Committee on Legal Education and Conduct, and the veto given in the 1990 Act to the four senior judges on any proposal to enlarge rights of audience in the higher courts. I note *en passant* the shift from a purely factual short title of the legislation in 1990 to the spin doctors' concoction of its 1999 successor.

Assigning the right to a government minister to decide who can, or who cannot, practise in the courts of law, poses in theory, if not in imminent fact, the risk that the advocate of the future, when not an employee of the state (as for example are Crown prosecutors or – in future – public defenders), but will be a state licencee. Lord Steyn, in particular, has exposed the constitutional consequences of such a development. But at a more mundane level there is a risk that the Bar will wither on the vine if its roots, if the new entrants to the profession, who (I should note) appear to me to be of ever increasing ability, are deprived of the soil in which they naturally grow – day-to-day litigation in the courts below the appellate levels, fertilised, if I may continue the agricultural metaphor, by adequate remuneration from the public purse. Silks do not spring fully developed like Athena from Zeus's head – and certainly would lack her wisdom if they did so.

Sedley J has articulated a 'real worry' about 'the eventual absorption by solicitors of all but the heaviest advocacy', because to the extent that solicitors exploit their new advocacy opportunities, 'the incremental experience which finally makes a reliable barrister will dry up and the Bar itself will finally die'. 'To let this happen,' he added, 'would … be a tragedy for a skill in which this country has for generations been a world leader'. May I add a piping note of my own to his sonorous reveille. The Bar should, indeed must, accept competition from solicitors: but solicitors should take steps to ensure that fair competition does not result in the elimination of an expert resource, which should, unless my other fears are realised, always be required.

There is, of course, no consensus among civilised nations that to do justice requires the court to enjoy – or endure – unrestricted or even extended oral advocacy. In the United States Supreme Court 30 minutes is the rule; and the Chief Justice, like some judicial Sweeney Todd, can cut the throat of the advocate in mid-sentence. And the European Court of Justice operates a similar practice, if a little less ruthlessly.

In both fora written briefs are the real weapons. Indeed, the English advocate who appears for the first time in Luxembourg may wonder if the Court is concerned with anything but time limits as a result of the charming pre-hearing encounter between Bar and Bench in the President's chambers, to quote from an essay by Richards J and myself.

> There may be some question about the order of speeches or some guidance from the reporting judge or Advocate General about points to address or not to address in the course of the speeches. But the real object of the exercise is to bargain for time. Before the hearing one has been asked to estimate the length of one's submissions. Thirty minutes as a maximum; it betrays naïveté to ask for more; one will be treated like some forensic Oliver Twist. The trick is to ask for something imprecise and qualified – 'I hope to be no more than twenty or so minutes' – which gives the impression of intended brevity, while – on close textual analysis – preserving one's right to the full half hour. But whatever one says, the President has a ready counter:
>
> – Twenty minutes, perhaps fifteen.
> – I will try, M le President.
> – After all [with a gallic shrug – the shrug will be gallic, irrespective of the provenance of the President] we have read it all already.

With luck, in a case involving English parties, the exchanges will take place in English. But it could be French, which is the working language of the Court – especially if there is a substantial number of interveners. A knowledge of the French numbers between 10 and 30 ('Vingt Minutes, M le President') is a great aid to confidence. But if in doubt about what has been said, seek confirmation in English rather than take the risk of stepping to the podium at the wrong time or presenting energetic submissions on a question that you have just been told it is unnecessary to address.

But even in that abbreviated procedure, the English advocate tends (if I may be chauvinistic) to outshine his continental colleagues. Lord Slynn has written, 'A stranger would quickly realise which lawyers come from a country where oral advocacy and debate between the judge and the lawyer is the norm.'

Some judges' vision of the future is expressed pithily by Lightman J. 'The trial procedure is abridged: the hearing is essentially limited to the briefest of openings and closing speeches (often little more than question and answer sessions between judges and counsel) and the examination of witnesses)'. I find the prospect an alarming one. I continue to believe that as Hankford J said in 1409, 'le ley per bon disputacion serra bien conus', and 560 years later

Megarry J repeated, 'today, as of old, by good disputing shall the law be well known'.

Lord Macmillan said, 'There are some who would malign the art of the advocate as dishonest and morally degrading. The charge is as old as Plato and so is its refutation.' Advocacy is not given free rein. It operates within a series of rules and conventions formerly passed down like tribal myths by word of mouth and example from one generation of advocates to another. They were codified in Boulton's classic, *Conduct and Etiquette at the Bar*, which ran for six editions from 1953 until 1975, and finally set out by the Bar Council from 1986 in a handbook.

Paragraph 601 of the contemporary Code of Conduct enshrines the nine cardinal rules over and above the barristers' 'a paramount duty to the court', which 'will require him to act in a variety of ways to the possible disadvantage of his client', that such barrister (and I paraphrase):

- has personal responsibility and judgment in respect of a case;
- must express no personal opinion of facts or law;
- must ensure that the court is informed of relevant decisions or legislative provisions;
- must adduce no evidence otherwise and from or through the professional clients;
- must devise no facts which will assist in advancing the lay client's case;
- must make no scandalous statements and ask no unwarranted questions;
- must avoid, if possible, naming in open court a third party whose character may be criticised.
- must not impugn any witness whom he or she has had the opportunity of cross-examining unless such witness has been given opportunity to rebut the allegations;
- must make no suggestion of fraud or misconduct unless such suggestion is supported by evidence.

The advocate who, for political or ideological reasons, too ardently identifies himself with his client's case violates the precepts of his profession as well as doing his client a disservice. Advocates may – indeed often should – simulate conviction in their client's case: but at all times the court should be aware that it is the client's case and not the advocate's which is before it.

Above all, a barrister must observe the cab rank rule which prohibits the advocates from picking and selecting their clients on political grounds, on the popularity of the client's cause, or on whim, and is to barristers what the Hippocratic Oath is to doctors. It is as important an element of the Bar's code of conduct as can be found – a matter of high constitutional importance, and the essence of the refutation of the criticism of advocates, as amoral mercenaries, which Lord Macmillan had in mind.

As Lord Pearce observed in *Rondel v Worsley*:

> It is easier, pleasanter and more advantageous professionally for barristers to advise, represent or defend those who are decent and reasonable and likely to succeed in their action or their defence than those who are unpleasant, unreasonable, disreputable and have an apparently hopeless case. Yet it would be tragic if our legal system came to provide no reputable defenders, representatives or advisers for the latter, and that would be the inevitable result of allowing barristers to pick and choose their clients.

Erskine put the matter unanswerably in justification of his defence of Thomas Paine, author of *The Rights of Man* and English supporter of the French Revolution, in 1792. His words are compelling more than two centuries later:

> I will at all hazards, assert the dignity, independence, and integrity of the English Bar, without which impartial justice, the most valuable part of the English Constitution, can have no existence. From the moment that any advocate can be permitted to say that he will or will not stand between the Crown and the subject arraigned in Court where he daily sits to practice, from that moment the liberties of England are at an end.

So it is that the Code of Conduct of the Bar for England and Wales can say of the barrister, that, subject to exceptions which in no way undermine the fundamental principle:

> He must in any field in which he professes to practice irrespective of whether his client is paid privately or is legally aided or otherwise publicly funded (a) accept any brief to appear before a Court … (b) accept any instruction … (c) act for any person.

Erskine's proposition is of course as memorable for the style in which it is couched as for the sentiments it articulates. In comparison, the Bar code is merely prose to his poetry. But the substance is more important than the style.

If advocacy can indeed be art, it is not art for art's sake; nor is its aesthetic quality its main, let alone its only, justification. In a society dedicated to the rule of law, advocacy is the shield of right, and the sword of freedom.

# 4

# 'Virtuous Voices – The Advocate's Contribution to the Rule of Law'

# MacDermott Lecture 2014*

IT IS A great privilege for me to be invited to deliver this annual lecture in honour of Lord MacDermott, one of the most eminent alumni of, and teachers at, this university, and a judge of international reputation. Unlike his august successors in the office of Lord Chief Justice of Northern Ireland, he took up that post *after* rather than before becoming a Lord of Appeal in Ordinary in what was surely an *upwardly* mobile career move.

Lord Kerr, last year's MacDermott lecturer, in his felicitous opening remarks, acknowledged how daunting it was to follow so long a line of distinguished lawyers to the lectern. I feel no less daunted in following Lord Kerr, not least because, whether I appeared before him in the High Court in Belfast, in the House of Lords, or in the Supreme Court, I cannot recollect ever having been the recipient of a judgment in my client's favour. I for my part fear that next year's MacDermott lecturer, whoever he or she may be, will feel absolved from any need to pay any tribute to his or her immediate predecessor.

I never had the pleasure of meeting Lord MacDermott, but, in 1964, as a recent history graduate converting to law and in search of a sound guide to law's fundamental purpose and principles, I read his Hamlyn lectures delivered in 1957 on the theme 'Protection from Power under English Law', the epithet 'English' being descriptive of the nature of the law being considered rather than imposing some geographical limitation. They included a prescient chapter on the power of the Executive, which looked forward to the modernisation of the supervisory jurisdiction, still at what Professor Sir William Wade QC has characterised as 'a low ebb' but whose engagement Lord MacDermott described as work frequently requiring 'skill of a high order'. That Delphic reference apart, Lord MacDermott did not comment on what contribution, if any, lawyers (other than judges) made to the protection from power which he regarded as an aspect of the Rule of Law. He contented himself only with the cautious observation that 'lawyers as a body are slow to depart from the settled way of things'.

* (2014) 65 *Northern Ireland Legal Quarterly* 429.

It is, however, the nature of that contribution which I wish to explore in your company tonight. While my theme, the advocate's contribution to the Rule of Law, is intrinsically perennial and knows no boundaries of time or place, my illustrations, to provide practical underpinning to otherwise theoretical and rootless musings, will be topical. They will focus from a barrister's perspective on recent events in England and Wales – that entity that, for the present at any rate, we can still describe as part, but not the whole of Great Britain. Rudyard Kipling penned the line 'What do they know of England who only England know?', to which my manifestly inadequate response has to be 'more at any rate of England than of the world beyond'.

At one level one may appreciate Lord MacDermott's abstinence from the theme. After all is it not elementary that law, where not made by legislation, primary or secondary, or in exercise of the ever diminishing prerogative powers, is made by judges, and not by those who argue cases before them? But that is surely not the whole picture.

In a letter to *The Times* on 10 February of this year from the Chairman of the Bar Council, sundry heads of Bar associations and a single female pupil barrister – the inclusion of the latter being a somewhat transparent forensic tactic – the signatories fulminated 'As the Lord Chancellor finalizes plans to cut legal aid even further, barristers are coming to voice a unified opposition to changes which, if implemented, would have a devastating effect on the public's access to justice and The Rule of Law' – the initials in the latter phrase being given, for emphasis, capital letters. One is tempted to comment, if unfairly, that, adapting Mandy Rice-Davies's legendary riposte when told that Lord Astor had denied having an affair with her, 'Well he would say that wouldn't he?' It requires no particularly penetrating insight to note that there will also be a devastating effect on counsel's fees, where dependent on the public purse, and on their expectations, whether legitimate or otherwise, of a certain standard of living whatever that might be.

On 11 July 2013 in an earlier, more measured response, as befits the second chamber, Baroness Deech, Chair of the Legal Services Board, introduced a motion to take note 'of the effects of cuts in legal aid funding on the justice system in England and Wales'. She ended her speech by saying that she was 'convinced that the protection of the profession and of the public that is enshrined in Section 1 of the Legal Services Act will be undermined by the proposals of the Ministry of Justice as they stand'. There was scarcely any speaker who did not invoke the concept of the Rule of Law to justify their assault on the Government's proposals.

This debate between the Ministry of Justice and the Bar Council has been played out in the public eye. The Justice Secretary wishes to cut £200 million from the legal aid budget by 2018/2019. He claims that expenditure on legal aid is in relative terms higher than in countries of equivalent size and standing. The Bar Council accuse him of dodgy dossiers, which seek to suggest that the earnings of the few so-called fat cats are trumpeted to distract attention from the multitude of starving kittens. One QC went so far as to argue that he could be charged with furthering his career by making false statements in contravention of section 2 of the Fraud Act 2006. Into that debate I shall not seek to enter save to say that the Bar Council seem to have currently the better of the general argument since Sir Andrew Dilnot, head of the UK Statistics Authority, has warned the Ministry of Justice that its figures 'were indeed calculated to mislead'.

The resistance of the profession to that proposed diminution in public funding came to a head when barristers declined either to defend alleged fraudsters whose cases fell within the category of so-called 'very high cost cases' in response to the Government's threat to impose cuts of 30 per cent in fees on top of a series of previous reductions, or to accept briefs for cases where colleagues were double booked – so called 'returns'. They intensified that resistance with a day of strikes on 6 January 2014, with a second round on 7 March 2014 – the efficacy of the former only somewhat impaired by the fact that one of a cohort of young female barristers, carefully posed for the mandatory press photograph, was carrying a Louis Vuitton handbag. On 27 March 2014 the Justice Secretary agreed to postpone implementation of the savings until after the election in 2015 – a truce, if not an armistice. Not this year, but next year, which could mean, depending on the vagaries of the popular vote, sometime, but not, I suspect, never.

To put these controversies over remuneration into some context, I read in a recent biography of Thomas Scrutton, the great commercial judge, that at the bar in the late Victorian era – well before the notion of legal aid was even a glimmer in the governmental eye – fashionable leaders were paid a brief fee whether or not they actually appeared in court – oh happy days! – and the reference in the law reports to juniors accompanied by the parenthesis (with Mr X QC) actually meant, not infrequently, 'without Mr X QC'.

But is the reference to the Rule of Law, whether in *The Times* letter or in the House of Lords, a mere rhetorical flourish or would the extinction of the professional advocate – to press the point to its limits – actually threaten the rule of law – a protean concept, but which I shall use in the narrow sense of ensuring that justice is done according to law rather than in the broader sense of ensuring that the law itself is just and, if so, why.

Let me start with a statement so obvious that it is often overlooked. While legal giants debate whether hard cases make bad law – Oliver Wendell Holmes taking one view, Lord Denning another – what is beyond argument is that it is *cases* that make law.

Disputes about what the law on a particular issue is, or should be, the stuff of academic commentary or of mooting competitions. Nonetheless, until some litigant, sometimes on the advice of counsel, sometimes against it, chooses to bring the matter to court, the issue will be undecided. (I have here omitted reference to the litigant in the dock, who lacks the essential element of choice.)

And the cases so brought have to reflect real issues. The civil courts will only exceptionally grant declaratory judgments about whether some person's conduct, actual or anticipated, would violate the law of the land, if the question is likely to come before, a fortiori is actually before, the criminal courts. In private law it is well established that the courts will not decide hypothetical cases, and even in public law, where there has been some relaxation of that stern rule; as Lord Slynn put it in *ex parte Salem*, 'Appeals which are academic between the parties should not be heard unless there is a good reason in the public interest for doing so'. It is no part of the judge's role to give unsolicited advisory opinions.

There are related restraints on what can or cannot be the subject of adjudication at the highest level. The Supreme Court nowadays has almost complete control over its docket, but can only select from cases, contested before the lower courts, and in which there is an application for permission to appeal; and even then, for the most part, maintains the practice that it will not decide points which counsel has not argued. In short, judges consume what the advocate cooks.

Advocates need not merely serve up a *table d'hôte* or even a standard *à la carte* menu. They can be more creative. Two of what are now standard interlocutory remedies in private law – the Mareva Injunction, which prevents dissipation of assets before judgment is delivered; and the Anton Piller order, which prevents potential destruction of evidence of infringements of intellectual property – were both the inventions of counsel in the respective cases which bear the remedy's name. In the former, Lord Denning MR said Mr Rix – later a senior judge in the Court of Appeal – 'has been very helpful'. In the latter case, Lord Denning MR attributed 'credit' or, as he said with uncharacteristic caution, 'responsibility' to Hugh Laddie – later a High Court judge in the Chancery Division. When these developments of the jurisdiction to grant injunctive relief were sought in association, they permitted one traditionally educated judge elegantly to make a classical pun by speaking of 'piling Piller on Mareva' in lieu – as you will all of course be aware – of 'piling Pelion on Ossa', which described, in the Greek myth, the use made of these mountains by the giants Otus and Ephialtes to storm Olympus. Since the use of Latin in our courts is now frowned upon, such gratuitous displays of judicial scholarship are, alas, unlikely to be repeated.

And even if sometimes an advocate seems to bend the bow too far, and provoke astringent judicial observations about his 'fertile mind' – on a par with the phrase 'with the greatest respect' which, in the court context, means its exact opposite – in other instances the fertility bears palatable fruit. *Ridge v Baldwin* stands out as one of the major cases which started to reshape public law in the swinging sixties, and where Lord Reid was able to chart how once lively concepts of natural justice had been diverted into a dark tunnel but could now be exposed again to light. But it was Desmond Ackner QC, later a Law Lord and the outstanding advocate of his generation, whose submissions, as the law report reveals, helped shape Lord Reid's speech. At the other end of the scale, one may instance Lord Nicholls' magisterial clarification of the law of resulting trusts in the Privy Council in an appeal from Brunei, where I was counsel for the victorious appellant, but where the most charitable reading of the summary of my submissions could discern no visible connection between them and the advice given by the Board to Her Majesty. Indeed, I confess that there was none!

These examples, whether of the sublime or of the ridiculous, remind one of another important matter. In England the adversarial process, even in the highest courts, is essentially, if not exclusively, an oral process. We have not yet replicated the procedures of the US Supreme Court where advocates are conventionally limited to half an hour with no injury time for the frequent interruptions usually caused by the Justices arguing amongst themselves. Still less have we replicated the processes of the European Court of Justice where the only golden rule is that the proceedings must conclude in time for a leisurely lunch, and the pre-hearing courtesy meeting in the judges' chambers resembles a bazaar in which the President will seek to bargain down the half hour presumptively allotted to each of the lawyers. Even in Singapore, a noted custodian of the colonial legal tradition, an appellate judge, Rajah JA, recently noted in an argument about whether overseas counsel Lord Goldsmith, the former Attorney General, should be admitted to plead a case, 'The appellate process in the Singapore Court of Appeal has evolved to be more writing-centred than that in many other common law systems.' It would be too austere to conclude that written submissions do not equate to advocacy, but nonetheless it is surely the dialogue between Bench and Bar which gives oral advocacy not only its savour but its strength.

For in a classic adversarial system it is appreciated that it is out of the clash of submissions that the judgments will be fashioned. Lord Eldon, twice Lord Chancellor in the early nineteenth century and for an unrivalled period of 26 years, said 'Truth is best discovered by powerful statements on both sides of the question', though (as is well known) he sometimes took an unconscionable amount of time to decide what the truth was. The essay on him in the *Oxford Dictionary of National Biography* refers to 'the arrears with which he was constantly reproached' – an odd literary epitaph for someone whose maxim was that 'a lawyer should live like a hermit and work like a horse'. Lord Pannick QC in his keynote address to the Bar Conference in 2013 put it more amply:

> the law is best administered by independent judges who hear arguments on both sides of a case before they make up their mind. The advocate exemplifies the valuable principle that there is always another point of view, a different perspective, an alternative explanation

and Mr Justice Megarry in his judgment in *Cordell v Clanfield Properties* more pithily 'argued law is tough law' citing in support a dictum of Hankford J of 1409, which he had excavated from the Year Books, and which, though in a mixture of medieval French and Latin, lost nothing in translation: 'Today, as of old, by good disputing shall the truth be known.'

And in such a system, in both criminal and civil cases, it is the advocate who decides what material is placed before the court. The common law system is not inquisitorial. The judge can rule on what evidence is or is not admissible – though rules as to admissibility are becoming ever more flexible – but he cannot compel an advocate to adduce particular evidence, nor can he search out evidence himself, nor, critically, must he enter into the arena in the way in which he did as an advocate – a habit that some judges find easier to foreswear than others!

And when there is a fact-finding body whom the judge must direct, his duty is to sum up the facts and identify the competing arguments, not to find facts, or fashion arguments of his own.

In the Channel Islands, the tribunal of fact is constituted by jurats, and the trial judge, the office-holder sometimes being a Commissioner, has a different role, but the basic principle of judicial restraint remains the same. In a recent case on an appeal from Jersey, the Privy Council said:

> Naturally, in Jersey, where the facts are decided by the Jurats (the Commissioner retiring with the Jurats but not joining in the fact-finding unless the Jurats disagree), the facts are not summed up. But that cannot begin to justify the Commissioner seeking to give the Jurats the benefit of his analytical powers by way of his own extensive examination of the witnesses, or indicating his thinking by the nature of his questions and comments.

The judge then is a referee, not a player. So it was that Sir Robin Dunn, who ended his career on the English Court of Appeal, wrote in his memoir, 'It was not until I became a judge that I realised how dependent the Bench is upon the Bar'. That realisation was not the less accurate for being somewhat belated.

Advocacy, the source of that dependency is, in so far as it is an art at all, a transient one. Even a transcript cannot capture the immediacy of its impact – assuming it has an impact upon its audience – the tribunal to whom it is properly addressed. Televised trials will capture it a little better and will at least add to civic understanding as long as advocates are not seduced into playing to the gallery rather than focusing their attention on those whom it is their function to seek to persuade; I confess that *I* have never been tempted in the Supreme Court to think that the object of my exercise is to provide entertainment to that quixotic group, who, for whatever inexplicable reason, while away their daytime in watching the court's dedicated channel.

'You cannot', as yet another retired judge Sir Peter Bristow said in his memoirs – autobiography is an occupational hazard of judges who have hung up their wigs – 'find the advocacy skills in the books. You have to learn them from your betters and think them through for yourself as you go along.' Dame Elizabeth Lane, the first woman to be appointed to the High Court Bench in England, in hers identified four pillars of advocacy, which can be summarised as good health, good temper, good voice and, last but by no means least, good luck.

Some adopt more subtle, even suspect, techniques. Peter Bristow recalled: 'In our Chambers we kept a drawer full of old school and club and regimental ties? Should we for example deploy service, club or old school tie?' This anachronistic advice is of limited utility, unless the advocate was appearing unrobed before a judge, and of no utility when he appeared in full legal fig before a jury – there are no old school bands – and, equally, utterly useless for the female advocate.

George Carman, the so-called silver fox – the vulpine metaphor being favoured for defamation lawyers – certainly had Dame Elizabeth's fourth *desideratum*; in no less than three of his major forensic triumphs, his case for the defence was rescued by the adventitious – or so one must assume – arrival of a critical piece of evidence midway through or even just before the end of the trial. In two of them he established that the TV journalist Jani Allen and TV soap star Gillian Taylforth, who each sued in respect of allegations of exotic sexual activity, were far from vestal virgins. (I must declare an interest as the unsuccessful counsel for the plaintiff in the latter). In the third he established that Jonathan Aitken MP, who defended a claim that, when a minister, he had allowed his bill at the Ritz Hotel in Paris to be paid by rich Arabs with whom he was dealing, on the basis that the bill had been paid at reception by his wife, was guilty of perjury since last-minute evidence from British Airways showed that, at the material time, his wife had actually been in Switzerland, of which judicial notice could be taken that Paris is *not* the capital city.

Yet other advocates rise to the top by techniques that *appear* counterproductive. Lord Devlin's account of the trial over which he presided of Dr John Bodkin Adams, accused but acquitted of murdering his patients in anticipation of a legacy, contains this cameo description of leading counsel for the prosecution:

> His disagreeableness was so pervasive, his persistence so interminable, the obstructions he manned, so far flung, his objectives so apparently insignificant, that sooner or later you were bound to ask whether the game was worth the candle, and if you asked yourself that you were finished.

This did not, however, impede the career of the object of judicial derision, Sir Reginald Manningham Buller, immortalised by the journalist Bernard Levin as 'Sir Reginald Bullying Manner', who held in succession both law offices of the Crown, ascended to the Woolsack and ended his professional life as a Lord of Appeal in Ordinary with the title Viscount Dilhorne.

How much influence advocates in fact have on the outcome of cases is not capable of exact measurement. According to Alan Paterson in his recent seminal study of how judgments have been and are reached in the Court of Final Appeal, a number of his interviewees from the ranks of counsel 'were sceptical as to how often in the final court advocacy had a determinative effect on the ultimate outcome of appeals', whereas, 'the Law Lords and Justices were in general rather more positive as to the impact of good advocacy', as he put it, 'fortunately'. Were it not so, many clients would be paying substantial fees to no purpose.

In *Torfaen Borough County Council v Douglas Willis Ltd*, a consumer protection case brought against the company for selling food past its use-by date, where the Supreme Court was deprived of argument on both sides from the Bar, Lord Toulson commented in his leading judgment:

> The company was not represented on hearing of the appeal. The reasons are understandable but the result is unfortunate. It is a small family company. In these circumstances the court asked a member of its legal staff to prepare a note of points

> which might have been made on behalf of the company. ... Nevertheless it is still unfortunate that the Court did not have the benefit of argument from both sides.

If the size of the contribution of the advocate to the resolution of civil cases may be debatable, it is all but dispositive in criminal cases with a lay, not legal, tribunal of fact – magistrate or jury. Lord Judge, the recently retired Lord Chief Justice of England and Wales, said:

> The administration of justice depends on the quality of the advocacy deployed on each side. The jury will do its conscientious best. The Judge will make the decisions and give the directions believed by him to be appropriate. But the analysis of each side's case and all the evidence, and its importance to the case, so as to enable both judge and jury to exercise their own responsibilities depends upon high quality advocacy. And we are not discussing some disembodied theory. This is the day to day stuff of reality. It is in the public interest that the guilty should be convicted. It is in the public interest, as well as the interest of the innocent defendant, that he should be acquitted. For a truly innocent defendant to be convicted is a disaster. These disasters happen even in the best run trials with the best quality advocacy. Poor quality advocacy by either side simply increases the prospects of the guilty being acquitted, or the innocent being convicted. In the process of adversarial trial before a jury it really is as stark and simple as that.

As Lord Pannick said in the same speech to which I have already referred, 'the work of lawyers on legal aid ... makes an essential contribution to the administration of justice, defending the innocent and validating the conviction of the guilty'. Nor is the matter of concern only to the particular prosecution or defence. It bears precisely on the confidence that the community has in the legal system as a public service.

Now, given that advocates have so vital a role to play, it is imperative that they are not free to pick and choose when to play it. In May 2012 the Legal Services Board, the legal regulator's own regulator, ever enthusiastic to bend the bow of its novel powers, commissioned two academics to analyse the impact on the market of the cab rank rule by which barristers are, in broad terms, obliged, subject to availability, adequacy of expertise and absence of conflict of interest, to represent any person who calls upon their services, however distasteful that person's character or cause. This duty has since at least the time of Henry VII been part of the creed of the profession. Nonetheless in their report published in 2013 the academics concluded 'the logic of our report argues that the rule serves no clear purpose ... while it can be lauded as a professional principle enshrining virtuous values, as a rule it is redundant'.

They based themselves first on pure economic literature, which they described as 'scant' and which they regarded as 'very sparse and ultimately not very illuminating', second on interviews with so-called 'stakeholders', whose testimony was given in exchange for a guarantee of anonymity, and third on sundry blogs and tweets. This may seem a fragile foundation on which to recommend abolition of a professional rule which dates back several centuries, but this is no way deterred the authors.

There were three main points of suggested substance argued by them against retention of the rule: first, that other providers of legal services are not subject to it, so why should the Bar be so subject?; second, that the rule has not been enforced and so is meaningless; and third that one of its purported rationales is devoid of force since there is no real problem with barristers being associated with their clients, and so being dissuaded from providing representation to those whose cases do not, for whatever reason, engage immediate, or, indeed, any sympathy.

As to the first – the fact that other providers of legal services do not adopt the higher standard of conduct required by the rule – can surely not be a reason for abolishing the application of the rule to the Bar which supports its retention. If anything, it is an argument for application of the rule to those other providers. To enshrine the lowest common denominator in the practices of all branches of the legal professions is not the most obvious way to promote the Rule of Law.

As to the second the assertion – that because 'there is no evidence that it has ever been the subject of enforcement proceedings' it serves no useful purpose and is not in fact adhered to – is likewise a strange piece of reasoning. The fact proceedings have not been brought to enforce a rule does not mean that it has no effect on conduct. Indeed, quite the contrary, conclusion will often flow: namely, that the rule *is* efficacious and *does* in fact guide conduct.

The rule contains an important statement of principle about the aspirations of the Bar and of the values which it, and indeed, society seeks to pursue.

As to the third, as explained by Lord Hobhouse in *Arthur Hall v Simons*, the rule protects barristers against being criticised for 'giving their services to a client with a bad reputation' as it negates the identification of the advocate with the cause of his client. It therefore assists to provide him or her with protection against Governmental or popular victimisation.

There is, contrary to the academics' premise, a real and present-day problem of counsel being associated, wrongly, with the cause they pursue for their clients. In 2012 two Asian barristers withdrew from the trial of a group of Asian men accused of running a paedophile ring (referred to by the media as 'the Rochdale grooming trial') after being intimidated and physically assaulted at the start of the case by far-right demonstrators outside Liverpool Crown Court.

The Delhi rape case and the Mumbai terrorist survivor case demonstrate further the difficulties faced by defendants in jurisdictions where representation *of* a client suggests association *with that* client, with the consequence that lawyers for those charged with such serious offences cannot easily be found.

Barely a month ago, a lawyer representing the former military ruler of Pakistan, Pervez Musharraf, in a treason trial arising out of the 2007 imposition of emergency rule, was threatened in an anonymous letter with beheading and the destruction of his children.

There is much anecdotal evidence that lay and professional clients in many areas of practice including defamation, seek to coerce sets of chambers into acting only for one or side, or other, by coupling an offer of instructions in a *particular* case with a threat to withhold further instructions in *future* cases if the set does not accede to such demands – an offer, which to borrow the dictum of Marlon Brando in *The Godfather*, is proposed as an offer they can't refuse. The cab rank rule not merely allows, but actually obliges, chambers, and counsel in them, as a matter of professional conduct, *not* to accept this position, even if, necessarily, to their financial disadvantage.

In a legal culture whose roots are the same, but whose branches have developed in wholly different directions, the USA, in the field of media law, an advocate will appear either for newspapers or against them; and it would regarded as inconsistent, rather than consistent, with professional principle and practice to switch sides from week to week. I submit that the approach of the English Bar is to be preferred.

Certainly, the judiciary appear to be in no doubt about the cab rank rule's continued vitality. In *Rondel v Worsley* in 1969, Lord Reid in upholding the barrister's traditional immunity from claims for negligence, said about the position and duties of a barrister or advocate appearing in court on behalf of a client.:

> It has long been recognised that no Counsel is entitled to refuse to act in a sphere in which he practices and on being tendered a proper fee, for any person however unpopular or even offensive he or his opinions may be, and it is essential that duty must be continued. Justice cannot be done and cannot be seen to be done otherwise.

In *Arthur JS Hall & Co v Simons* in 2002, when the same immunity was overturned, Lord Hobhouse of Woodborough said of the rule:

> It is (in fact) a fundamental and essential part of a liberal legal system. Even the most unpopular and antisocial are entitled to legal representation and to the protection of proper legal procedures. The European Convention for the Protection of Human Rights and Fundamental Freedoms (1953) (Cmd 8969) confirms such right.

In *R v Ulcay* the Lord Chief Justice Lord Judge stressed the importance of the rule despite its claimed evasion:

> The cab-rank rule is essential to the proper administration of justice. We simply emphasise that if the cab-rank rule creates obligations on counsel in civil proceedings, it does so with yet greater emphasis in criminal proceedings, not least because to a far greater extent than civil proceedings, criminal proceedings involve defendants charged with offences which attract strong public aversion, with the possibility of lengthy prison sentences, when more than ever, the administration of justice requires that the defendant should be properly represented, so allowing the proper exercise of his entitlement at common law and his Convention rights under article 6.

Nor is the rule just an English legal curiosity. As observed by Brennan J in the High Court of Australia in *Giannarelli v Wraith*:

> If access to legal representation before the courts were dependent on counsel's predilections as to the acceptability of the cause or the munificence of the client, it would

be difficult to bring unpopular causes to court and the profession would become the puppet of the powerful.

Sir Sydney Kentridge QC, speaking of his experience of acting for opponents of the Apartheid regime in 1986, expressed the importance of the rule in eloquent and practical terms as follows:

> [I]n some types of cases – particularly in treason trials, of which there are many in South Africa – defending counsel is sustained and strengthened by the understanding of his professional colleagues – among whom for these purposes I include the judges – that what he is doing for his client, however much it may hurt or offend persons in authority, is no more than his duty. The rule also ensures that the independence of the advocate is generally recognised even by the public at large – the advocate is not necessarily associated with the views of his client. This may seem pusillanimous. Why should we care what anyone thinks of us? If we all had the courage of an Erskine or a Clarence Darrow, we should not require that sort of protection. But I assure you that for ordinary mortals the support of this professional tradition can be very comforting indeed.

While Sir Sydney is himself no ordinary mortal, but fit to be ranked with those with whom he declines to compare himself, his observation loses nothing in pertinence because of his modesty.

So as explained by Lord Bingham in his chapter on 'A Fair Trial' in his book on *The Rule of Law*, 'scarcely less important than an independent judiciary is an independent legal profession, fearless in its representation of those who cannot represent themselves, however unpopular or distasteful their case may be'.

The academics' analysis appeared oblivious to the fact that the legal profession, while it inhabits a market, is not only a participant in a market, and mercifully the report has, at any rate for now, disappeared into the *oubliette* of history.

The fact that a barrister is not identified with his or her client has the *additional* advantage that the *court* will repose greater confidence in his or her submissions than if such identification were perceived or perceptible.

Judges themselves are by tradition and training expected to suppress – as far as is possible – their personal or political predilections when ruling on cases that come before them. But over the last year several members of the Supreme Court have yielded to the temptation of expressing their views on a topic of extreme sensitivity, the extent to which the domestic courts should defer to the Strasbourg Court's interpretation of the European Convention on Human Rights in applying those of its key provisions – and they form a substantial majority – that have been incorporated into domestic law by the Human Rights Act 1998. The issue has achieved salience over a range of cases including the exclusive use of hearsay evidence to achieve a conviction, the rights of prisoners to vote, and whole life sentences.

The basic law is clear enough. The Human Rights Act provides only that British courts must 'take into account' the decisions emanating from Strasbourg.

In *Ullah* Lord Bingham said that they should apply them 'no more but certainly no less' which in *Al-Skeini* Lord Simon Brown countered in 'no less but certainly no more'. The gap revealed by these obscurely differing emphases has widened into a chasm. On the one side, Lady Hale is an outrider in the Bingham camp, contending for *Ullah* plus, advocating that the domestic courts should be free to adopt a more generous construction to convention rights than the European Court of Human Rights. On the other side, Lord Justice Laws argued that domestic courts should be free to adopt a less – generous or native – interpretation to those rights; and Lord Judge proposed that the Human Rights Act be amended to make that clear.

Meanwhile Lord Sumption was concerned that the European Court had 'gone well beyond the language, object or purpose of the Convention' in a manner which posed a threat to democracy', a view which Lord Mance elsewhere described as 'apocalyptic'. (Lady Justice Arden – in private life, Lady Mance – has advocated a three-year stay on the rulings of the European Court of Human Rights which lay down new law.) To cap it all, Lord Neuberger has stated, 'The idea of courts overruling decisions of the UK Parliament, as is substantially the effect of what the Strasbourg and Luxembourg Courts can do, is little short of offensive to our notions of constitutional propriety.' Truly a court divided against itself – and one whose revelations of judicial philosophy will inform the approach adopted by advocates who appear before them.

Advocates, by contrast, do not enjoy even such limited licence in their professional role. Their beliefs are irrelevant to the arguments they present. Indeed, for an advocate to state to the courts his or her belief is a solecism; advocates neutrally submit. Such convictions, as they may have, are parked outside the doors of the court. Their independence is in that sense of a purer variety than that of the judges.

But is the advocate's devotion to a client's cause an unqualified benefit? In a speech last year to the St Petersburg International Legal Forum on the theme 'Learning from Each Other', the Dean of the Oxford Law faculty explained that in teaching law 'We have to focus on dispute resolution, because of the way in which the common law has developed over centuries, through the decisions of judges in trials and appeals'.

But, he added, provocatively,

> there are drawbacks to a common law legal education, even to a good one. We never put this on our university publicity materials but let's face the facts; we teach students how to make bad arguments sound plausible ... We equip students to become part of an industry in which they can charge high fees for legal services in support of claims that should not be brought and in making defences against claims that should not be resisted. This form of education supports the Rule of Law. But the Rule of Law is not altogether a good thing,

and supplied an alleged example – 'If a murderer has a good defence lawyer and a fair trial, the lawyer may prevent justice from being done' – while referring in the same sentence in deaconal paradox to the counter case, 'yet our country is worse off if a murderer cannot get a good lawyer'.

While I would acknowledge the Dean's analysis as superficially plausible, I would also describe it as misguided. For intrinsic to it is a sense of omniscience which, while it may be understandable in an academic, is alien to a practitioner. It confuses hindsight with foresight. It assumes that, before a case has even been argued, the answer to it is certain. Yet it is for the judge, not the lawyer, to provide that answer. As Lord Denning observed in *Tombling v Universal Bulb Co Ltd*, 'Cicero makes the distinction that it is the duty of the judge to pursue the truth, but it is permitted to the advocate to argue what only has a semblance of it.' Norman Birkett, one of the pre-eminent counsel in the golden age of advocacy, in a famous 'Face to Face' television interview with John Freeman said that he had not infrequently defended clients whom he believed to be guilty, but never one who he knew to be so. In a democracy subject to the Rule of Law, it is no business of counsel to judge his client. As Baron Bramwell observed, 'A client is entitled to say to his counsel "I want your advocacy, not your judgement", I prefer that of the Court.'

Alex McBride's recent literary *jeu d'esprit*, *Defending the Guilty*, an account of the professional life of a criminal barrister, is a book with a title which abbreviates rather than illuminates the truth. Defence counsel is representing someone who, however formidable may be the prosecution case, until convicted enjoys the presumption of innocence. Indeed, if defence counsel was in receipt of an admission by the client that he had done that of which he was accused, the ambit of the defence would be restricted to putting the prosecution to proof rather than advancing a positive case inconsistent with his client's instructions. A fairer but less engaging title would be 'Defending a person who, notwithstanding my arguments, was found by the tribunal of fact beyond reasonable doubt to be guilty as charged'. As an exercise in sales promotion such title would, of course, be less attractive to the publishers!

So, to the Dean of the Oxford Law School, I would make the riposte 'The Rule of Law is altogether a good thing': and the fact that in litigation the right result is not always achieved does not make it less so. Advocates, even judges, are only human!

But whatever techniques they deploy, how far should advocates go in their desire to promote their clients' interests? The parents of the murdered 13-year-old Milly Dowler had their own sex lives subjected to prolonged scrutiny by defence counsel for Levi Bellfield, ultimately convicted of Milly's murder – as well, of course, of having their voicemails hacked by journalists for the *News of the World*. Frances Andrade committed suicide after giving evidence against a former music teacher, Michael Brewer, accused of having sexually assaulted her when she was his pupil, apparently in consequence of her ordeal in the witness box, which she confided in a text to a friend made her feel that 'she had been raped all over again'. Domestic goddess Nigella Lawson, a prosecution witness in the trial of the Grillo sisters, accused of defrauding her former husband Charles Saatchi, was herself accused of being a habitual user of drugs by the sisters' defence counsel, to sustain a line of argument that she had licensed such payments from his bank account as a price for their silence. Prosecutors are under a professional obligation not to seek conviction at any cost. It may be that a similar restraint should be imposed on defence counsel rather than that they should enjoy, subject only to control by the court, what Nigella's brother, the prominent journalist Dominic Lawson, described as an 'unchecked destructive licence'?

The degree to which the court's control is effective is itself controversial. Judge Robin Johnson, who had reversed an earlier ruling to exclude evidence about Ms Lawson's alleged drug taking, was compelled to abort questions by a Ms Arden, counsel for Francesca Grillo, only when she asked Ms Lawson whether she had received a Mother's Day card with a spliff attached to it and the words 'To enjoy later' with the direction 'That ends your cross-examination. I'm not having any more. You have exhausted my patience' – a not entirely principled or satisfactory safeguard.

Sometimes the boundaries of forensic propriety, if not transgressed, may be thought to come close to being so in ways other than the harassment of witnesses. In the three-week trial of two Al-Qaeda sympathisers for the murder of Fusilier Rigby, the advocate for Michael Adjebolo reminded the jury that it was for the prosecution to prove their case: 'The onus is on the prosecution to prove intent to kill or do really serious bodily injury', a submission correct in law, but somewhat ambitious given that his client had been seen to kill the soldier on the public highway, and had been photographed with the murder weapon – a blood stained machete – in his hands. Counsel also argued that his client was a soldier in war believing himself to be engaged 'in a legitimate armed conflict against an odious regime' and therefore could not have breached the Queen's peace – a submission, as the judge held, incorrect in law.

The same advocate's dramatic and eloquent introduction – 'There is no greater honour than to stand up for someone who is innocent of a charge' – savoured of exaggerated optimism, and was also inappropriate insofar as it implied his belief in his client's innocence – which was no more relevant than would have been his belief in his client's guilt.

In *R v Farooqi and others*, a terrorist case, the conviction of Mr Farooqi and his co-accused were challenged last year on the basis of 'flagrant misconduct and alleged professional incompetence' of Mr Farooqi's advocate. The catalogue of misconduct included giving evidence himself (his client having declined to do so); making submissions about facts not themselves adduced in evidence; making critical comments about the prosecution police witnesses, notably that they had been guilty of entrapment, which they had been given no opportunity to answer; and making unwarranted personal attacks on the judge, the prosecution, and even other defence counsel who were said to be guilty of 'sucking up' to the judge because they conducted their cases in a manner different to his own.

In stressing that 'the trial process is not a game' the Court of Appeal emphasised as well that

> the advocate is not the client's mouthpiece. In short the advocate is bound to advance the defendant's case on the basis of what his clients tells him is the truth, but save for

> well-established principles … the advocate, and the advocate alone remains responsible for the forensic decisions and strategy. That is the foundation of the right to appear as an advocate with the privileges and responsibilities of an advocate, and, as an advocate burdened with twin responsibilities, both to the client and to the court.' It added only that 'in the course of any trial, like everyone else, the advocate is bound ultimately to abide by the rulings of the court.

*Farooqi* itself has re-emphasised the well-known principle that lawyers' duties to the court may conflict with duties owed by lawyers to their clients. The reconciliation is also well known. As was said by Mason CJ in *Giannerelli v Wraith*:

> It is not that a barrister's duty to the court creates such a conflict with his duty to his client that the dividing line is unclear. The duty to the court is paramount even if the client gives instructions to the contrary.

This paramountcy is justified by reason of the court being the representative of the public interest in the administration of justice. As Lon Fuller, the noted Harvard legal philosopher wrote:

> The lawyer's highest loyalty is at the same time the most intangible. It is a loyalty that runs, not to persons, but to procedures and institutions. The lawyer's role imposes on him a trusteeship for the integrity of those fundamental processes of government and self-government upon which the successful functioning of our society depends.

This proposition is well illustrated by the precept and practice that counsel must, if the other side is unrepresented, even draw the court's attention to what the other side might have said. In the *Torfaen* case Lord Toulson mentioned that the note prepared by legal staff had been disclosed to counsel for the local authority and added:

> This was disclosed to Mr Jonathon Kirk QC, who represented the council. In addition, mindful that he was appearing for a public authority against an unrepresented respondent, Mr Kirk himself invited the court to consider those points which we would have regarded as fairly capable of argument if he had been instructed on the other side. This was in accordance with the best tradition of the bar and we believe that it has enabled us fairly to evaluate all the arguments.

David Ipp, a Singaporean judge wrote:

> The administration of justice requires the processes of the court to be protected from abuse and particular duties enable courts to police their own procedures. They must not countenance the use of litigious procedures for purposes for which they were not intended, and from excessive zeal.

But advocates should also be astute to police themselves.

It has always been necessary to ensure that only those who enjoy the privileges of advocacy deserve it. Historically the Bar was subject to sanctions for professional misconduct imposed by judges of the High Court acting as visitors to the Inns of Court. As I have already mentioned, advocates are now subject to the same liability for negligence if they breach their duty of care as other professionals, although still enjoying absolute privilege from the perspective of the law of defamation as do other participants in judicial proceedings.

Nonetheless a sea change occurred with the coming into effect of the Legal Services Act 2007, which substantially reformed the provision of legal services in England and Wales. At its heart were eight regulatory objectives which included 'supporting the constitutional principle of the Rule of Law' and 'promoting and maintaining adherence to the professional principles … which themselves required that … authorised persons should maintain proper standards of work'. Part 2 of the Act established the Legal Services Board (LSB), whose domain extended to oversight of, amongst others, the Bar Standards Board, to whom the Bar Council had delegated its own regulatory functions.

The LSB determined to drive forward a Quality Assurance Scheme for Advocates (QASA). There were no less than four rounds of consultation, and commissioning of further reports. The mountains laboured, and produced not so much as Horace's ridiculous mouse, but an animal of an entirely different nature – an evaluation scheme by the judges for all advocates to be introduced in stages with the criminal bar being the first target. Market forces were no longer deemed sufficient to weed out the incompetent, nor the acquisition of points for continuing professional development – a euphemism if ever there was one – to improve them.

It was unsurprising that the Bar should challenge the scheme, and no less surprising that the challenge has been at any rate to date unsuccessful, given the support of the majority of the senior judiciary. The impetus behind the challenge, based on the thesis that for judges to have to mark advocates who appeared before them would compromise the integrity of both, is to be found in a lecture by Lord Justice Moses, where he posed the question: 'Can anyone who has spent any time in Court listening to advocacy really believe that a system of marking will encourage, influence or inspire, or will it deaden and crush in pursuit of a bland and colourless uniformity?'

Lord Denning said succinctly, 'Courage and courtesy should go hand in hand'. Lord Justice Moses clearly thought that a courtesy might survive but courage would not; and, in consequence, the court be deprived of the quality of uninhibited argument that it required to reach the right result, whereas for their part judges might hesitate conscientiously to criticise advocates for fear of being sued.

The Administrative Court rejected all these arguments. While recognising expressly that the independence and impartiality of the criminal Bar, both prosecutor and defence, enshrined 'values to the great advantage of the Rule of Law in this country', they considered implicitly that QASA promoted rather than impaired it.

Let me now seek to weave the threads of this lecture into something that more closely resembles a seamless robe than a patchwork quilt, and hark back to Lord MacDermott's lectures on protection from power. For coupled with the albeit postponed reduction in legal aid is the imminent curtailment of judicial review – through the vehicle of the Criminal Justice and Courts Bill currently before the Westminster Parliament. Since judicial review is concerned with ensuring that government itself is not guilty of abuse or misuse of power, it has never been popular with governments of whatever political complexion. Whilst the Lord Chancellor was himself a judge, he could and did defend the judiciary against attack. The present incumbent – a politician, not a lawyer – has no judicial role.

But although complaints about judicial overreach by ministers, where the objects of unfavourable judgments are legion, the target of the Lord Chancellor, who retains statutory responsibility for judicial independence and is properly mindful of that particular constitutional duty is the advocates, not the judges.

In the foreword to his response to the consultation on judicial review he wrote:

> I believe in protecting judicial review as a check on unlawful executive action, but I am equally clear that it should not be abused to act as a brake on growth. In my view judicial review has extended far beyond its original concept, and too often cases are pursued as a campaigning tool or simply to delay legitimate proposals. That is bad for the economy and the tax payer, and also bad for public confidence in the Justice system.

He added in the substantive part of the document:

> [T]he Government's view is that the better way to deliver its policy is through a strong package of financial reforms to limit the pursuit of weak claims, especially but not only by aiming to deprive parties and interveners of protective costs orders unless permission has been granted.'

The devil is in the detail – it amounts to death by a thousand cuts!

But what is notable is that the case against what are perceived to be extravagant applications for judicial review is couched in economic, not constitutional terms. Yet the Lord Chancellor had another relevant obligation under the Constitutional Reform Act 2005, which is set out in its initial section but assumed in its very language to be of far greater vintage: 'This Act does not adversely affect the existing constitutional principle of the rule of law, or the Lord Chancellor's existing constitutional role in relation to that principle.'

The same monocular approach informs the Lord Chancellor's explanation for postponement of his legal aid reforms: 'I wanted to do what I could to ease their effect on lawyers'. The Lord Chancellor, with the greatest respect, has wrongly focused on the singer, not the song; who lawyers are, not what they do. In the words of Lord Henry in Oscar Wilde's *The Picture of Dorian Gray*, his department knows the price of everything, but the value of nothing.

For these two streams of reforms, curtailment of legal aid and of judicial review are interrelated, not distinct. As Lord Faulks QC said in the House of Lords debate on the former,

> what is at stake is not just the standard of living of lawyers; but the ability for members of the public to obtain competent representation when facing criminal charges, the

> consequences of marital breakdown, abuse of power by public authorities, threats of repossession of their homes or deprivation of contact with children or grandchildren. The cuts affect the most vulnerable; asylum seekers, prisoners, the mentally ill.

Lord Faulks has himself been since promoted to the Ministry of Justice and hence presumably disabled from reprising his critical observations; better no doubt, as Lyndon Johnson once said of a critic, to have him doing something inside the tent outwards rather than outside the tent inside – in a public lecture I bowdlerise the verb which the former President actually used.

Lord Neuberger, President of the Supreme Court, has added in a newspaper interview this melancholy reflection: 'cut price litigation leads to unrepresented litigants and worse lawyers'. The direct consequences are elongation of hearings and increase in costs of the courts themselves, but more importantly the indirect consequences are the risk of judicial error and hence of injustice.

For, there is, alas, a limit to which courts can assist litigants in person. In a decision in the Jersey Court of Appeal last week, in an appeal on a charge of grievous and serious assault, the Court noted:

> The applicant was of course a litigant in person. Obviously a court will seek to assist such a litigant in his presentation but not at the expense of the rules of evidence and proper procedures appropriate to lawyers.

It can be said of the Bar, not only that it presents arguments better than litigants in person – an under-ambitious aspiration (not that it does it perfectly) – but rather as was said of James Bond in the Carly Simon lyric 'Nobody does it better'.

In short, my thesis is that the fulfilment of the forensic function by a profession, educated, conscious of its plural duties and the balance to be struck between them, subject to proper education, monitoring, and where necessary discipline, and ever faithful to its fundamental principle – the cab rank rule – is necessary for the prevention of injustice and the protection of the rule of law.

The many changes to which the Bar of England and Wales has been subjected over the last 20 years may appear to deflect its attention from some of its core values. An increasing number of qualified barristers in an age of austerity prefer the security offered in the employed sector. Yet, as Sir Ivan Lawrence, one of the diminishing number of lawyers active both in the Commons and in the courts, said, 'The independence of the self-employed lawyer owing allegiance to his client not to an employer telling him what is in the best interests of the firm is of particular importance to the integrity of the justice system' – an independence put at particular risk if the employer is the state. The vision said by sceptics to be prevalent in the Ministry of Justice of a future where a Crown Prosecution Service is confronted by a state defender system is not one calculated to inspire public confidence.

Concurrently the emphasis on marketing and branding of sets of chambers, as if they were de facto if not *de jure* partnerships, *rather than* an association of independent practitioners; the imminent ability now to convert chambers into partnerships and even to become subsumed in commercial entities – as well as the deliberate withholding of labour by barristers – suggests that, paradoxically, they are adopting features both of business and of trade unions. The possibility for a barrister to practise as a limited company with consequent tax and limited liability advantages, and even with his or her spouse as a shareholder, has been advertised in a recent brochure by a firm of chartered accountants. This, if nothing else, would add new hazards to the phenomenon of 'conscious uncoupling'.

A trial, is not, as was said in *Farooqi*, a game: nonetheless, Grantland Rice, the American sports journalist, penned a quatrain which is usually attributed to cricket, in fact refers to basketball, but would be equally appropriate to advocacy:

> For when the one Great Scorer comes.
>
> To write against your name,
>
> He marks – not that you won or lost –
>
> But how you played the game.

A trade, profession, or a vocation? That is, as it always was, the choice for the Bar. On how it exercises that choice will depend in part on the future of the Rule of Law itself.

# 5

# *'Looking at the Locus'**

> A view is an observation undertaken out of court during the course of a trial … when the tribunal visits a place so the witnesses can show where they were standing at the relevant time, the court is being asked to act on real evidence … such a demonstration may be distinguished from a visit to a relevant public place to appreciate better the evidence adduced in court.

(Evidence by Rupert Cross, my former law tutor at Magdalen)

There is only one modern authority where principles governing whether or not the view should be undertaken were fully discussed – *Tito v Waddell*. Mr Justice Megarry, in a claim brought by the islanders against, amongst others, HMG, to compel them to replant trees in areas razed for phosphate mines, gave prolonged consideration to whether he should visit Ocean Island. He said:

> The matter is dealt with by RSC, Ord 35, r 8(1). This provides as follows:
>
>> 'The Judge by whom any cause or matter is tried may inspect any place or thing with respect to which any question arises in the cause or matter.'
>
> This language could scarcely be more simple or more general: but there seems to be little in the reported cases which affords such guidance on the principles to be applied in exercising this jurisdiction. However, I think I can properly act on the following propositions. First, there seems to be nothing to restrict the rule to cases in which the place or thing to be viewed lies within the jurisdiction; and no suggestion that there has been any such restriction made … Second, the rule plainly appears to confer a discretion on the judge … No litigant is given the right to prevent him from holding a view …
>
> Third, where … the parties disagree about whether or not a view should be held, the judge should weigh the advantages of holding a view against the disadvantages …
>
> One matter, I think, should be left wholly out of account, and that is inconvenience to the judge. A view of Ocean Island would, of course, be far removed from being a pleasant holiday trip to the South Seas. The journey would be long and exhausting, and a proper inspection of the rugged terrain of the island would in all probability involve a considerable degree of strenuous agility in a high temperature. Nevertheless, although there must be some limits to the degree of judicial wear and tear that can be expected, I do not think that I should give any real weight to what is involved in this case; for this seems to me (though by no great margin) to fall within the bounds of what a litigant is reasonably entitled to expect from the judge.

* *Verdict* (Oxford University law student newsletter) (2003).

> I have already referred to three propositions based on Ord 35 r 8. There is a fourth, which seems to be of fundamental importance, and that concerns the juridical nature of a view ... What a judge perceives on a view is itself evidence, in the same way as what he sees and hears in the courtroom. Just as a portable object may be brought into court and, being made an exhibit, become real evidence, so if the judge duly views a place or object which cannot be brought into court that place or object provides real evidence through the medium of the judge's eyes, ears, touch, tongue or, as in one recent case before me, his nose ... On this footing the tendering of real evidence no longer depends upon the res being portable ...
>
> True, it is evidence the abduction of which is, by virtue of Ord 35 r 8, made a matter of judicial discretion; but still it is evidence. Quite properly, it has not been suggested that this evidence is irrelevant or inadmissible: the contention is merely that it is unnecessary and too expensive in terms of time and money. Nevertheless, I think that the court ought to exercise some caution in refusing an application for a view. In some cases it may be clear that to hold a view would achieve nothing save waste both time and money. But except in reasonably plain cases of this kind I think the court ought to incline in favour of granting any such application. In short, in my judgment the proper approach is to consider not whether a sufficient case for holding a view has been made out, but whether there are sufficient grounds for rejecting the application to hold a view.

I myself participated in one of the most talked about (and photographed) views in recent legal history when I appeared for the actress Gillian Taylforth in her case against *The Sun*, who had accused her of – to put the matter shortly – giving her boyfriend a blow job in a slip road off the A1 (what I have subsequently taken to calling, more decorously, 'A stationary traffic offence'). On the second day of the trial a reconstruction took place in the car park in the precincts of the Royal Courts of Justice in order to demonstrate whether or not it was actually possible to perform such an act in a Range Rover.

First Gillian and her boyfriend, and then two *Sun* reporters, acted out their rival versions. The somewhat unhelpful conclusion was that it all depended upon whether the seat belt (and, for that matter, the boyfriend's trousers) was (or were) not undone. You can read all about it in Gillian's autobiography.

That fell into Cross's first category of demonstration; into the second category fell my walkabout in South London, following in the wake of Lord Scarman (rather as the page followed Good King Wenceslas) who was investigating the Brixton riots of 1981 (I had a small role as counsel for the Lambeth Borough Council for Community Relations Committee).

It is, however, not unusual for counsel and solicitors to visit the *locus in quo* (since Lord Woolf's reforms we have to anglicise it and call it 'the scene of the action') simply to get a feel for what might have happened. I say 'a feel', though in the case of *West Oxfordshire District Council v Beratec*, it was my nose rather than eyes that were engaged, since the issue pivoted around whether or not the respondents were in breach of an undertaking not to commit a nuisance by smell in their factory for conversion of chicken offal into chicken feed. And I have made such visits both home and away.

At home, in pursuit of the truth, I have visited the refrigerated bowels of a 'ro-ro' (roll-on, roll-off) cargo vessel moored in the Thames estuary wearing a pink padded overall rather like the Michelin man; scouted out a site where my client proposed to build riding stables in the vicinity of Lloyd George's grave; and, in the context of a claim brought by Indian employees of British Steel for discrimination in refusing to employ them because they could not read safety signs in English, together with my leader, Anthony Lester QC (later Lord Lester of Herne Hill), and the other side's leader, Alexander Irvine QC (later the Lord Chancellor alias Cardinal Wolsey), trekked out to the company's manufacturing HQ in Suffolk I have a fading photograph from the local newspaper, showing us all in our hard hats.

Competition issues were said to arise when my client Sealink decided to launch a catamaran-cum-hovercraft on the Holyhead–Dublin route. I was invited to see the Holyhead harbour, and promised a ride in the company executive jet. Alas, when I arrived at Gatwick I was told that our team was too small to justify the expense, and offered an alternative trip in a small single-engine propeller plane piloted by someone whose aeronautical career seemed to have peaked during the Korean War. Fear of seeming a coward won out over actual cowardice; we clambered aboard in single file; and the little craft valiantly fought its way through the clouds. We navigated apparently, by occasional sight of the land below, and landed on a runway in Wales otherwise used for military jets, performing later a series of hair-raising manoeuvres which delayed our departure back.

Sometimes, however, it has not been feasible to pay a site visit. In the only murder trial I ever did, my client had killed a woman in the public lavatories in St Giles – and decency as well as squeamishness inhibited me from going down stairs which were firmly marked 'Ladies'.

My most recent – and bizarre – sortie to a *locus* was when I was instructed by Spearmint Rhino, the curiously named international business, which is to lap-dancing what Exxon is to oil. Their licence to supply alcohol to their customers was under threat by reason of a complaint made by the Metropolitan Police that 'lewd and indecent' acts were taking place at their various outlets (the clubs', not the Met's).

According to their American attorney, who educated me via a telecom from Los Angeles, the appeal raised high issues of principle focusing on the freedom of expression guarantees in the First Amendment to the American Constitution. (In the Highbury Magistrates Court they talk about nothing else.) At the end of the conference the clients suggested that I could best appreciate the classy nature of their enterprise by a visit. I struck while the iron was hot, and suggested we go at once, insisting only that my solicitor come too, so as to interpose himself between me and the roving lens of any paparazzi. After a cursory glance at the lavish, if ornate furnishings, the well-stocked bar, and the naked ladies posturing by the poles, I said that I was satisfied that I had the flavour of the enterprise. But my host insisted that I enjoy, as it were, the Full Monty: and I was hustled into an empty booth, guarded by a large bouncer, to be entertained by a striptease performed by a youthful blonde from South Africa (who told me that she had ambitions to be a ballet dancer) while I sat, trapped against a wall, with a gaze necessarily fixed at a level midway between her belly and her knees. At the end of her Salome-like performance she said, noticing my apparent discomfort 'Don't worry, my dear, you'll be properly warmed up by the end of the evening', and kissed me lightly on the forehead. I realised then, if not before, that she thought I was a punter, not a lawyer (though the two statuses may not be incompatible). I made, as they say, my excuses and fled. It was, I supposed, all in a day's – or night's – work.

Away I have travelled to various parts of the globe. When acting for the Church of Scientology (in the great tradition of Lord Hailsham, subsequently Lord Chancellor, their first UK QC) I had to visit their Los Angeles HQ and then journey into the outlying countryside to the boat whence L Ron Hubbard, the Church's founder, guided his flock.

The case under discussion was an application by Mr Hubbard to enter the UK: the object to test whether the one-time ban on Scientologists, lifted in the wake of a report by Sir John Foster QC, still applied to the Church's leader. The Home Office, astute to avoid reviving the public policy issue, disputed that Mr Hubbard was still alive or, accordingly, that he needed an entry permit. Our response was, if you believe he is dead, what is the objection to giving him one? Impasse. In the end the case was compromised.

I was also briefed on behalf of the Port of Singapore Authority in an inquiry into an accident which took place when the mast of a converted drill ship snagged an overhead cable connecting mainland Singapore and the island of Sentosa, and caused the deaths of several unfortunate persons catapulted out of a cable car *en route* between the two places. It was not the easiest of briefs.

First the inquiry had already been afoot for more than 12 days. Secondly my clients were already receiving rough treatment at the hands of the presiding judge, and, in consequence, of the local press. Thirdly my knowledge of matters maritime (at that stage) was such that I would have been hard pressed to differentiate between port and bow. (The QC originally instructed, Michael Thomas, a 'wet shipping' expert, had just been elevated to the position of Attorney General of Hong Kong.) But I received a crash course from my instructing solicitor, Pathma Selvadurai of Rodyk & Davidson, and by the end of the three months, I had learnt enough to be briefed back in England in a number of scuttling cases which were usually reserved to members of the Bar in specialist Admiralty chambers, whose hobbies were (like Toad of Toad Hall's) mucking about in boats. I inspected the Singapore harbour, but not the cable car, which was still out of commission.

I also journeyed to Kuwait in connection with an arbitration presided over by Lord Justice Kerr, Lord Griffiths and Judge Schwebel – subsequently President of the International Court of Justice, on behalf of the insurers of a number of major car dealers in Kuwait whose showrooms had been looted by locals during the (first) Gulf War. I was instructed to advance the unpromising argument that the looting was not a consequence of war, and that accordingly the insurers were not entitled to rely upon the war risks exclusion clause in the policy.

My visit to the Gulf state, by no means recovered from the ravages of the invasion, convinced me that one of the hardest jobs in the world at the time would have been to be chief executive of the Kuwaiti Tourist Board. No doubt the country has many charms, but they did not repose in vandalised retail outlets for automobiles. Precisely what we gained from the experience (fees apart) may be a matter of some doubt. I do remember, however, that it was Ramadan; and that when we were offered coffee in the offices of one of our clients, the young lady receptionist who seemed to be a very orthodox Muslim, looked at us with such hostility that I was convinced that she would call the police to charge us with the offence of drinking between the hours of dawn and dusk. I declined the proffered cup, and distanced myself in the forecourt from the rest of the lawyers, whose thirst appeared more potent than their fear.

Still it was an ill-wind (or sandstorm) which blows no one any good: and in consequence I flirted briefly with another specialist subject – war risk exclusion clauses. Another case which turned on such a clause was that of Grell-Taurel, in which, in this instance, I had the happier task of representing the insurers initially before the delightfully named Mr Justice Kangaloo. In Trinidad an attempted *coup d'état* by the Muslimeen (a militant group of Muslims), resulted in the capture of the Parliament building, the holding hostage of the Prime Minister and other senior ministers, in a siege which was only ended after an amnesty (subsequently upheld as valid) offered to the insurrectionists. Locals took every advantage of the diversion of the civilian and military authorities to seize everything and anything from the neighbourhood shops. My opponents' ambitious argument, rejected both at first instance and in the Court of Appeal, was that this looting was not even the indirect consequence of the insurrection. But once again we solemnly trooped around the pink-coloured Parliament building, reminding us of the virtues of fragile democracy, but giving us a superficial insight only into the cause and effect of burglary in less salubrious areas of Port of Spain.

I well recall, however, a delightful Sunday excursion with my Junior on the island of Tobago (Trinidad's little – and lovelier – sister), which was, by coincidence, paying host that day both to a CARICOM conference chaired by Madeleine Albright, the US Secretary of State, and the inaugural flight of BA. These two huge jets on the tarmac (Airforce 2 and BA Jumbo) flanked and dwarfed our little propeller plane. The stewardess, clipping our return boarding passes, said (somewhat superfluously), 'Yours is the one in the middle'.

Site views have had their little compensations.

# Part II

# Judges

# 6

# *'Towards a Supreme Court? The British Experience'*

# John M Kelly Memorial Lecture*

TO THE BEST of my recollection, I only had one brief encounter with John Kelly, in whose memory this lecture was inaugurated. If I *had* met him *more* than once, I am sure that I *would* have remembered it, so vivid was the personality that impressed itself on all who knew and cared for him. Yet, if one believes the 'Cleopatra's nose' theory of history, it was *his* decision to accept a Chair *here* that led *me* to my position as President of the Oxford College, which bears the same name as this university's Dublin rival. For had Trinity College, of which Cardinal Newman was an eminent alumnus, not needed the services of a lecturer to bridge the gap between his departure from the fellowship in jurisprudence and the arrival of Dr Alan Milner, his successor (who had outstanding commitments at Yale to teach the law relating to witchcraft – amongst *other* subjects) – I would never have found myself 30 years later a candidate, let alone a successful candidate, for my present office. While I am confident that my subject matter would have been attractive to John Kelly, spanning as he did so expertly the realms of the law and of politics, I only hope that this audience will not feel that my lecture is a poor means of repaying to his memory so considerable a debt.

In an obituary evocation in *The Times* of William Brennan, who served on the US Supreme Court for 34 years, entitled in post-Murdoch style 'The Lawman who moulded America', the author referred to Brennan's English judicial contemporaries as persons who 'unlike America's Judges, … have never been in a position to shape our civilisation. That is a role only American Judges are allowed to play – and play it they do with gusto'.

I do *not* suggest that the writer either overestimated the power, or the manner of its exercise, of the American judge in that country's highest appellate court. I *do* suggest that he underestimated the power, and manner of its exercise of his modern English counterpart. The thesis that I wish to develop before you is that, imperceptibly in *Great Britain* – and I use *that* concept deliberately – there

* (1998) 2 *Irish Jurist*.

is developing a constitutional court, even a Supreme Court. Lord Devlin once wrote 'The Supreme Court, like the vines of France is not for transplantation … it needs two things which Britain has not got: first a Constitution as a source of life; secondly a legislative vacuum for it to fill. Britain may still have neither.' But despite their absence and in, what, according to Lord Devlin should be wholly barren soil, the green shoots of such a court can be detected.

The respective roles of the judiciary, the Executive and the legislature in the British Constitution are nowhere expressly delineated. In the realm of private law there are a large number of areas which are a product of judicial creativity, and in respect of which parliamentary intervention has been, if growing, incomplete. As Lord Steyn said:

> Sometimes politicians seem surprised to hear that judges make the law. The answer is that, without the creative function of judges, we would have no common law: the common law is entirely judge made law.

In the realm of public law, matters stand differently. Judges are involved in adjudicating upon matters which are *primarily* the fruit of legislative or executive action. Judges' decisions in *public* law excite acute controversy because it is in *that* area, where their rulings collide with the orders or decisions of the administrators and politicians, is located the raw material of politics – housing, welfare, education, immigration, transport and city regulation.

Sir John Laws, one of the leaders of the new judicial generation, has said about the spreading territory of modern judicial review:

> Within that jurisdiction the Judges do, and must, adjudicate upon cases which involve questions of acute political controversy. The ban on viva voce broadcasts by terrorist sympathisers (ex p. Brind); the rights of persons claiming refugee status (ex p. Bugdaycay); local government finance (ex p. Hammersmith); a local authority's ban on hunting across its land (ex p. Fewings); grant maintained schools (ex p. Avon); the disposal of nuclear waste (ex p. Greenpeace Limited); the government's decision to ratify the Maastricht Treaty (ex p. Rees Mogg); you cannot construct the litany of this matter of modern judicial review without being struck by the fact that time and again it engages questions upon whose merits the politicians (and others) are in rancorous disagreement.

How far the position has changed in 50 years! In the post-World War II era academics and judges were united in their perception that public law was dormant, if not dead.

Lord Devlin described the (wartime) decisions in *Liversidge v Anderson* and *Duncan Camell-Laird* as showing that during the first half of this century the courts were 'quite anxious not to tread on the executive toes', coinciding 'with the tendency on the part of the courts to restrict rather than to enlarge their jurisdiction in all matters in which questions of policy might arise', and said in 1956:

> The common law has, not, I think, no longer the strength to provide any satisfactory solution to the problem of keeping the executive, with all the powers which under

> modern conditions are needed for the efficient conduct of the realm, under proper control. The responsibility for that now rests with Parliament.

What contemporaries witnessed, legal historians have verified. Professor Sir William Wade described the period as 'the great depression'.

But the lean years were followed, in best biblical fashion, by the fat years. The seeds of modern judicial review were planted in the 1960s during the first two Wilson administrations in the cases of *Ridge v Baldwin*, *Padfield* and *Anisminic*. During the next two and the subsequent Callaghan administration, Lord Denning MR, the Lord Woolf of his era, presided over a Court of Appeal, which dealt a series of blows to a variety of government decisions – *Congreve*, *Laker Airways*, *Thameside*. But it is in the last two decades of primarily Conservative administrations that judicial review has added so signally to its stature, belying the theory that, if the Church of England was (as once said) the Tory Party at prayer, the High Court was the Tory Party in wig and robes.

How did this come about? The judges *have* had, to an extent, to fill a vacuum left by the lack (until the accession of the present Prime Minister to the leadership of his party) of an effective political opposition. For the bulk of that period, certainly during the three Thatcher administrations, the Government of the day enjoyed a substantial majority Parliamentary opposition that was more formal than real; Thersites blowing off steam, not Coriolanus poised for power. Parliament had become the instrument of the Executive, not its instructor.

The Conservative Government, nominally dedicated to the lighter touch on the tiller, and the rolling back of the frontiers of the state, was paradoxically responsible for more legislation of an intrusive and regulatory nature than any of its predecessors. No area of national life, education at all levels, the National Health Service, the welfare state, local government, energy, the legal professions, the city, was exempt from statutory measures. And the more material there is for Governmental interference, inevitably the more scope there is for error, and, therefore, for judicial review.

There has been a marked change in public attitudes towards the establishment. The citizenry is less supine; and the very publicity accorded to judicial review makes people consider, in a way they would not previously have done, the possibility of legal remedy rather than political action or simple protest. There has been a growth of dedicated pressure groups, such as Greenpeace, Friends of the Earth, or the Joint Council for the Welfare of Immigrants – not to speak of such statutory creatures as the Equal Opportunities Commission with the expertise, legal knowledge and funds necessary to mount such challenges effectively.

Practising lawyers have adapted to the new culture. There are sets of chambers in the Temple and Grays Inn which specialise in judicial review and its satellite disciplines. Professor Harlow of the London School of Economics has written flatteringly of this development: 'A flourishing and prestigious public law bar has developed, to its credit very professional concerned with standards and active in publication'; Robert Stevens of Oxford more astringently: 'The prosperity of the Bar in the late 1960s undoubtedly changed attitudes … no longer was the Bar dominated by the rather childish high jinks of circuit life.' But their conclusion is the same: there is a more professional profession.

Academics have not only recognised, but themselves have contributed, to the new structure of public law. No systematic treatises on administrative law were published until 1959, when Professor de Smith wrote his seminal work, *Judicial Review of Administrative Action*. That book is now in its fifth edition under the august joint editorship of Lord Woolf MR and Professor Jeffrey Jowell QC (symbolising a new relationship between the gowns of court and campus), while *Wade* is in its seventh.

There have been influential procedural changes, both indirect – the power granted to the House of Lords to overrule itself in 1966 – and direct – the reforms of RSC Order 53 in the late 1970s and early 1980s and the creation of a Crown Office list of specialised judges. This innovation was itself stimulated by the House of Lord's decision in *O'Reilly v Mackman* that, as a general rule, all applications against public bodies for abuse of power had to be brought by way of judicial review rather than by way of writ or originating summons, or risk being struck out for abuse of process. This exclusivity principle was neither recommended by the Law Commission nor vouched for by legislation. It provides an impressive early example of the judges implementing their own agenda without Parliamentary encouragement, indeed (arguably) contrary to Parliamentary intent.

Judges have developed experience in, even a taste for, public affairs in a number of different ways. The Lord Chancellor has a hybrid role as a member of the Executive, legislature and judiciary. The Law Lords are legislators as well as judges. Service on the Restrictive Practices Court or Employment Appeal Tribunal has involved judges in decisions of a not purely legal nature, and judges such as Lord Nolan and Lord Justice Scott continue to be seconded to extra-curricular activities: to inquire into political scandals, major public calamities, and crises of regime and legitimacy. Judges have even been promised by the new Lord Chancellor a role in policy making. The relaxation of the Kilmuir Rules (which sought to insulate judges from broadcasting) have allowed them the opportunity, not often spurned, to pronounce on matters in the public domain. We now enjoy not mute, but, as the title of David Hare's play has it, *Murmuring Judges*, even clamorous ones.

Above all the judges *themselves* have simply become more interested in the exercise of judicial power. I yield to no one in my admiration of the English judiciary. The present House of Lords is the strongest in my 30 years at the Bar. They are persons of intelligence, education and integrity entitled, though not elected, to see themselves as an elect. I do not suggest that they are power-hungry, only that they are not, despite their training, wholly immune to the seductions of wielding authority, even if less than those over whom they exercise it – a simple point, but one usually, but unreasonably, overlooked in discussions on this subject. Judges have, for example, extended the range of circumstances in which administrators must give reasons for their decisions precisely so as to enable the judges to police those decisions more efficiently: they have been candid, not covert about their ambitions. Robson's comment in 1951 – 'The attitude of the judicature seems also to be partly due to a diminished confidence in their own ability to scrutinise and control administrative justice' – seems to, and does, belong to – in terms of public law – a prehistoric age.

Judicial review has developed an energetic momentum. The extension of supervisory jurisdiction is well recognised. It has expanded into areas hitherto uncolonised by judicial intervention, notably the exercise of prerogative powers, the contractual activities of statutory bodies where they have a public dimension, the self-regulatory functions of private bodies which themselves supervise economic and related activities within a framework of government policy. According to Sir John Laws:

> We now possess a jurisdiction in which every body, is in principle subject to the supervision of the court as regards every decision it makes. The only true exception in the present state of the law, is the Queen and Parliament exercising the function of enacting primary legislation and this exception is now constrained so as not to apply the legislation on its face is credibly asserted to be inconsistent with the law of the European Union. ... all other exceptions are apparent, not real. The dicta in CCSU about national security, diplomatic relations of foreign sovereign states and so forth only describes cases where it is thought (rightly or wrongly) jurisdiction cannot sensibly be exercised, not cases where there is no jurisdiction at all.

and yet more has been contemplated. Sir Stephen Sedley has written that

> the sub legal regions of constitutional convention (are) at present a no man's land, regulated, neither by parliamentary privilege nor by the common law, but capable both of invading the democratic process and of infringing legal norms of good government. It may yet become an area in which public law has to take an interest.

This would involve considerable audacity: the subjugation of what is by definition *not* law to legal norms.

Despite the acutely political nature of so much of the stuff of modern judicial review, judges constantly state that they are politically detached *or* that certain issues raised before them are ones of political judgment, not law from which they should abstain on pronouncing or that, in the name of constitutional responsibility, they should practise the virtues of restraint from undue interference with the acts of government.

The traditional view, which reflects such self-justifying sentiments, is that the judges, even when controlling the Executive, are only seeking to execute the will of the legislature – to exercise a subordinate, not co-ordinate role. In public law this exercise extends beyond the mere construction of individual words and phrases. When Parliament confers a statutory discretion it is often unfettered. But the courts have constantly said that there is no such thing as an unfettered discretion. The considerations that the minister should take into account are not usually specified. But the courts have said they must nonetheless ascertain what considerations would impliedly be relevant, and what irrelevant, to the exercise of such powers.

In *Padfield*, it was held that every power must be used to promote the purposes of the Act of Parliament itself. But these purposes are rarely spelt out. So, from such diverse sources as the background to the Act, the Green or White Papers which precede it or, since the case of *Pepper v Hart*, clear ministerial statements in Parliament – if such there ever are – as well as the language and structure of the Act overall, the court purports to discern what the statute's purposes are. Open textured legislation gives scope for choice enabling judges to decide that Parliament's intention was what the judges would wish it to be. Even the classic cases themselves show how controversial can be their conclusions. Sir Stephen Sedley has asked '*was* it perfectly all right for *Wednesbury* corporation to use its licensing powers to stop young people going to the pictures on Sundays?'.

The grounds of judicial review are well established: decisions must be taken lawfully, fairly, rationally, influenced by material considerations only, supported by some evidence. But the boundaries between legitimate and illegitimate judicial review are imperceptibly blurred: Courts may consider not whether a decision was reached fairly, but whether it was fair; not whether a decision was irrational, but whether the decision was one that the judge dislikes: not whether there was failure to take account of a material consideration, but whether there was a failure to weigh it appropriately. A requirement of 'no evidence' as a condition precedent to judicial review can become one of 'no sufficient' evidence.

In my view to describe the ascertainment of Parliamentary intention as the object of the judicial exercise is a legal fiction of public law on a par with the invention of those well-known private law legal personalities, John Doe and Richard Roe. Judicial review lies, as I have mentioned, to the activities of central government still carried on by prerogative powers; and to quasi-governmental organisations not established by or under statute, eg a university visitor, or the take-over panel. Judges are also increasingly impressing upon powerful organisations in the private sphere obligations, for example of fairness, equivalent to those imposed on public bodies. There can be no question that any *parliamentary* intention is at play in *any* of these areas. In truth, the standards of judicial review are autonomous: and many judges now openly admit that they are *not* seeking to ascertain intention of Parliament at all.

To quote Sir John Laws again:

> It cannot be suggested that (all these) principles which represent much of the bedrock of modernistic law, were suddenly interwoven into the legislative intention of the 1960s and 70s, in which period they have been articulated in force by the Courts. They are, categorically, judicial creations. They owe neither their existence nor their acceptance to the will of the legislature. They have nothing to do with the intention of Parliament, save as a fig-leaf to cover the true origins. We do not need the fig-leaf anymore.

Not that there is anything entirely novel in such statements. It was in 1863 in *Cooper v Wandsworth Board of Works* that Byles J said 'the justice of the common law will supply the *omission* of the legislature'.

And were the judges to decide to adopt wholeheartedly the proportionality ground for judicial review – the subject of my predecessor's lecture – it is hard to see how they – or anyone – could identify precisely at what point in time Parliament had determined that powers conferred by them on executive bodies had to be exercised proportionately rather than merely rationally.

The best testimony to the power of the courts – but also to their capacity to say that Parliament meant things which may never have crossed its collective mind and were certainly not meant by the departmental authors and Parliamentary draftsmen is the frequency with which Parliament reverses judicial decisions: *Anisminic* was followed by the Foreign Compensation Act 1969; *Pulhofer* by Section 14 of the Housing and Planning Act 1986.

At a prizegiving in *The Times* Law Awards 1997, the then Lord Chancellor Lord Mackay cautioned judges against taking it on themselves to overcome defects in the law. He expressed his 'firm view' that the judge's duty was 'to apply the law as he finds it, not to seek to rectify perceived inadequacies by the use of creative interpretation.' When deficiencies were revealed 'it is for Parliament to respond'.

Just how far can creative interpretation lead?

The former Conservative Government was concerned about the huge influx of persons claiming political asylum to the United Kingdom. They believed that a substantial number of the claimants are not refugees from persecution, but 'economic refugees'. They sought to distinguish between those who claimed asylum on arrival (who were assumed for the most part to be genuine) from those who claimed asylum only after arrival (who were assumed for the most part to be bogus). The Social Security Act 1986 had delegated to the Secretary of State power to define by regulation the class of persons entitled to social security. He used that power a decade later to deprive asylum-seekers of their benefits, pending determination of their asylum applications under the Asylum and Immigration Appeals Act 1993. Although the regulations had been the subject of two Parliamentary debates, in *ex p JCWI*, the Court of Appeal by a majority of 2:1 held that their object could not be achieved without primary legislation. They struck the regulations down on the basis that they deprived asylum-seekers of the rights to remain in the United Kingdom pending determination of their applications by confronting them with a stark choice of destitution or departure.

It is, however, clear that the intention of Parliament, in *approving* these Regulations, was indeed to pose the very dilemma to the asylum-seeker of the kind identified by the Court of Appeal; and that Parliament *was* prepared to take the risk that a few asylum-seekers might suffer in order to deter a perceived bogus majority.

At the same time, the Court of Appeal in another case held that the housing departments of local authorities had been wrong to refuse asylum seekers the status of a person having a 'priority need' for accommodation under Section 59 of the Housing Act 1985.

Faced with two decisions of the Court of Appeal, which undermined their immigration policy, the Government laid before Parliament, and Parliament duly enacted, the Asylum and Immigration Act 1996, which blocked out any access for such asylum-seekers either to social security benefits or to priority accommodation.

But their lawyers lacked nothing in ingenuity. They resorted to section 21(1a) of the National Assistance Act of 1948 – a central element in the welfare legislation of the first post-war Labour Government – which obliged local authorities to make arrangements for the provision of residential accommodation (board, food and other necessities) for persons who by reason of age, illness, disability 'or other circumstances' were in 'need of care and attention which is not otherwise available to them'.

Now it was the foundation stone of the reasoning of the Court of Appeal in *ex p JCWI* that the asylum-seekers were ineligible for, still less entitled to, support; for if they had such a facility, the entire premise of that judgment, namely that the Government were by regulations seeking to starve or expel them, would have been unsound. This did not impress a differently constituted Court of Appeal who were prepared to identify the asylum-seekers as persons who *were* in need of care and attention by reason of 'other circumstances'; those other circumstances being the very lack of access to income support and accommodation, which Parliament had deliberately sought to deny them.

The Court stressed that the 1948 Act was 'a prime example of an act which is always speaking and so should be construed on a construction that continuously updates its wording to allow for changes since the Act was initially framed'. It is *not* quite tantamount to saying, as does the Queen in *Alice Through the Looking Glass*, that words mean what one wishes them to mean; but it comes perilously close. It is *doubtful* whether Parliament in 1948 ever envisaged that the provisions of the National Assistance Act should be used for the benefit of the huge numbers of persons from abroad without rights of residence – the House of Lords may yet have to pronounce on this issue. It is *certain* that Parliament in 1996 would never have intended to leave so large a loophole in the comprehensive barrier it sought to erect against asylum-seekers. To invoke the intention of Parliament as a justification of those judgments stretches the concept far beyond breaking point.

Another example of judicial imperialism is the *Pergau Dam* case when the Divisional Court quashed the grant of aid to fund the construction of the Pergau Dam in Malaysia – as political a decision as can be conceived. There are many remarkable features about that case. Firstly, the proceedings were brought by a pressure group, who were waging a campaign in the court, which had been unsuccessful outside it. Secondly, the Court in determining whether the grant was, in the statutory language of section 1(1) of the Overseas Development and Co-operation Act 1990 'for the purpose of promoting the development of 'Malaysia' chose to read in the word 'sound' before development. Thirdly, the Court then took upon itself the task of assessment of the soundness of the development – an economic matter. Fourthly, having preferred its analysis of that soundness to that of the Secretary of State, the Court determined that all other considerations – diplomatic, strategic or political – were irrelevant. In this way the judges conducted a significant part of the Far Eastern foreign policy of the nation.

The tensions created by this creative decision-making is revealed by the significant number of occasions in which the House of Lords in recent years has split into two camps on issues of public law – truly a House divided against itself.

In *Woolwich* the majority of the House of Lords held that taxes paid by a citizen to a public authority in response to an unlawful demand were *prima facie* recoverable as of right. This was a novel, if desirable, development in restitutionary law. Lord Goff for the majority however noted: 'However compelling the principle of justice may be it would never be sufficient to persuade a government to propose its legislative recognition by Parliament.' 'Caution', he added, 'otherwise known as the Treasury would never allow this to happen.'

That is not fulfilling legislative intent, but outflanking it.

In the *Fire Brigade Union* case the House of Lords held that a minister who had a *discretion* to bring into force a statutory scheme for the compensation of victims of crime, could not (in the interests of economy) substitute for it a scheme without a statutory basis. To put it shortly, where Parliament had given the minister a power, the House found that he had a duty.

Lord Mustill for the minority said:

> Some of the arguments addressed would have the court push to the very boundaries of the distinction between court and Parliament established in, and recognised ever since, the Bill of Rights 1689.

In *Pierson* the House of Lords split on the issue of whether the Home Secretary was entitled to increase the penal element in the sentence of a mandatory life prisoner. Lord Browne-Wilkinson for the minority said:

> Parliament having chosen to confer wide powers on the Secretary of State intends those powers to be exercised by him in accordance with his standards. If the Courts seek to limit the ambit of such powers so as to accord with the individual judges concepts of fairness, they will be indirectly attribute to the court a right to veto a decision conferred by Parliament on the Secretary of State.

In *Venables* the House of Lords split again on whether the Home Secretary could set a fixed tariff for the period of detention to be served by a young offender. There was in particular a 3–2 division on the issue of whether the Home Secretary was entitled to take account of the *vox populi* in form of petitions. Lord Lloyd for the minority said:

> It is to the Home Secretary that Parliament has entrusted the task of maintaining confidence in the criminal justice system and as part of that task gauging public concern in relation to a particular case when deciding on the earliest release date. I do not regard it as the function of the Court to tell him to perform that task.

The majority took a different view.

This capacity to outrun the legislature can be detected in related fields of private law. Bills to introduce a right to privacy into English law have never prospered; nor has any government ever subscribed to the introduction of such a right. The Court of Appeal indeed recently regretted in the Gordon Kaye case their inability to provide relief for a gross invasion where photographs were taken of a then heavily sedated actor lying with severe head injuries in a hospital bed: but said that 'a right of privacy has so long been disregarded that it can be recognised only by the legislature'. But in an article last year, Lord Bingham LCJ, bending the bow of Warren and Brandeis, wrote

> if, for whatever reason, legislation is not forthcoming, I think it almost inevitable that cases will arise in the Courts in which the need to give relief is obvious and pressing: and when such cases arise I do not think the Courts will be found wanting.

So the Courts *will* tiptoe in where Parliament declines to tread.

The powers of the judiciary have, of course, been enlarged in kind, and not merely degree, as a result of the subscription of the United Kingdom to the Treaty of Rome in 1971. In that sense: creativity is thrust upon them. By the medium of the European Communities Act 1972, section 2, all directly effective community law is part of the national legal system; and community law has a long arm. In consequence the courts have identified the power, indeed duty, to apply community law, and to disapply, dramatically and abnormally, conflicting domestic legislation. They have indulged in major departures from conventional constitutional law – suspending the operation of statutes, rewriting legislative provision, granting injunctions against the Crown. Hence the famous – or infamous – decision in *Factortame* in which provisions of the Merchant Shipping Act 1978 were first suspended and finally struck down as discriminatory against Spanish fishermen. Lord Bridge said

> whatever limitation of its sovereignty Parliament accepted when it enacted the European Communities Act 1972 was entirely voluntary. Under the terms of the Act of 1972 it has always been clear that it was the duty of a United Kingdom court, when delivering final judgment, to override any rule of national law found to be in conflict with any directly enforceable rule of Community law.

But was this truly so? In a case of irreconcilable conflict between a later statute and Brussels legislation, it was always in theory open to the courts to give effect to the latest expression of Parliament's will and treat the later statute as having impliedly repeated the earlier inconsistent community law. Moreover, English judges did not haul down the Union Jack and run up the blue and gold standard of the European Community only where EU law was directly effective, that is to say, passed the test for being capable of being relied upon against organs of the state in domestic courts. They also yielded to non-directly effective EU law and regarded themselves – after initial resistance – as bound to construe English statutes in order to harmonise with Community legislation even where *subsequently* enacted. So that Parliamentary language, chameleon-like, changed meaning under pressure of external forces (as in *Webb* where the issue was whether to dismiss a pregnant employee constituted sex discrimination): one of the younger school of amphibious practitioner-academics has written that the House of Lords' acceptance of the supremacy of Community law in *Factortame* and the *Equal Opportunities* cases, and of indirect effect in *Webb*, 'goes far beyond anything which can plausibly be justified in terms of the ECA 1972'.

But even if English judges had no choice, they have shown no reluctance to exercise the new power. In the EOC case (which concerned the validity of domestic constraints on the ability of part-time workers to claim employment rights), Lord Keith not only held that community law trumped domestic law: he poured scorn on the Secretary of State's effort to justify the minimum two-year period before which a part-time employee could claim for compensation for unfair dismissal or redundancy:

> Then as to the threshold provisions being requisite to achieve the stated aim, the question is whether on the evidence ... they have been proved actually to result in greater availability of part-time work than would be the case without them. In my opinion that question must be answered in the negative. The evidence for the Secretary of State consisted principally of an affidavit by an official in the Department of Employment which set out the views of the Department but did not contain anything capable of being regarded as factual evidence demonstrating the correctness of these views.

He refused to accept the implicit judgment of Parliament or the explicit opinion of the Secretary of State. For ministers to have to justify proposed legislation to Parliament is one thing: for them to have to justify it to judges whose training and experience lies in law, not policy you may think quite another. It was of this case that *The Times* concluded that 'Britain may now have, for the first time in its history, a constitutional court'.

Nor has the impact of EU law been confined to cases with an EU element. In *M v Home Office* the House of Lords reconsidered purely domestic law, and held that there was power in judicial review cases to grant injunctive relief against the Crown. The reinterpretation of section 31 of the Supreme Court Act 1981 was stimulated by a recognition that it would be odd if there was disharmony in this sensitive area between cases where citizens relied on EU law and where they relied on domestic rights only.

Power may have passed from Westminster to Brussels and Luxembourg – but at the same time it has passed to The Strand. The judicial appetite for innovatory jurisprudence in a purely domestic sphere has obviously been stimulated by experience of community law.

Through the gateway of community law, the European Convention on Human Rights has already infiltrated domestic law as a governing and not merely guiding instrument. The principles of the Convention form an integral part of the EC law to which English domestic (including statute) law is subject. The infiltration is on a significant scale. To quote Lord Browne-Wilkinson:

> How big is that area? At present it is in broad terms limited to areas of economic activity. But that is no mean area and affects life far wider than one would expect. Employment law, sex discrimination, food, medicine, the organisation of professions, road traffic, shipping and many other areas already the subject of EEC regulation.

But quite apart from propulsion by the EU Treaty, the resourcefulness of the judiciary in making use of the European Convention, even in the absence of incorporation, has been impressive: as an aid to construction of ambiguous primary or delegated legislation; as an aid to construction where Parliament has legislated in order to fulfil the United Kingdom's obligations under the ECHR; to resolve uncertainty in the common law; to supplement certain, but incomplete, common law; to determine the way in which judicial discretion should be exercised; to resolve *uncertainty* in, to buttress principles *already found* in, to supplement incomplete, or to judge the efficacy *of* the common law; as a source of public policy; and as stimulant of increased sensitivity to fundamental rights.

In a recent case dealing with the subject of disclosure of information in child adoption proceedings, Lord Mustill said that there was no need

> to engage the important general question which would have arisen if the conclusions dictated by English legislation and decided cases had differences in important respects from the jurisprudence of the European Tribunals.

This was a tantalising, even mischievous hint, that the court might in due course have given the Convention paramount status on their own, had New Labour not pre-empted them.

English judges are now freely using the vocabulary of fundamental rights. Lord Hoffmann said in this very lecture last year:

> [D]espite the fact that the United Kingdom has no written constitution, its principles of judicial control do not in practice differ from those applied in countries like the United States or Ireland which have constitutionally guaranteed rights.

Indeed, they are claiming to make the incorporation of the Convention otiose in a number of areas, primarily those concerned with freedom of speech (the First Amendment issue in American terms) or access to the courts. In *Derbyshire CC v Times Newspapers*, the House of Lords concluded that public bodies had no right to sue in defamation: considering that citizens should not be muffled in their power to criticise elected bodies. It was only just over 10 years ago that Lord Diplock doubted the utility of 'this evocative phrase' constitutional right in the context of another case, *Guardian Newspapers v Secretary of State for Defence*, which touched on another aspect of press freedom, the confidentiality of sources.

This use of the concept of constitutional right is no mere verbal garnish. It has a significance in substantive law. The courts have held there is a *lower* threshold of review where executive action interferes with fundamental human rights. As Sir Thomas Bingham MR put it in *Smith* – the case about the bar on homosexuals in the armed forces – 'The more substantial the interference of human rights, the more the court will require by way of justification before it is satisfied the decision is reasonable'. This sliding scale of judicial review owes again everything to the courts and nothing to Parliament.

Of course, the Convention is now to be incorporated: and even if the Government's apparent intention is not to give its overriding force, it cannot but encourage the developments to which I have referred. After all, if the judges can achieve so much by way of entrenchment of the fundamental rights which *it* enshrines without its incorporation, we can scarcely expect that they will do less with it. And sceptics have stressed not only the shift of power involved, but the risk of further politicisation of the judiciary in consequence.

The English judiciary are not without experience in adjudicating on issues arising in the context of a paramount constitution and Bill of Rights. The jurisdiction of the Privy Council once extended over pine and palm. But even if its geographical reach is now limited, its power to intrude upon matters of high sensitivity is still undoubted: the constitutionality of the death penalty; the effectiveness of a pardon given to rebels who sought to overthrow the Government of Trinidad and Tobago; the validity of the prolonged detention of the Vietnamese boat people in Hong Kong. The introduction of a Bill of Rights in Hong Kong provided further, if finite, clay for the judicial potter.

In all these areas, for two decades or more, the Privy Council have applied the approach canvassed by Lord Wilberforce that constitutions 'call for a generous interpretation and avoiding what has been called the austerity of tabulated legalism'. And in the same body's history lies the experience of determining conflict between states' rights and federal government at the time when it policed the federal jurisdictions of Canada and Australia.

In my view, there has been inadequate consideration of the degree to which devolution, on whose political merits I do *not* propose to pronounce, will cede further power to the judges. There was always the possibility of constitutional tension over the respective standings of the Act of Union with Scotland 1707 and Westminster legislation: but over the intervening centuries the courts have managed neatly to bypass it.

But if power is devolved to Scotland, there *will* necessarily be boundary disputes, patrolled by the judiciary. The question of what is within the remit of the Scottish Assembly, what is within that of the Westminster Parliament, will provoke questions similar to those which continue to arise in the Federal Constitutions of the Old Dominions and of the United States. There will be, as one recent commentator observed 'federalism in all but name'. The Consultation Paper says delphically:

> 4.15 The Scottish executive and UK government may from time to time take different views of the Scottish Parliament's legislative powers. There will therefore be procedures for identifying and resolving any such difficulties.

Apparently, such *vires* disputes will be resolved by the Privy Council – the Law Lords, English and Scots, by another name. But these warm words disguise the variety of circumstances in which such conflict can arise. It will not merely be a question of an advance dispute between the executives north and south of the border. The Scottish Assembly may pass laws whose legality is subsequently challenged directly or (for example, by way of defence to a criminal charge) indirectly. The genie cannot be kept in the box as easily as the Government appears to believe.

The expansive tendencies of conventional judicial review already encroached, as I have sought to illustrate, on the authority not only of the Executive, but also of the legislature – the separation of powers becoming close to a superiority. From time to time judges have exhibited too scant respect even for politicians who purport to respond to the will of the electorate particularly at local level. The manifesto of the Labour group, which they sought to implement in the *Fares Fair* case (free transport for pensioners in the Greater London area) was held by the Law Lords to be a legally irrelevant consideration in a decision, in which it has to be admitted, worked against the Law Lords' own interests since most were, and those who were not, would soon be, of pensionable age.

One last step remained to be taken: that is, to assert in certain extreme situations, unaffected, I stress, by EU law, that the will of Parliament could be ignored. Some judges seem prepared to take it.

It is constitutional orthodoxy that Parliament can act unjustly, but not unlawfully.

But three members of the English judiciary, in particular, have developed a thesis of judicial control which harks back to the seventeenth century and Sir Edward Coke: All three spoke extrajudicially: and all their lectures were, by coincidence, published in *Public Law* (1995) – not usually thought of as a revolutionary tract.

Lord Woolf said:

> As both Parliament and the courts derive their authority from the rule of law so both are subject to it and cannot act in a manner which involves its repudiation … There are even limits on the supremacy of Parliament which it is the Courts inalienable responsibility to identify and uphold. They are limits of the most modern dimension which I believe any democrat would accept. They are no more than necessary to enable the rule of law to be preserved.

Sir John Laws said:

> The doctrine of Parliamentary sovereignty cannot be vouched by Parliamentary legislation: a higher order law confers it and must of necessity limit it.

Sir Stephen Sedley said:

> We have today … in this country … a new and still emerging constitutional paradigm, no longer of Dicey's Supreme Parliament to whose will the rule of law must

> finally bend, but of a bi-polar sovereignty of the Crown in Parliament and the Crown in its Courts, to each of which the Crown's Ministers are answerable – politically to Parliament, legally to the Courts.

The English judges were treading cautiously down a path mapped out by more radical Antipodean judges, in particular Lord Cooke. Even in Australia, where there is no bill of rights, the courts have discerned implied boundaries to the power of the Commonwealth Parliament and held sections of Commonwealth legislation invalid on free speech grounds.

The path from subordination, through coordination, to control, may find not only example from the south, but inspiration from the north. The origins of the concept of Parliamentary sovereignty are found in English rather than in Scottish constitutional theory, and in *MacCormick v Lord Advocate*, Lord President Cooper questioned, obiter, the application of the doctrine to the Parliament of Great Britain. 'The principle of unlimited sovereignty of Parliament is a distinctive English principle which has no counterpart in Scottish constitutional law.'

I confess to a degree of scepticism about the impact of judicial supremacism: since it seems to me that if the position were ever to be reached in Great Britain where Parliament sought to perpetuate its powers indefinitely, or to introduce torture as a legal method of public interrogation, any orders of the judiciary seeking to reverse such acts would be writ in water. The assumption that government will accept judicial verdicts, encapsulated in the civilised practice that declaratory rather than coercive orders are normally made against it, would hardly be maintained in an age of even *elective* dictatorship.

There is, however, one instance in which the courts have already determined simply to ignore an unambiguous legislative rule. Section 4(4) of the Foreign Compensation Act 1950 stated that the Commission's decisions were not to be 'called in question in any Court of law'. A clearer provision it would be difficult to conceive. Parliament had stipulated that the Commission, right or wrong, was immune to judicial supervision. But in *Anisminic*, the House of Lords held that the exclusionary formula did not apply to a *purported* decision because it was one which the Commission had *no* jurisdiction to make. They then defined the Commission's jurisdiction in such a broad form that, as de Smith says, 'it was not easy to identify errors of law which in the light of their analyses would *not* be held to go to jurisdiction'.

The importance of *Anisminic* cannot be exaggerated. The House of Lords may not have said expressly that they were ignoring the legislative prohibition on judicial review by reference to a fundamental right of access to the courts, but their verbal legerdemain and decorum cannot conceal that they were doing precisely that.

As Sir William Wade has observed:

> The Court had been forced to rebel against Parliament … the intention of Parliament was clear … in refusing to enforce it the Court was applying the presumption that

> jurisdictional limit must be legally effective. This is tantamount to saying that judicial review is a constitutional fundamental which even the sovereign parliament cannot abolish.

*Anisminic*'s influence is still powerful. In the case of Mr Al-Fayed, the Court of Appeal (again by 2:1) held that a duty on the Home Secretary to voice his concerns to an applicant for naturalisation so that the applicant can seek to deal with them is to be implied into the British Nationality Act of 1981. The Act, however, provides expressly that the decision of the Secretary of State if refusing naturalisation 'shall not be subject to appeal or review in any court'. But because of *Anisminic* the Treasury Counsel for the acting Secretary of State did not even argue that judicial review was barred.

I would finally remind you that in the USA the powers of the courts to declare federal legislation unconstitutional (the badge of its Supreme Court) was something not expressly envisaged in the Constitution but in the creation of Chief Justice Marshall in *Marbury v Madison* in 1803. In his view, the authority of a court to pronounce on constitutionality flowed ineluctably from its judicial duty to determine the law: 'It is emphatically the province and duty of the judicial department to say what the law is.'

There are a number of risks run by the increasing involvement of judges in decisions of political impact, if not intent. Firstly, that they venture into areas outwith their expertise, even though limited to analysis of the evidence placed before them by contending parties, which may fall far short of the material relevant to a truly informed decision. Secondly, that they become embroiled, albeit unwittingly, in unseemly controversy with appointed officers, or elected representatives of the people spurred on by an enthusiastic media. Thirdly, that they themselves become judged by the same criteria as politicians, and may be compelled to submit to a kind of selection process which has affected the composition of the United States Supreme Court. Were the ordeals of Robert Bork and Clarence Thomas to be replicated in England, any diminution in status or salary would pale into significance as a disincentive to accepting judicial appointments. Fourthly, that they diminish their capacity to command respect in areas within which they both and are should be supreme. Fifthly, that they may even find themselves unable to sit as judges because of a conflict of interest caused by earlier public utterances. Judges, in an ideal world, must not only be (as they are) non-political, but be seen to be non-political. The tension between the Lord Chancellor's various roles can seem as a warning about too great an erosion of the separation of powers.

The sensitivity of the judiciary to the criticism that they are acting exorbitantly is marked. In the Al-Fayed case, the Court of Appeal, presided over by Lord Woolf, the Master of the Rolls, took a course, unprecedented in my experience, of issuing a press release. In that remarkable document published at the very same time as they ruled that Mr Howard had acted unlawfully, they stated that 'no *criticism* can be made of those who advised that the procedure followed was appropriate, nor of those that followed that advice'.

The present Lord Chief Justice, and former Master of the Rolls, Lord Bingham said at the Mansion House Dinner for Her Majesty's judges in 1996:

> Judicial review, my Lord Mayor, is not a novel phenomenon, as the Latin names of the principal remedies there witness. No constitutional democracy governed by the rule of law could function without it. Far from challenging the authority of Parliament, as is sometimes suggested, judicial review buttresses the authority of Parliament by ensuring that powers conferred by Parliament are used as Parliament intended. Nor does it involve any usurpation of ministerial authority. Judges are concerned with the lawfulness of administrative decisions, not there wisdom or advisability. It was after all a great judge, the late Lord Devlin, who reminded us that the British no more wish to be governed by judges than they wished to be judged by administrators.

These words of wisdom sit not wholly comfortably with present realities.

So there, as we approach the Millenium, is the picture. A court with powers to disapply statute in conflict with EU law and including in areas within the reach of community law the rights guaranteed by the Convention; an assertion that judges may inherently enjoy such a power and a prime example of its exercise (even if *sub silentio*) in the avoiding of judge-proofing clauses; control over executive action which, on analysis, uses the intention of the legislature as a cloak for the imposition of judicially ascertained values; an application of ever-widening principles of review to ever-widening areas of executive activity, now to be fortified by incorporation of the Convention; and the prospect of a judicial role as referee over the respective competences of Parliaments of Westminster and Edinburgh.

My thesis, then, is that the constitutional landscape has changed. It is a cliché of political scientists that power has leached away from Parliament to the Executive, and within the Executive from cabinet to Prime Minister. Less visible, but no less important, has been the accretion of judicial power at the expense of both. I do not suggest that judicial power is like lava from a suddenly erupting volcano streaming across a hitherto unaffected land mass: it is rather, like a glacier, moving by stealth into the same zones. But in substance, if not in form or name, the outlines of a Supreme Court are discernible.

I am conscious – and have been conscious throughout – that I address an audience well familiar with the Court's enjoyment of jurisdiction to consider the constitutional validity of laws enacted by both Houses of a legislature, whose proper name I shall not dare to try to pronounce. But this is the product of deliberate choice of those who brought to fruition the Constitution of Ireland of 1937: itself based on an earlier instrument of 1922. The judges in Ireland do what the Constitution invites, indeed obliges them to do.

By contrast it is essentially of its own volition that the power of the *English* judiciary has increased and is increasing. It is not my case that it ought to be diminished: it is only that the phenomenon be recognised, and the people, the ultimate repository of authority in a democracy, be entitled to pronounce it good or no.

# 7

# *'Neither Cloistered nor Virtuous? Judges and their Independence in the New Millennium'*

## The Atkin Lecture 1999*

It is a great privilege for me to be invited to give this lecture which commemorates one of the outstanding common law judges of the century, whose family are so happily represented here today, and to follow, like a solitary page behind a line of Wenceslases, in the footsteps of the far more august speakers who have preceded me in this role. I know how much the invitation pleased my father, Lord Beloff, a faithful member of this Club, and only regret that he did not live long enough to save me from errors and infelicities that, in the absence of his usual wise guidance, it will inevitably contain.

I have chosen as my title a corruption of one of Lord Atkin's most celebrated dicta, 'Justice is not a cloistered virtue', uttered as part of the advice of the Privy Council to His Majesty in *Ambard v Attorney-General for Trinidad and Tobago*. The case revolved around the conviction for contempt of court of the editor for a leading article in the *Port of Spain Gazette* entitled 'The Human Element'. The editorial criticised in a manner that would have astounded the editor of *The Sun*, both for its polysyllabic vocabulary and for its moderate tone, the alleged inequality of sentences passed in the islands for certain criminal offences.

Lord Atkin's observation was apt for my purposes in a number of overlapping ways. It is not, I hasten to assure you, that I intend to verge on the contemptuous in my remarks about the judiciary of England and Wales. Many of my best friends are judges and I hope that this situation persists beyond the conclusion of this lecture – and at least as long as I remain a practising member of the Bar.

But I wish to raise some questions about them with, of course, the greatest respect – a phrase that, I will explain for any non-lawyers present, when uttered in court, bears the precise opposite of its literal meaning.

I wish to suggest that contemporary criticism by others than myself of judges would stretch even the tolerance of Lord Atkin. I wish to examine whether and to what extent, judges, either as volunteers or as conscripts, have now emerged

* Archived in the Reform Club Library.

so far from the cloister into the arena as to put in jeopardy the independence which is their single most precious virtue.

And I wish to consider how the process of erosion can be halted, if it has not already gone too far.

Let me start, as so much discussion about the role of the contemporary judiciary in England must start, with the case of General Pinochet. For I have little doubt that the case and its consequences will have had as dramatic an effect on perception and, as a result, treatment of the judiciary as any other single happening in the recent past.

The bizarre sequence of events in the *Pinochet* case, which led to the three decisions indexed blandly in the Law Reports as *Ex p Pinochet Ugarte Nos 1 2* and *3*, is well known. In the first case the House of Lords split three – two in favour of the proposition that the General was not immune for reasons of sovereignty from extradition to Spain on charges of torture. In the second, the House unanimously set aside that decision on the grounds of apparent bias of one of the Lords involved, Lord Hoffmann, who had not disclosed his links to Amnesty International, an intervener in the proceedings. In the third, the House split five ways on the same issue as had been raised in the first hearing and, while favouring, again by a bare majority, extradition did so on extremely limited grounds, indeed advised the Home Secretary to reconsider whether to exercise his discretion to extradite. The case is now poised on a journey from the Bow Street Magistrates to the Divisional Court. There were some obvious lessons to be learned.

The first and foremost was the critical importance of the twin precepts that justice not only be done, but be seen to be done, and that, for that purpose, no man may be a judge in his own cause. As Lord Hope observed, 'One of the cornerstones of our legal system is the impartiality of the tribunals by which justice is administered'; and as Lord Nolan, the most recent, if not the only begetter of the standards which should guide those in public life, added, 'In any case, where the impartiality of a judge is in question the appearance of the matter is just as important as the reality.'

The second was that our judges can nowadays be involved in decisions freighted with political implications of the highest sensitivity: it indeed may strike someone not versed in the niceties of extradition law as odd that English judges should have any role in deciding whether a former leader of a friendly foreign state must stand trial in the courts of another friendly foreign state.

The third is that a result of litigation can often depend upon the composition of the tribunals. One could construct, what I shall loosely call a pro-Pinochet majority out of the members of the appellate committee who sat in cases one and three. *Quot judices tot sententiae*, if I may surreptitiously make use of a language now barred in the age of Woolf – the Lupine era – from the vocabulary of our courts. This proposition, familiar even to pupil barristers, let alone the subscribers to the American realist school of jurisprudence, may not have made hitherto a similar impact upon the general public. On the Clapham omnibus, they are said to speak of other things. But the attention of that public is now inevitably focused upon who selects the Law Lords, and who indeed selects the panels in any particular appeal, and, more generally, how senior judges are chosen for their distinctive constitutional role.

The fourth, and maybe most doleful, is that judges can make mistakes. Lord Hoffmann has never explained publicly the circumstances of his non-disclosure; but his failure has been expensive in terms of his own reputation and the reputation of the judiciary as well as to the public purse. I lack nothing in admiration for him. He was in a former incarnation my Roman law tutor at Oxford. He is nowadays recognised as an intellectual powerhouse among even the present Law Lords. But as Homer nodded, so, alas, did Hoffmann.

I want to develop some further thoughts from this point of departure. Judges share with other lawyers the unpopularity which inevitably stems from involvement in other people's disputes – if there were no disputes, there would be no need for judges – and the exercise of dispute resolution touches the lives of citizens on a micro, if not a macro basis, more intimately than the activities of other organs of government. From the very nature of their function springs the very imperative for their independence. But we take it as axiomatic that our judiciary not only should be, but are, independent – by which we mean broadly that the judges approach cases before them, untainted by any interest in their outcome, free from any outside pressure to reach a decision in a particular way, and excluding from their consideration, so far as is humanly possible, any of those prejudices which are the product of class, race, gender or genes. As Lord Saville has recently written, the best judges are 'people who will apply the rule of law, people who are able, and seen to be able, to put aside their personal feelings and views'.

We institutionalise judicial independence by immunising the higher judiciary from dismissal other than by address to both Houses of Parliament; and by legislation which prevents judicial salaries from being diminished other than by statute itself. It is well settled for the same policy reasons that judges as well as other participants in the forensic process are immune from action for statements made in the course of proceedings, even if made maliciously, and certainly if made foolishly!

We view with a sense of distaste, but also of comparative satisfaction, stories from overseas such as – and I take them at random from the last 12 months – the attack by the Government of the PRC on the decision of the Court of Final Appeal to give mainland children born to Hong Kong residents a right of abode in the former colony; the invitation extended by President Mugabe to three Supreme Court judges of Zimbabwe to resign because they pointed out in a judgment that Armed Forces are not entitled to arrest civilians; the unconvincing verdict on bizarre sexual charges against former Deputy Prime Minister Anwar in Malaysia; and, least remarked in this context but maybe the most telling of all, the acquittal of President Clinton on charges of impeachment, where the requisite dispassionate analysis by the Senate, *pro tem* constituted as a court of law and fact, curiously led all Democrats to one conclusion and all Republicans to another. No better example could be furnished of politics trumping law.

But though such gross aberrations would not conceivably occur in this jurisdiction, is any sense of complacency about the domestic state of judicial independence completely justified? Let me start with the *casus belli* in the Hoffmann case. I very much doubt that conflicts of interest in the personal sense are a pervasive problem in this country. And hitherto there has been a hallowed customary way of dealing with them if and when they arise. The case of *Megacorp International v Worldwide Plc* is called on; and the judge says to counsel before it starts, 'I should mention that my aunt Agatha has a parcel of 10 shares in the Plaintiff company in case either side has any objection to my sitting.' Counsel have a purely formal whispered interchange with their instructing solicitors and say in chorus, 'My Lord – or it may be my Lady – my clients are perfectly content for you to hear this matter.' The judge groans inwardly at the prospect of an eight-week reinsurance trial, spanning as it does, Lords, Wimbledon, Henley and the Open Golf Championship, and the case continues. It is recorded that when Russell LJ made a similar statement in the Court of Appeal, at the start of what threatened to be a lengthy and tedious hearing, Lord Denning, the then Master of the Rolls, leant over and said, 'If my brother Russell thinks he avoids sitting in this matter on as flimsy a pretext as that, he should think again.' But we live in more sensitive and less civilised times.

The Lord Chancellor wrote in stark terms to the Senior Law Lord in the wake of *Pinochet No 2* urging 'every effort to ensure that such state of affairs would not occur again' and requiring appropriate consideration and, if need be, disclosure of any such potential conflicts of interest. And the word has gone out at lower levels too. Judge Henry Pownall, retired from the Old Bailey, said in his valedictory a fortnight or so ago that he found it

> sad, even offensive, being bombarded by bumf from on high telling me that I must disclose my personal interest I may have or might have, which might be seen to have some effect on my judgment – as if I had not complied since pupillage.

The *Sunday Times* somewhat tendentiously purported to identify judges, including three in the High Court, who were said to have flouted the rule that commercial directorships should be surrendered on appointment.

In truth, there was far more smoke than fire. But judges have become wary, in circumstances of some perceived potential partiality, shunning even the traditional way of seeking parties' waiver of objection to their sitting, to which I have already referred, and have recused themselves on a number of grounds; not only of shareholding (however small) in a corporate party, but of an Oxford degree where the University was a litigant, membership of the same set of Chambers as one of the advocates, and, in one of my own cases, the fact that the judge had the day before received communion from a Dean who was a member of the relevant committee of the respondent quango! Judge Hooton, who famously adjourned a criminal trial to ensure his presence at the Wimbledon semi-finals (which he was, despite the predictable press hullabaloo, contractually entitled to do), chose not to sit in a case involving a hunt saboteur because of his own interest in rough shooting. Caesar's wife might have regarded some of these reactions as over-sensitive.

Patrick Bartle, the stipendiary magistrate who heard the application to extradite General Pinochet, was revealed in *The Times* as a member of the Conservative Party. While this might make him an endangered species, it could hardly by itself disqualify him from hearing the case, – and did not, in the event, prevent him from making an extradition order. Many judges have been or are members of or voters for political parties. If such membership or sympathy were held to disqualify from sitting in any case with political implications (as distinct from a case actually involving that political party) we should soon have no eligible judges at all!

But, more important, the notional cure is becoming more malign than the supposed disease. Challenges multiply as the so-called Hoffmann card is played. A golden opportunity is given to unscrupulous litigants to affect the make-up of their court by asserting a lack of independence, while fearful in fact of independence itself. By coincidence, this very week the Court of Appeal consisting of the Lord Chief Justice, the Vice-Chancellor, and the Master of the Rolls – Tom, Dick and Harry, if I may be familiar – are deciding a series of appeals which may result in guidelines to curb what the Lord Chancellor has trenchantly termed 'a legal industry'.

Interestingly few, if any, have sought to question whether it was appropriate for a judge such as Lord Hoffmann to be a member of even so apparently admirable a body as Amnesty. The present Lord Chief Justice in a book edited by the present Solicitor General wrote only a few years back: 'In this country a judge will undoubtedly expect to exercise considerable discretion about the bodies with which he will allow himself to be associated, and in avoiding involved in any campaigning organisation of even a non political kind.'

After all, one person's political prisoner is another person's terrorist.

Judges have also become more public and therefore publicised since the abolition of the Kilmuir Rules, which prohibited them from media contact unless specifically authorised by the Lord Chancellor. The rationale was that silence greatly enhanced their reputation for wisdom. At a time when we are now becoming as familiar with the media judge as we once were with the media don, the jury is out on whether it has been further enhanced by their speaking out. In my view, judges should be judged on their *ex cathedra* judgments, not their extra-curricular pronouncements, and should seek to confine themselves to the former.

Yet looming on the horizon is the insidious phenomenon of televised courts. I say 'insidious' because, quite apart from the potential for perverting what purports to be educational into what is envisaged as entertaining, the presence of television can necessarily affect judicial behaviour: no one behaves in the same way on camera as in camera. The performance of Judge Ito at the OJ Simpson trial should stand as a warning signal. It is not only advocates, but judges who can be tempted to play to the gallery. Immunity from such infection of their independence should, in my view, be preserved. Comprehensive coverage of cases would stupefy. Edited coverage would distort. All television corrupts; selective television corrupts absolutely.

There are a number of other ways in which the judiciary become involved in political controversy via extra-curricular activities, though as a result of compulsion, not free will, through their recurrent chairing of enquiries of a political character which (significantly) become known by the name of the presiding judge – Nolan, Scott, Saville, Phillips – something (interestingly) only permitted in the United States in situations of national emergency, as exemplified by the Warren Commission inquiry into the assassination of President John F Kennedy. The canons of judicial conduct promulgated by the ABA are hostile to such involvement unless the inquiries are law-connected.

The Scott Report was actively undermined by the former Government – through leak and spin, the modern methods of character assassination. The Executive by such political attacks increases the danger of destroying the very reputation for impartiality that judges need to perform their judicial functions, and underscores the undesirability of their initial involvement in such non-judicial activity.

Lord Saville – to take a contemporary example – is not only required to investigate the correctness of the conclusions of an earlier inquiry by Lord Widgery, the Lord Chief Justice, an exercise which by necessary implication involves his predecessor inquisitor in criticism, but has himself been subjected to judicial review in relation to his decision to refuse anonymity to army witnesses. It is in one way admirable that Lord Saville's status as a Law Lord does not save him from review when sitting in a non-judicial and subordinate capacity as chairman of an inquiry. However, the spectacle of a High Court or even appeal judge impugning his judgment is not calculated to promote confidence in the hierarchy of tribunals; and the problem is compounded by the calls for his resignation in the right-wing press (broadsheet as well as quasi-tabloid) attendant upon his initial defeat in the Divisional Court. His participation in his important exercise, in my view, damages (though no fault of his own) his future image as an impartial arbiter above the fray. And now the Hoffmann defence has intruded even into this sensitive area. The families of the deceased are contemplating a challenge to the Court of Appeal's decision to restore anonymity on the grounds that Lord Woolf, who presided, had served for two years in the army on national service – although why this should necessarily be thought to predispose him to the military is not by any means obvious.

The media, of course, are not slow to leap on bandwagons, even when they do not set them rolling. Another by-product of *Pinochet 2* was an extraordinary intrusion into and exposure of Lord Hoffmann's private life – or a version of it. Headlines in the press about 'Legover Lennie' and 'Lennie the Loin' may sufficiently give the bitter flavour of the witch hunt. Ministers and MPs are prevented by Parliamentary rules from attacking the character of judges. The press labour under no such restraint, external or internal. The right of free expression – the familiar justification – provides no excuse. The European Convention on Human Rights itself qualifies such right by considerations of the need to maintain 'the authority and impartiality of the judiciary' (Article 10(2)); equally the various considerations listed in Article 8(2), which would override the right to respect for private life, do not appear to be in play in any way in the case of Lord Hoffmann. There was in short no link between press punishment and judicial error: the interest of the public and the public interest were fatally confused. When Lord Atkin spoke in *Ambard* of the need for justice 'to suffer the scrutiny and respectful, even though outspoken comments of ordinary men, I doubt he would have had in mind something akin to Hoffmania.

The demystification of the judiciary is, of course, a phenomenon and by-product of our age. The sugar coating to the burdens of office dissolves: the pomp and circumstance depart. Cyril Hare in his 1930s classic, *Tragedy at Law* reminds us of the glories that were the old Assizes:

> A Rolls Royce of cavernous size purred at the door of the Lodgings. The High Sheriff, faintly redolent of moth balls but none the less a shining figure in the full-dress uniform of a Volunteer Regiment long since disbanded, strove to bow respectfully and to avoid tripping over his sword at the same time. His chaplain billowed in unaccustomed black silk. The Under Sheriff gripped his top hat in one hand and in the other the seven foot ebony wand, surmounted by a carved death's head, ... Behind, the Judge's Clerk, the Judge's Marshal, the Judge's Butler and the Marshal's Man formed a sombre but not less satisfying group of acolytes.

His Lordship's peevish complaint 'No trumpeters!' reminds us that these were times not only past, but *perdu*. I do not suggest that it is in any way necessary to reconstitute the glories of a bygone age. I merely surmise that if judges lodged in a motel, and lunched at McDonald's, people might be less prepared to accept that the law still had any majesty, or the judges' rulings any authority.

If judicial independence depends in part on the illusion that judges were different from the mere mortals whose fate was in their hands, the illusion is all but shattered. The demands on them of the bureaucrats are rampant as in every walk of modem professional life. As George Bernard Shaw might have said – a little unfairly it may be – those who can do; those who can't regulate.

The civil service interpreting and applying government policy compel judges to do less than full justice by taking account of considerations which extend beyond doing right in the particular case. Only last week, Lord Justice Rose, no silent spokesman for the judicial cause, warned that the recent proposals from the Lord Chancellor's department for 'planned work which begins at 9am and finishes not before 5pm', and for performance targets to be set, had 'very serious implications which the authorities have not appreciated in relation to the role of our independent judiciary'. I am not a campaigner for judicial indolence – although I suspect that those who have not participated in litigation have only a shallow notion of the stresses involved for the professional players – judges as well as advocates. But I do recognise that cases cannot be treated like guests on the bed of Procrustes with portions lopped off at either end to suit the diktats of some bureaucratic notion of an ideal timetable.

No profession is ever enthusiastic about regulation from outside; but the activities of, for example, dons and doctors, who voice equal resentment, do not have a constitutional dimension. The tension is palpable. Lord Steyn said 'The Judges do not share the modem adoration of the deity of economy, on the whole they put justice first.' A distinctive form of pressure upon judicial independence is a move towards positive discrimination. Earlier this year the *Labour Research* magazine analysed 652 judges, including the 85 appointed since the start of 1997, and concluded that the majority were white males and largely the product of independent schools and Oxbridge. Two celebrated campaigning solicitors then wrote an article in *The Times* suggesting that this was unacceptable. They argued that in environmental cases in particular, 'the judge's natural instincts ... are to protect property and the interests of the corporate world rather than those of the ordinary citizen' – the opposite analysis, I note, to that conventionally contained in the editorial columns of the *Daily Mail.*

I do not subscribe to the shallow view that evaluation of fact or analysis of law is a robotic exercise; what, for example, a judge regards as a credible explanation given by a witness for some event may be affected by cultural considerations; what is or is not the appropriate legal principle to apply, and of what it consists, may be so likewise. As Lord Hoffmann himself has said in a recent speech, 'Since judges are also people, this means that some degree of diversity in their application of values is inevitable.' Many legal problems have a range of potential solutions – Pinochet, I repeat, illustrates the point. But although fact-finding is an important aspect of the judicial act, it is not distinctively so. In England, after all, we conventionally assign to non-legally trained persons, lay magistrates and jurors, fact-finding functions. The distinctive quality of a judge is knowledge of the law and its application.

Such quality is not particular to, nor dependent upon, gender or race or social class. But giving all due weight to such factors, it would be intensely damaging to judicial independence if any factor other than perceived judicial merit were to be the criterion for judicial appointment. As the Lord Chancellor himself has put it, 'Our higher courts should not be sculpted to conform to some notion of social, political, sex or any other balance.' I mention *en passant* that one of the reasons why members of the Bar may be well (if not uniquely) qualified to be appointed to the Bench on the basis of their previous professional experience arises from the fact that years of acting, faithful to the cab rank rule, as the mouthpiece of the client, in the sphere of public law where I practise, sometimes for citizen against government, sometimes for government against citizen, has bred an habitual ability to see and appreciate both sides of any argument. The necessarily correlative disadvantage, I should in candour add, is an inhibition as to choosing between such arguments and an erosion of any sense of what is right and what is wrong, as distinct from what can or cannot plausibly be argued.

I do not suggest that appropriate efforts should not be made, as they are being made, to encourage applicants for judicial office from all sectors of the legal profession, nor that it was other than entirely sensible for the Lord Chancellor to appoint Sir Leonard Peach to review the whole system of judicial appointments. But the judge who owed appointment to positive discrimination would be the prisoner of the circumstances of such appointment. The current gender and ethnic imbalance in the judiciary reflects no more than the historic imbalance in the Bar, the pool from which candidates from the Bench are overwhelmingly selected. As the Bar broadens its intake (as it has done), so will a growing number of women and ethnic minority persons ascend to the Bench. If the constituency of potential appointees broadens – solicitors; even academics for appellate positions – this tendency will be encouraged. It would be as unwise to accelerate this natural and inevitable process as it would be to interfere with the timetable of childbirth. It is only to spare their blushes that I decline to name at least two women who, within 15 years, and two members of ethnic minorities who, within three decades, will surely be members of whatever apex court we then enjoy.

I draw an analogy from my experience at Oxford. The fact that the number of independent schools-educated students at Oxford is disproportionately high, occurs despite genuine and strenuous efforts to reach out to a wider world of applicants, not because of a desire to keep a closed academic shop. If critics wish us to discriminate positively in favour of the under-represented, they should say so, and be prepared to debate the implications of that strategy. They should not claim, fallaciously, that we ourselves are guilty of discrimination: refusal to discriminate positively is not itself discrimination.

I turn from the issue of who should be appointed – I shall return to the 'how' later – to the issue of how they should be paid. A reasonable remuneration for judges is in principle justified as a bulwark against the risk of corruption. Mercifully the debate about the level of judicial salaries in this country needs to take no account of that factor. But there are more subtle ways in which pay issues intersect with issues of judicial independence.

At present judges are ranked in groups from 1 to 7.2 – Lord Chief Justice through to district judge – and have their salaries uprated annually by statutory instrument laid before Parliament. Account is taken of the recommendations to the Review Body of Senior Salaries, who provide inter alia, 'independent advice to the Prime Minister and the Lord Chancellor on the remuneration of the holders of judicial office'. I am presently Chairman of the Judicial Sub-Committee of that body, and indicate that nothing I say should be regarded as other than provisional – indeed I raise questions rather than provide answers – and certainly does not represent conclusions of the body itself.

But I note performance-related pay is now common in the senior civil service; it is due in the foreseeable future for the senior military. At some future time the question is bound to be posed: is it feasible to introduce the same system for judicial salaries? In such a system of performance-related pay, judges within a particular group could have a variety of salaries, reflecting (no doubt within bands) their relative performances. But there are a number of problems which would necessarily arise in the context of any such scheme. By what criteria is judicial performance to be judged? Is a judge's performance to be assessed by his throughput – the number of cases decided – or the extent to which his judgments are appealed, unsuccessfully or at all? Who would exercise the judgement? Critically, on the basis that such judgement could be translated into pay differentials – a technical matter, no doubt as capable of achievement in this area as in others – what would be the consequences for judicial independence?

None of these questions, I suggest, is susceptible of any easy answer. It can be said cogently that the Lord Chancellor makes evaluations for promotion: that if X is elevated to the Court of Appeal, it is on the basis that he or she is assessed as a better candidate than Y, so that differentiation is not itself impossible. Against that, the impact on judicial independence of a division of judges within a single tier into sheep and goats would have to be most carefully weighed. The public might ask whether the favoured judges had not earned their salary spurs by their amenability to the powers that be.

I have spoken so far of fetters imposed upon judges from without. I tum now to judicial behaviour from within. Judges cannot be held responsible for many aspects of the enhancement of their purely judicial role – the accession to the European Community; the enactment into domestic law of the European Convention on Human Rights; the ascription of functions to the Privy Council in consequence of devolution of policing the type of conflicts familiar to the judiciary in federal jurisdictions. But judges have also become authors of their own misfortune, unnecessarily attracting accusations of overreaching themselves, not showing that 'judicial restraint', publicly proclaimed as a virtue last week by the Prime Minister's wife. Accession to the European Community gave judges legitimate power to set aside Acts of Parliament as contrary to a higher law – an experience customary for judges operating in a state with the written constitution, but alien to the domestic judiciary since, in the seventeenth century, Sir Edward Coke asserted a similar power by reference to a higher order of natural law. It was, however, unwise for some judges to assert, even if theoretically, a power to do the same merely because the legislation offended against what they see as fundamental rights. Lord Woolf and Lord Justice Laws in particular have hinted that parliamentary sovereignty may not be absolute.

Incorporation of the European Convention on Human Rights will give the judges legitimate power to invalidate executive action as violating its provisions. It is, however, unwise for some judges to proclaim that they should make judgments as if the Human Rights Act were which, by design it is not, already in force. Judicial review provides a salutary discipline against abuse or misuse of executive power. It is, however, unwise for judges to proclaim themselves as consciously filling a political vacuum left by an ineffective opposition. It is sensible that judges have sloughed off the barren literalism of traditional methods of statutory construction in favour of a purposive approach which seeks to discern the true intent of the legislation. It is, however, unwise for judges to seek to impose – and avowedly so – their own values upon a legislative framework so as to reach results which the legislature would never have contemplated, and which, had it contemplated them, it would surely have opposed. The areas of treatment of refugees and of prisoners serving life sentences provide a wealth of illustrations from recent law reports.

Ultimately, it must be accepted that judges lack democratic legitimacy. As unelected persons it is not their role, except where compelled to do so, to subvert the sovereignty of Parliament. The more involved in political issues they become, the more important it is that they should be then seen to be non-political.

This then engages the question of the infringement of separation of powers in our historic Constitution, the relevant part of which – the House of Lords – is under scrutiny by Lord Wakeham's Royal Commission.

In my view, irrespective of either the personal qualities of the individuals involved, or the contributions that Law Lords can make to the legislative (and, in the case of the Lord Chancellor, also the executive process) in an era when the judicial function has become inextricably involved in politics, it is no longer appropriate that judges should police laws in whose making they have a constitutional role.

The overriding disadvantage, in my view, of the possession of membership of Parliament on the one hand, and judicial functions on the other, relates to the appearance (as distinct from actuality) of judicial partiality – and consequent confusion in the public mind about the role of judges. Judges must not only be independent, but be seen to be independent; they should fulfil – and be thought to fulfil – the aims of the judicial oath 'without fear or favour affection or ill will'. If judges are members of a political institution, the perception of their necessary independence from the political process is blurred. When the Fire Brigade case, which involved the then Secretary of State, Michael Howard's, proposals to make cuts in the Criminal Injuries Compensation Scheme, came on before the Appellate Committee it was difficult to find five Law Lords to sit judicially, since so many of them had already spoken out, in debates and elsewhere, against the proposal. (And had they spoken out in favour, the problem would have been equally visible and actually worse, since judges should not appear to be creatures of the other branches of government.) The fact that the Law Lords split 3:2, with the minority suggesting that the majority were trespassing into the province of the legislature, underlined the danger of the status quo.

Constitutional conflicts of interest seem to me to provide a far greater cause for concern than personal ones. Section 13 of the Defamation Act 1996 was introduced by way of amendment by Lord Hoffmann to rectify the position by which an MP, who chose to sue for libel a newspaper who had impugned his parliamentary conduct, could have his action dismissed because the newspaper could not, on account of Article 9 of the Bill of Rights, defend itself in justifying its allegations, by referring to proceedings in the House, with the result that a fair trial was impossible. But how far Section 13 entrenches upon parliamentary privilege is a moot point; and fell for decision earlier this month when the case of *Neil Hamilton v Mohammed Al-Fayed* reached the House of Lords. Would it have been possible for Lord Hoffmann to sit and determine the objective meaning of Section 13 when he had, no doubt, a fixed subjective view about its purpose?

I turn to the position of the Lord Chancellor, that earthly three-in-one, with some trepidation, since I stand in the very room where he made his notorious, if humorous, comparison of himself to Cardinal Wolsey. He is not only the senior judge, and the head of the judiciary in England and Wales. He is also a politician who serves in the Cabinet and has a responsibility for a major executive and spending department.

The Lord Chancellor's involvement in politics has an unavoidable effect on the assessment of the independence of his judgments. Lord Chancellors may sit less frequently than they once did (in the same way as Attorney Generals appear far less in court as advocates for the Government than they did). But when they do sit, their role is compromised. It may have been coincidence that in *Pepper v Hart* (which established that, within limits, ministerial statements in Parliament were legitimate aids to construction of statutes) Lord Mackay dissented on the pragmatic ground that resort to such grounds would increase the cost of litigation. Was it the judge who spoke or the politician, Cabinet colleague of the Chancellor of the Exchequer? More important would the public be convinced that it was the former, not the latter?

Lord Irvine has sat equally sparingly, but one of his two (so far) reported cases concerned the right to use the highway for protest, a sensitive issue with obvious political overtones and one whose legally controversial nature was exemplified by the 3:2 split in the House. The Lord Chancellor ought sensibly to be ruled out of membership of the Appellate Committee whenever, for example, a decision of a Cabinet colleague is under challenge. But what if it were a decision of a local authority? Would it make a difference if the authority were of the same (or different) political stripe to that of the Lord Chancellor? The moment it is appreciated that the boundary lines between the indefensible and defensible are not fixed, but fluctuating, pragmatism as well as principle suggests that it is better (and simpler) for the Lord Chancellor not to sit at all. Given that even a Lord Chancellor with the legendary energies of the present incumbent has only been able to sit twice in two years suggests that the sacrifice involved is more formal than real. Lord Irvine does not, however, accept that he is *hors de combat* even for constitutional cases, and even with his back to the wall – I do not say wallpaper – has made throughout the year a formidable, but I believe ultimately unpersuasive case, for retention of the plurality of his powers. The European Commission of Human Rights has ruled that the position of the Bailiff of Guernsey, who, in a smaller world by far than that in which the Lord Chancellor holds triple sway, has legislative, executive and judicial roles, violates, if he sits judicially, Article 6 of the European Convention on Human Rights (itself scheduled to the Human Rights Act 1998) which guarantees, inter alia, 'an independent and impartial tribunal'. If the European Court of Human Rights (which has recently heard the case) reaches the same conclusion – and the matter is presently under consideration – reform may be the only option.

I confess that I reach these conclusions without relish. I do not believe that nations with a long history of evolving democratic government should lightly discard traditions or images which have served them well. A sense of history, even a *soupçon* of ceremony, is no bad thing. If l may adapt what Oliver Wendell Holmes said about the law, the life of constitutions is not logic, but experience. Rules often matter less than practice; convention and compromise have valuable roles. But if perceptions of the essence of justice have become more sensitive, then the institutions which provide that justice must adapt to those perceptions.

I return lastly to the question of judicial appointments. The statutory protection of the higher judiciary against arbitrary dismissal or diminution in benefits because of offence caused to the Government of the day contrasts vividly with the fact that though in form the Queen's judges in substance they owe their appointment to the Government, the Lord Chancellor – or in the case of the Law Lords the Prime Minister – acting inevitably on his advice, which allows for political calculation to inform the minds of the appointer, though not the appointed.

There are, it must be recognised, nowadays no more appointments as a reward for political service. At the start of the century, membership of the House of Commons was often seen as a springboard to judicial office. By its end even the reversionary right of the Attorney General to the Lord Chief Justiceship – indeed to any judicial post – had long since atrophied. The reasons lie partly in the inability of any one any longer to enjoy a career in politics simultaneously with a career in law of sufficient distinction to make an appointment to the Bench credible; partly because of an increased scrupulousness in the Lord Chancellor. However, the fact that the power is not abused does not mean that it is not capable of abuse; nor can it eradicate the perception for potential abuse.

No judges rightly stand higher in the esteem of their colleagues, the profession and the public at large than Lord Bingham LCJ and Lord Woolf MR; but it is not without interest that each ranks among the handful of judges who were actually supportive of the Mackay and Irvine legal reforms; nor that Lord Justice Rose, the judges' candidate for the office of Lord Chief Justice on the untimely death of Lord Taylor, had been an outspoken critic of the then Home Secretary's sentencing proposals as well as having suggested that some female appointments to the High Court Bench owed more to a policy of political correctness than of selection on merit.

In December 1973, when Sir John Donaldson, a High Court Judge, was sitting as the First President of the Industrial Relations Court, 187 Labour MPs called for his removal for 'political prejudice and partiality'. Donaldson ended his career as Master of the Rolls, but not until there had been a change of administration. What was unpalatable to the Labour MPs *was* appetising to Mrs Thatcher. Lord Steyn has suggested that separation of powers can only be ensured if the Lord Chief Justice is head of the judiciary. One might logically add (though Lord Steyn does not) if he – or she – appointed the judges. I doubt, however, that such bird would fly.

On the contrary, any move is likely to be in the other direction. Lord Patten, the former Education Minister, has already suggested that in so far as the judicial role has become objectively politicised, so the elected politicians must have a role, like Congress in the United States, in appointment of the judges.

The leader of the Conservative Party, William Hague, has developed that thought to its logical conclusion by calling for a House of Commons' veto on senior judicial appointments. Dr Liam Fox has suggested that newly appointed candidates should appear before a new joint committee of both Houses of Parliament where his or her views could be sought on a range of political and legal matters. Any such schemes would be the fatal blow to the independence of the judiciary. That our potential judges should be Borked and Thomassed will add to the haemorrhage of talent which the High Court Bench is already sustaining. Lord Browne Wilkinson, the Senior Law Lord, will apparently say in an interview in *The Times* tomorrow that, while willing to sacrifice several million pounds of income in advancing from Bar to Bench, he would not have accepted office if he had had to undergo such a cross-examination.

I cite only the most notorious recent examples of Congressional inquisition, which were fuelled by a heady cocktail of political partisanship and political correctness, so that one nominee was never appointed and the other is a maimed presence on the Bench. Indeed, as disquieting as the treatment meted out to such nominees, is the reason why they were nominated, that is to say, to sustain a particular philosophical majority on the Supreme Court Bench? The US Supreme Court Bench contains judges of surpassing ability; but their method of selection is something which should not lightly be transplanted. In my view, it is even less acceptable that nomination should be the plaything of a multitude of elected politicians than that it should be the perquisite of a single unelected one. I would prefer some form of appointments commission whose membership and whose functions should be legislatively defined so as to ensure that merit alone was the touchstone of elevation to the Bench.

I appreciate that it will be asked: *Quis custodiet ipsos custodes?* –Who will appoint the appointers? – and that this will only remove at one stage potential political influence on any appointment. But there is no perfect solution. What is important is that my proposal increases, not narrows, the distance between the politicians and the judiciary. Accountability – the favoured buzz word of those who take the other view – is in my view, a euphemism for control. From my perspective the virtues of an Appointments Commission is not that it exposes judges to, but that it protects them from, the excesses of democratic or popular selection.

Lord Atkin had strong belief in the separation of powers between Executive, legislature and judiciary. Like Lord Denning, several of his most memorable judgments upholding the rule of law were dissents, more valuable for the principle they asserted than the precedent they set; *Liversidge v Anderson*, the subject of two distinguished Atkin lectures, being the best-known example.

But in a private letter to Sir Herbert Evatt written in 1940, Atkin touched a broader chord:

> How *little the public realise how dependent they are for their happiness on an impartial administration of justice. I have often thought it is like oxygen in the air: they know and care nothing about it until it is withdrawn.*

I have sought to ventilate my own concerns in this historic club to a more sentient and sophisticated sector of the public. If my lecture has been more patchwork quilt than monochrome cloth it is because the concept of judicial independence admits of no solitary or universally accepted definition. But we can legitimately seek to preserve and protect that which we cannot precisely describe. I fervently hope that the enemies of independence that I have identified can be kept at bay; and that all four estates of the realm (for I will accept the media into that category in terms of actual, if not legal power), but also the wider public will recognise the value of judicial independence, and strive to diminish the dangers to it. It is not in the people's interest to have the people's judges.

# 8

# *'Paying Judges: Why, Who, Whom, How Much?'* Neill Lecture 2006*

My Lords, Ladies and Gentlemen, it is a great privilege for me to be invited to deliver the fifth Neill Lecture following in the footsteps of such legal giants of our time as Lord Bingham of Cornhill, Lord Woolf of Barnes, Lord Steyn and Lord Hoffmann, just as the page followed in the footsteps of Good King Wenceslas in the snowy wastes of Bohemia. After four aces the Fellows of All Souls have clearly opted to play the Joker.

Pat Neill, the honorand, is fit to be ranked with Tom and Harry, not to speak of Johann and Lenny, in the annals of the law although he abstained from taking judicial appointment in this country. Instead, like a modern Pooh Bah, he became Lord High everything else, notably – I make a judicious selection – Warden of All Souls, Vice Chancellor of Oxford University, Chairman of the Press Council, Chairman of the Committee on Standards in Public Life and Treasurer of Gray's Inn.

My path has crossed with Pat's at several junctures. We appeared against each other in court, most memorably in a case in the Privy Council, *Ng Enterprises v Urban Council*, which involved an issue of major constitutional importance, namely whether my client could continue to sell 'Mister Softie' ice cream in Hong Kong from mobile vans. There were no Mr Softies in the Privy Council and they acceded unanimously to Pat's argument that regulation of an activity could sometimes, if not always, include its outright prohibition.

When Vice Chancellor of Oxford, Pat invited me to chair a committee which investigated a unique piece of alleged plagiarism in a thesis submitted and approved by this University for the degree of doctor of philosophy in the field of public international law. Our report determined that the charge was, alas, made out; but Pat's successor prevailed upon us not to give wide currency to our conclusion since it showed that the system was as potentially vulnerable to fraud as are postal ballots at municipal elections, and opened up vistas of headlines in *The Mail on Sunday*: 'The dumbing down of the doctorate'.

* (2006) 18 *The Denning Law Journal* 1.

Finally, I followed Pat in what is now becoming the Oxford 'head of house' slot in the Appeal Courts of Jersey and Guernsey, if a sequence of two can create a precedent, in the same way as certain places have become reserved to members of particular ethnic groups or genders on the Supreme Court of the United States of America, a tribunal which enjoys a somewhat more extensive jurisdiction.

I should add, before warming to my theme, that I understand that in recognition of Pat's abilities as a pianist, this lecture takes place only on alternate years, the intervening ones being the occasion for a concert. I make no great – or indeed any – claims to the merits of my address, but I can say with a supreme measure of confidence that it will at any rate be better than my performance on the piano.

It is axiomatic, so Halsbury recites, that 'the independence of the judiciary is essential to the rule of law and to the continuance of its own authority and legitimacy'. Some of the mechanisms to ensure this are historic, for example security of tenure; others more modern, ie prospective appointments by a Judicial Appointments Commission. The principle that judicial salaries may be increased by administrative action, but may not be reduced except, presumably, by Act of Parliament, has its origins in the Act of Settlement 1701 and has been linked with immunity from removal as one of the guarantors of such independence.

In a decision last year in the sensitive area of immigration control, *R (on the application of G) v Immigration Appeal Tribunal*, Lord Phillips of Worth Matravers, then Master of the Rolls, and now Lord Chief Justice, said expressly:

> It is the role of the judges to preserve the rule of law. The importance of that role has long been recognised by the Parliament. It is a constitutional norm recognised by statutory provisions that protect the independence of the judiciary such as Sections 11 and 12 of the Supreme Court of 1981, which are the recent descendants of the Act of Settlement. The same norm is now enshrined in the Constitutional Reform Act 2005 s 34(4).

A more sonorous reference to the original statute featured in a speech by one of Lord Phillips's predecessors on a less formal occasion, a provincial Law Society Dinner in Hastings in 1935, when Lord Hewart said:

> It might be useful sometimes to remind persons who have forgotten, or who never knew, that there is still in existence an instrument called the Act of Settlement, and that the independence of judges is the protection of the people. 'That speech incidentally forms part of a collection of ephemera by that less than radical figure entitled 'Not Without Prejudice' – an all but unrivalled example of lawyerly meiosis.

The principle that judges' pay should not be diminished while they hold office is reflected in the constitutions and laws of many jurisdictions, not all of which are based on the common law, such as Brazil, Egypt and Japan as well as in common law-based jurisdictions, such as the USA, Bangladesh, India, Australia, Canada, Ghana, Ireland, New Zealand, Malta and Singapore – indeed generally throughout the New Commonwealth where constitutions retained their original Westminster hallmark.

However, the principle is not universal. In Finland there is no law to that effect. An academic commentator noted, 'There are no regulations against decreasing salaries', adding somewhat primly, 'but it is out of the question and no one has, perhaps, even thought about it' – and more primly still, 'a judicial proceeding is not the way to solve problems relating to salaries'. Norway, Italy, Portugal, Spain, Uganda, Uruguay, France and Greece supply other examples of the principle's exclusion. In Israel, the Basic Law provides that a reduction in judicial salaries may be made only if it does not apply solely to such salaries in the public sector. In Germany, the Basic Law stipulates that, in the extraordinary event of changes in the structure of courts, judges may be transferred or removed 'provided they retain their full salary', but in ordinary circumstances judges' salaries are linked to the annual rate of inflation in the same way as the pay of other civil servants.

In Russia too there is no such guarantee. China is another notable exception. A standard commentary refers to 'the relatively low social and bureaucratic status and pay of the PRC Judges'. Ominously, Article 93 of the Basic Law of the Hong Kong SAR confirms only the irreducibility of present pay and allowances for judges who served at the time of the hand-back. No similar provision is made for subsequent appointees. It has been bleakly observed: 'There is no guarantee that salaries or other benefits of subsequent appointees would not be reduced.'

In other countries the principle, once applicable, has been abandoned. In Sweden, the Constitution was modified in 1966 to allow for such reduction; likewise in Belgium in 1980. In the Netherlands, indeed, where law also fixes the salaries of judges, it is expressly provided that 'the legislature can reduce judicial salaries'.

Nor is this altogether surprising. The common ground identified in international instruments, such as the IBA Minimum Standards of Judicial Independence, is that judges' salaries can be reduced only as part of an overall economic package, not that they cannot be reduced at all. So whereas in England, we consider the principle of the protection of judicial salaries to be a necessary but not, of course, a sufficient guarantee of judicial independence, in the wider world it is not always seen as necessary.

I wish to explore the prehistory of the domestic principle, its development from the Act of Settlement onwards, its rationale, and the contemporary issues surrounding judicial pay in this country.

The inspiration for any form of judicial payment was rooted in the consideration that judges who were not paid could be bought. Wilfred Prest has written, 'The spectre of judicial corruption haunted the west from classical times onwards.'

Corruption was certainly a problem in England during the reign of Henry III when, in Holdsworth's words, all royal officials, judges included, were 'both poorly and irregularly paid'. The short-lived Provisions of Oxford in 1258 were introduced to ensure that the Chief Justiciary 'Takes nothing unless it be presents of bread and wine, and such things, to wit food and drink, as have been used to be brought to the tables of great men.'

The oath administered to newly appointed Justices of the Courts of King's Bench, Exchequer and Common Pleas from 1344 onwards included an undertaking to abstain from receipt of gifts 'except meat and drink and that of small value' at the same time a promise to 'do equal law and execution of right to all … rich or poor', whose value, if not vocabulary, has persisted into modern times.

The history of judges' pay prior to the Act of Settlement has been recounted, amongst other places, with characteristic detail and humour – as befits a Trinity graduate – in an article by Theobald Mathew, who identified as his chief source of information Sir William Dugdale's *Origines Juridiciales*. The records begin in the eleventh year of Henry III when William Insula and R Ducket, Kings Justices, received 'X (ten) marks' (a mark being 13 shillings and 4 pence, if I may cross-refer to another obsolete currency) each out of the Exchequer. The trend was generally upward although there was shrinkage in the reign of Edward III in the salary of the Chief Justice of the King's Bench Division.

In the reign of Henry VI, judges were required to pay taxes on their income for the first time. Mathew comments, 'This novel and disagreeable demand was probably the explanation of the subsequent raising of judicial salaries.' During the reign of Elizabeth I, The Lord Chief Justice in England was paid for Reward and Robes £208.68, Wyne: 2 tonnes at £5 per tonne: £10.00, allowance for being justice of assise: £20.00.

The assessment of the judges for taxation purposes in the reign of Henry VIII shows, however, that they had sources of income apart from official pay: presents, fees, perquisites under a system 'in full swing', as Mathew puts it,'during the sixteenth century'. The right to sell legal office, or to bestow it on some penurious relation was prime among them.

The Lord Chancellor up to time of Lord Eldon in the nineteenth century had a surfeit of sinecures to bestow. Mathew dwells with palpable relish on the exotic nature of these creatures inhabiting the undergrowth of the law in a kind of legal bestiary: the Keeper of Her Majesty's Hanaper, the Clerk of the Custodies of Lunatics and Idiots, the Prothonotary of the Court of Chancery, Chaffwax, whose duty it was to bring the wax to the proper state of liquefaction when the Government Seal was in use. As Mathew comments wryly: 'These posts were alike in two respects – the emoluments were large and the duties could be performed by a deputy.'

The offices in the gift of the Chief Justices were fewer, but by no means insignificant.

But even these benefits were perceived as insufficient to make bribes otiose and in the sixteenth and early seventeenth century the satire directed at the judiciary increased. In the middle of the sixteenth century, Bishop Hugh Latimer had inveighed against judicial bribe-taking. Curiously, the reputation of Chancery judges was inferior to that of their common law counterparts, as they sat solo and without juries, and did not take the common law oath.

As Prest puts it, 'By the reign of James I the inflation-stricken salaries for judges in the three ancient common law courts hardly provided a significant deterrent to impropriety.' Bacon's fall from office as Lord Chancellor in 1621 for accepting gifts from litigants is not the only, if it is the best-known, example of judicial corruption. In 1641 the charges on which Lord Keeper Finch was impeached included two for such corruption, which dated back to the time when he was Chief Justice of the Court of Common Pleas.

In the same year, 1641, the House of Commons ordered John Pym to include in the Grand Remonstrance a clause attacking the buying and selling of judicial office as 'being among the causes and remedies of the evils of this kingdom'. The remedy for judicial corruption was perceived to be adequate pay for judges out of public revenue openly declared.

In September 1645 a massive 500 per cent increase from under £200 to the £1,000 pa in the salaries of the common law judges was effected by Resolution of the House of Commons. In present day values the uplift was from approximately £23,000 to approximately £116,000. Prest suggests that the increase in financial provision after 1645 was of 'prime importance' in improving judicial integrity.

But the restraint on judges supplementing their salaries with fees was expressly abandoned in January 1660, even before the Restoration: 'The important if unforeseen result', adds Prest, 'was that post 1660 judicial income did not fall quite so far behind those of leading counsel as they might otherwise have done.' However, payments remained at the same level until the judges' next pay rise in the next century.

The day after the House of Commons resolved that James II had abdicated in 1688, the Parliamentary Committee drew up its agreement to be presented to a new king, which contained provisions for security of tenure and for payment of judges' salaries out of the public revenue only. These provisions, however, did not appear in the Bill of Rights 1688. In 1693 in *Bridgman v Holt* three puisne judges of the Court of King's Bench, faithful to the old ways, upheld the right of their Chief Justice to the very valuable sinecure office of Chief Clerk of the King's Bench.

But in 1701 the Act of Settlement, as I have already indicated, gave judges secure tenure and secure pay. It provided: 'Judges commission to be made quam diu se bene gesserit and their salaries ascertained and established', then interpreted to mean that judicial salaries should be fixed by Parliament and not left to the discretion of the Executive. GN Clark notes in his volume in the *Oxford History of England*:

> It should be simply regarded as the formal termination of that control of judges by the executive which had died with the Stuart system. It removed the possibility of a new attempt to subject judges to Royal control: judicial independence has been a central fact of the constitution from the fall of James II.

Nonetheless in the early eighteenth century, judicial salaries still frequently ran up to three terms in arrears and while increasingly stringent ethical sensibilities percolated among the common law judiciary from 1650 onwards, the practices of judicial favouritism, receipt of fees and sale of legal offices persisted long after.

Lord Chancellor Macclesfield increased the honorarium charged by his predecessor for the sale of the Chancery Masterships by so much that the newly appointed Masters felt obliged to recoup the premiums they had had to pay from the litigants who appeared before them. In 1724 the same Lord Chancellor was duly impeached, convicted and fined £30,000.

At the end of the seventeenth century the salaries of the puisne judges were £1,000 per year (approximately £118,000 in present-day values) complemented by an equivalent amount of fees. Although the salaries were increased in 1714, 1760 – described as 'noble improvements' by no less a figure than Blackstone – 1779, 1799 and 1809, while the value of money diminished, the problems of extra-curricular remuneration remained.

Two further developments were noteworthy. First the rule was established that, unless Parliament had provided (or promised) a salary, no judicial vacancy could be filled. Secondly, judicial salaries were charged to the consolidated fund, created in 1767, so further protecting judges against the vagaries of politicians.

In 1815, puisne judges were paid £2,400 (approximately £135,000 in present-day values), but still drew much of their income from fees – something that, according to the former Chief Justice of Australia, Sir Anthony Mason, in a throwaway line in a judgment concerned with cycling selection procedures for the Sydney Olympic Games, explained the longstanding judicial opposition to arbitration:

> As formally the emoluments of Judges depended mainly or almost entirely upon fees, and they had no fixed salary there was great competition to get as much litigation as possible into Westminster Hall for the division of the spoils. Therefore they saw that the Courts ought not to be ousted from their jurisdiction and that it was contrary to the policy of the old law.

In 1826 two Chiefs lost the whole of their patronage and fixed, enhanced compensatory, but above all tax-free salaries replaced the old method of remuneration, with a range from the Chief Justice of King's Bench at £10,000 per annum through to judges and barons at £5,500 – an enviable £346,000 in present-day values – notwithstanding the opposition from some, on one flank, who regarded the power to dispose of offices as a necessary prerogative of a Chief Justice, and on the other the radical Brougham, but for whose oratory the basic figure would have been £6,000.

This tax-free annual salary was trimmed to £5,000 – still no pittance at £338,000 in present-day values – in 1832, the same year in which the Lord Chancellor lost his sinecures – but not, for reasons of constitutional propriety, of those already appointed at the higher salary. It remained at that level (astonishingly) for over 100 years.

In 1851 by the Court of Chancery Act the salary of the Master of the Rolls was fixed at £6,000, and those of two new judges of the Court of Appeal in Chancery at the same sum, but when in 1873 the number of Lord Justices was increased to five the salary was lowered to £5,000. The judges, consulted on whether the newly titled Lords Justices should be distinguished from mere puisnes by a further £500 per annum or by a Privy Councillorship, preferred glory over gold.

Gladstone's efforts to cut judicial salaries in his first administration was resisted by the judges who refused to discuss the forthcoming Judicature Bill while such a threat existed, Chief Justice Bovill of Common Pleas arguing that 'since judges' salaries were fixed, everything especially house rents, servants and horses have become much more expensive'. Their salaries were, however, confirmed to be subjected to income tax in Judicature Act 1873 following on the Income Tax Act 1842. The Privy Council later opined in a Canadian case in 1937 – with what suppressed reluctance I can only speculate – 'Neither the independence nor any other attribute of the judiciary can be affected by a general income tax which charges their official incomes on the same footing as the incomes of other citizens.'

It is arguable that during nineteenth century the real value of the High Court judges' salary did not decline, but it is indisputable that there was a dramatic increase of 250 per cent in the cost of living between 1900 and 1920 so that, when tax was taken into account, judges, in the view of that most sapient and learned diagnostician of the judicial condition, the former Master of Pembroke, Robert Stevens, 'really were suffering serious diminution in status'.

Lord Birkenhead, Lord Chancellor from 1920 to 1922, himself a notorious over-spender, was sympathetic to High Court judges, but the governments of which he was a member were not persuaded to favour increases since the average earnings of QCs in 1920–21 were £6,814 whereas judges had not only their £5,000 pa but also an attractive non-contributory pension, a knighthood and concomitant prestige. The 1920s were indeed a time when High Court judges did not question their salaries or pension since the cost of living was dropping and the Bar's prosperity was at best erratic.

But the Great Crash at the turn of the next decade reverberated inside, as it did outside, the courts. The National Economy Act 1931 authorised Crown by Order in Council to make economies in remuneration of persons in the service of the Crown and it reduced by 20 per cent salaries of judges which had been – I repeat, been – static at £5,000 pa since 1832 and were worth in present-day values £220,000. By that time the only judges who received more than £5,000 (less income tax) were the Lord Chief Justice (£8,000), the Master of the Rolls (£6,000) and the six Lords of Appeal (£6,000).

Mathew commented sadly:

> It is melancholy to realise that the Judges, with a salary of £5,000 diminished by 20% and the deductions of tax and surtax were worse off than they were in 1799 when they had £3,000 p.a. 'free and clear of all taxes and deductions whatever'.

A deputation of judges complained to Lord Chancellor Sankey, who in consequence addressed the Cabinet with the following plea: 'I must point out that their (ie the Judges) prestige will be lowered. They will be addressed in Court by leaders of the Bar who sometimes make in 2 or 3 days as much as a judge makes in a year.' *Plus ça change*!

There were threats of resignation, and representations which ranged from the dignified to the extreme such as those of Mr Justice McCardie, who spoke of 'pecuniary sacrifice to which there is no parallel in the world'; of Mr Justice McNaughten, who said that 'the judges were now in the power of civil servants and he considered his position was no better than that of an office boy', adding as a final thrust 'at the Home Office'; and of Mr Justice Maugham, who complained that the judges had been treated 'as if they were policemen or postmen'. With few exceptions, the vehemence with which judges expressed their views was in inverse proportion to their judicial reputation.

There was talk of a Petition of Right, raising the interesting issue of the reach of the principle *nemo judex in causa sua*. The Government had a defensive bill drawn up by George Schuster, the Lord Chancellor's Permanent Secretary who wrote to the Parliamentary draftsmen with the cunning of a Machiavelli, even of a Mandelson,

> begin with a recital which should be as long and pompous as possible, asserting the independence and all the rest of it, negating any idea that the Economy Act or Order by Council affected that in any way … then declare that notwithstanding all this they are affected by the cut.

Academics entered the fray. Sir William Holdsworth proposed that judges' salaries be made tax-free but ventured, additionally, the observation that on its true construction, the National Economy Act did not apply to judges at all who were not 'persons in his Majesty's Service'. Professor Sir William Wade QC has since expressed a contrary view shared by his no less eminent namesake, Professor ECS Wade. In that clash of the titans I prefer the views of the junior Sir William. Service takes many forms. Its meaning in public law differs from that in private law. and to suppose that the Wade analysis threatens their independence is truly to elevate form above substance.

In the end the judges did not strike – strikes are left to the modern Criminal Bar – and in 1934 the judges' salaries were quickly restored. Schuster's biographers have written, 'Looking back on this convoluted conflict as a piece of legal history, it is clear that Judges who protested were concerned about money rather than constitutional principle.'

I should add that the Invergordon Mutiny in 1931 resulted in a Government commitment that no salary reductions for servicemen, police or teachers would exceed 10 per cent, proving, if nothing else, that politicians were – and doubtless still are – more fearful of revolt among the British navy than among the British judiciary.

In the post-World War II years under both Labour and Conservative administrations, issues about the scale of judicial salaries continued to surface, but the time for an increase never seemed ripe: egalitarianism and economics both militated against it. Not until 1954 was there an uplift from £5,000 to £8,000, about £143,000 in present-day values. Lord Maugham, the ex-Lord Chancellor, as the former Mr Justice Maugham had by now become, was as querulous in the 1950s as he had been in the 1930s, suggesting that for a judge on the net salary, 'it is impossible to support a wife and children with dignity and to send his sons to public school' – an observation whose unspoken premises could justify a thesis in itself.

By 1960 the cost of living had risen 400 per cent since 1913/14, High Court salaries by only 60 per cent, and the rate of tax had *grow'd like Topsy*. In real terms, judges' salaries had peaked more than a century and a half earlier, and were on an accelerating downward curve.

To hasten this brief history to its conclusion, the Judicial Remuneration Act 1965 provided that judges' pay could be increased, but not reduced, by Order in Council with concurrence of both Houses of Parliament. It also raised High Court judges' salaries to £10,000: £126,000 in present-day values. The Administration of Justice Act 1973 authorised the Lord Chancellor acting with approval of the Prime Minister to increase judicial salaries in the light of (but not bound by) the recommendation of the Top Salaries Review Board (established in 1971) – to give the Senior Salaries Review Body its original and strikingly politically incorrect appellation. (I note, however, that similar sentiments have led the New Zealand equivalent, previously the Higher Salaries Commission, to be re-titled more neutrally the Remuneration Authority).

As a by-product of this new regime, which had switched ultimate control from legislature to Executive, in 1972 a High Court judge salary became £15,570 (worth £134,000 in present-day values).

There were pleas in 2005 for further uplift of judicial salaries, which had taken place over the intervening three decades more in fits and starts than in smooth curve and now for a High Court judge amounted to £155,404. When it was realised that the Lord Chancellor would inevitably fail to persuade Parliament to enact a Judicial Pensions Bill designed to exempt judges from the legislation in force in April of this year, which will impose a lifetime limit of £1.5 million on the tax relief allowed on pension benefits, the judges asserted that since their pensions position was statutory, they were, in the words of Lord Woolf, the then Lord Chief Justice, 'excluded from opportunities available to other professionals to take action to protect themselves against the new legislation' and that the forthcoming cap breached the legitimate expectation that they had entertained in accepting judicial appointment. Moreover, the convention is that judges cannot (unlike in some other countries) return to the Bar – although it is rumoured that an opinion obtained by a former Lord Chancellor can point to no legal foundation for it – so depriving them of the one post-judicial career for which they are most obviously suited.

The Parliamentary arithmetic suggested that were such a bill, positively discriminatory in favour of the judges, to be introduced, it would fail to attract sufficient support among Blairites, Cameroons, Lib Dems and certainly Old Labour and a *quid pro quo* of a 20 per cent salary uplift, only obtained twice in the last 30 years, could logically be anticipated to engender similar objections. It was reported that judges were ready to take legal action and had instructed pension specialist counsel to advise. Some had even (it was rumoured) threatened to resign. The new concordat between Executive and judiciary, brokered by Lord Woolf and Lord Falconer, seemed fragile.

And then on 15 December 2005, the Lord Chancellor, donning the seasonal garb of Santa Claus, announced that he would spend an extra £9 million a year on judges' pay and pensions in a complex package whose provisions, announced in Parliament and on the website without the usual illuminating concomitant explanatory statement or interview, were capable of being understood, save for the concept of a long service award for judges nearing retirement, only by revenue specialists, as illustrated by the diverse descriptions of its elements in the serious press. This was government not so much by spin as by stealth, but as in 1931, so in 2005, by an act of political *legerdemain*, a constitutional crisis was averted.

But England is not the only country where controversy has erupted over judicial pay. In Israel there have been several skirmishes. During the mandate period, the Courts Ordinance 1940 had authorised the High Commissioner to fix judicial salaries. After the establishment of the State of Israel this power was transferred under the Law and Administration Ordinance to government as a whole. The first Minister of Justice, DP Rosen, had promised that salaries of judges should equate to those of ministers, but salaries were low, and 'The final insult came when one minister demanded that the judges' salaries be made to 10 Lira less per month than that of the ministers in order to symbolise the Executive's superiority over the judiciary.' This proposal was defeated and in 1950 it was decided that judicial salaries were to be determined by the Knesset (or Parliament) rather than the Executive.

Nonetheless, in 1978 Israeli judges were primed to go on collective vacation to protest over the linkage of their salaries, together with those of all other government employees, to the cost of living index. It was somewhat imaginatively claimed on their behalf that this gesture evidenced their independence. Proceedings were commenced by a dissenting but bold lawyer to restrain the judges. An injunction was refused. The President of the Supreme Court, to whom an approach was made, negotiated a solution. Henceforth judges' salaries were linked to the average wage rather than based on the cost of living.

But in 1985 emergency regulations were introduced to combat inflation and all wages in the public sector, including those of the judges, were frozen contrary to the provisions of the Basic Law Adjudication of 1984. The dispute was resolved by awarding an increase to the judiciary of 20 per cent; the rest of the public sector gained, by contrast, nothing.

In Canada during the Depression the same issue arose as in contemporary England. A Canadian constitutional lawyer has witheringly described the argument then advanced on the judges' behalf that even non-discriminatory reductions affected judicial independence as 'fantastic'.

Half a century later in the same dominion a contributory pension scheme was introduced for federally appointed judges and applied retroactively to judges who were appointed on the day the bill was introduced. In *Beauregard v Canada* in 1986 a challenge to the legislation failed. While it was recognised that it is a condition of judicial independence that a judge's right to salary or pension should not be subject to *arbitrary* interference by the Executive, only laws which were indeed 'arbitrary', 'colourable' or 'discriminatory' would be vulnerable to attack. And in *Re Public Sector Pay Reduction Act* in 1996, it was held that there was no threat to judicial independence when provincial judges' salaries shared in a pay cut in common with other public officials.

In Ireland a novel point was taken in *O'Byrne v Minister of Finance* when the widow of a deceased judge claimed that taxation payments deducted from his salary while he was in office were breaches of the conventional constitutional guarantee. A minority of the Supreme Court actually agreed, but Maguire CJ said sensibly: 'The purpose of the Article is to safeguard the independence of judges. To require a judge to pay taxes on his income on the same basis as other citizens and thus to contribute to the expenses of Government cannot be said to be an attack on his independence.'

In the USA the authors of the Declaration of Independence complained of George III who had 'made judges dependent on his will alone for the amount and payment of their salaries', but the boundaries of the consequent constitutional guarantee to protect the salaries of judges in office have frequently been tested in the court themselves. In broad terms the outcome has been that direct interference (that is to say, outright reduction) is unconstitutional: indirect interference (that is, erosion) is unconstitutional only if two criteria are satisfied: that the erosion is discriminatory; and that it amounts to an attack on independence of the judiciary. In *The Federalist*, Alexander Hamilton, a founding father, stated: 'Next to permanency in office, nothing can contribute more to independence of the judges than a fixed provision of their support.' Mr Justice Breyer, a serving Justice, has said by reference to these historic statements, 'The framers also understood that steady judicial compensation would help to secure that necessary independence.'

The issue was most recently revisited in *Williams v USA* in 2002. It had as its backdrop the Reform Act 1989, which applied to federal judges and had two objectives. First, a strict limitation in the amount of outside income that any judge could earn, leaving only writing books or teaching as an alternative source, together with a strict cap on the latter; but second, by way of *quid pro quo*, the maintenance of the judicial compensation at a nearly constant level, with the right to automatic annual adjustments in judicial pay to take account of inflation.

In each of the relevant fiscal years – 1995, 1996, 1997 and 1999 – Congress legislated to prevent those adjustments taking effect for that year. A minority of the Supreme Court (Justices Breyer, Kennedy and Scalia) held this to be unconstitutional, arguing that the special nature of the judicial enterprise should immunise them from cuts in the salaries of other branches of government. They proclaimed: 'Independence of conscience, freedom from subservience to other government authorities, is necessary to the enterprise.'

In 1981 the Prime Minister of Australia requested the 'Justices of the High Court to accept a reduction in their salaries because of the economic situation. The judges refused although they made separate individual arrangements'. Judges internationally have not been shy to contest in court any perceived diminution in salaries including a decrease in real value. There are examples from Brazil, Greece and Spain as well as those I have already cited.

Before turning to more contemporary and domestic issues, I should now belatedly declare an interest. I served as Chairman of the Judicial Sub-Committee of the Senior Salaries Review Body from 2001 to 2003 before Nolanisation compelled me to surrender my seat on the SSRB and hence on its subsidiary body. I recall that when I mentioned my role to an audience of Indian judges and lawyers in Chennai – Madras as it then was – they expressed astonishment that a practising QC should enjoy a status which would, as they saw it, confer such a forensic advantage in court. I am bound to say that I never noticed any particularly restrained treatment of my submissions by the judges, and was more conscious of the loss of income sustained by performing an unpaid service to the state at the expense of my practice! This service, however, gave me a particular perspective on the matter under consideration as well, of course, as a particular fascination with the subject.

I turn first to the question of method. There are various possibilities as to who should decide how judges are paid.

Firstly, it could be the judiciary itself. But there would surely be principled objections to judges determining how much they themselves should be paid.

Secondly, it could be court users. But since the legal system provides a vital public service, it ought to be substantially financed by state budget, and not by payments of those requiring its services.

Thirdly, it could be the legislature as is the case in Brazil, Australia, Belgium and Greece. But this, while it has the advantage that the process is in the hands of a democratic body, has the concomitant disadvantage of cumbersomeness.

Fourthly, as is typical in some states in the USA, it could be by a court system responsible for its own budget, within the limits of a sum of money allocated to it by the legislature – a notion which attracted the former Senior Law Lord, then Vice-Chancellor, Sir Nicholas Browne-Wilkinson. But this is inconsistent with British constitutional practice, as he recognised.

Fifthly, it could be the Executive without third-party intervention as in Spain and Sweden. But since the Government is often party to the litigation, this could compromise the independence of the process. As David Pannick QC, Fellow of this College, put it succinctly: 'Pay rates for an independent judiciary should not be set by the Executive, the most frequent clients of the courts.' And on this issue LSE is at one with Oxford. Kate Malleson wrote: 'The way in which judges are ... paid ... provide the potential means for punishing or rewarding judges for their decisions.'

Sixthly, there could be automatic adjustment of salaries by reference to the price index, as in California and some Australian states, or to the average wage as in Israel. But, while this would have the virtue of certainty it would have the concomitant vice of inflexibility.

The British compromise, imitated incidentally in New Zealand and South Africa, is in my view the best solution. It seems to me a sensible method of reinforcing the constitutional guarantee to distance the Government as far as possible from the determinations of judicial salaries, while also allowing a measure of judicial and outside input. An analogous philosophy is belatedly mirrored in the concept of the Judicial Appointments Commission.

I say as 'far as possible' advisedly, since it must be for the Government of the day to enjoy the last word, always within the constraints of the constitutional guarantee, on what may be affordable at any particular time. Lord Williams of Mostyn QC, then Chairman of Bar Council, later a poacher turned gamekeeper as Attorney General and finally, before his premature death, Leader of the House of Lords, called it 'dangerous to have an allegedly independent body which is then overruled by politicians'. As a matter of record, governments have rarely declined to take the SSRB's advice, if from time to time they have decided only to stage the increases proposed.

I have, however, always thought it incongruous that the SSRB's terms of reference include an obligation to have regard to the funds available to departments as set out in the departmental expenditure limits. This blurs the boundary between the role of the adviser and the advised. But since the obligation is only to '*have regard to*' rather than to be bound by such consideration, this may be of less significance than at first sight appears, and it does remind the SSRB that their function is not simply to accept judges' estimation of their own value.

The customary processes of consultation are (or were during my time on the body) well established. An advance guard of senior civil servants from what was then the Lord Chancellor's Department (now renamed the Department for Constitutional Affairs) would come and explain the Government's view to the sub-committee. At a later plenary meeting the Lord Chancellor would arrive in all his glory accompanied by his Permanent Secretary. Either between or after, depending on the respective party's schedules, the Lord Chief Justice would have an audience as spokesman for the judiciary, accompanied by one other judge, usually Sir Andrew Morritt, now Chancellor – shop steward and shepherd. After exchange of the usual courtesies, more elaborate in the last two meetings than in the first, carriage of the debate was left largely to the judicial sub-committee, three in number, all then lawyers, as the judiciary had originally insisted as the price for their participation in the process.

In a little-noted change, after my retirement from the Chairmanship there was a temporary purge of lawyers; although now the body has been afforced by Sir Peter North QC, Lord Neill's successor as Vice Chancellor of Oxford. How and why this happened will have to await revelations in political memoirs or (less likely) in response to a precisely targeted request under the Freedom of Information Act 2000.

For several years I enjoyed some brief encounters of the forensic kind with Lord Irvine on the one hand and Lords Bingham and Woolf on the other. The Lord Chancellor would plead poverty; the judges need. We would formulate proposals for our parent body, and recommendations would go forth to the Prime Minister in due course in immaculate civil service prose with my more rhetorical flourishes sternly sub-edited out. Never underestimate the power as well as the skill of the accomplished civil service draftsman!

For the future under the new constitutional settlement the amount of salary in point of law 'is to be determined by the Lord Chancellor with the agreement of the Treasury', the one with responsibility for the rule of law, the other for the wealth of the nation. The SSRB's role will continue to be to square the circle.

I turn to the question of criteria. There is no definitive way of measuring what judges should be paid. To claim that they are worth such-and-such a figure is to make a judgment more appropriate to the divine than to the human. Justice Breyer of the United States Supreme Court wisely said, making a case for an uplift in judicial pay to the National Commission on Public Service, 'In this world I can find no pay scale that measures an individual's just desserts.'

No such inhibition, incidentally, affected the judge sitting in Clarksville Tennessee, where the court transcript records the following dialogue:

Judge: All right. I sure would feel better if you had a lawyer. You can afford one, can't you?

> Defendant: No, I can't, Your Honor. I cannot afford an attorney.
>
> Judge: Are you drawing your salary from the fire department?
>
> Defendant: Yes, I am.
>
> Judge: That is a pretty good salary, isn't it? I mean by that, firemen get paid pretty well.
>
> Defendant: Well, it is not comparable to yours.
>
> Judge: Well, it ought not to be comparable to mine. I mean, after all, we are the highest in the State. We are God!

Axiomatically, the Constitutional guarantee must be respected: it sets a floor, not a ceiling. It may be thought by some invidious to protect judges against financial risks to which others in the community are vulnerable, but I cannot regard it as anachronistic or anomalous. Where the administration of justice is concerned, perception is important. Judges must not only be independent, but must be seen to be independent.

It has been argued that there is a need to avoid reduction, not only in formal but in real terms. Otherwise judges' independence can be compromised by a side wind. Shetreet writes: 'Withholding salary increase may be an indirect method of interfering with independence at times of higher rates of inflation.'

If so, the pass has long since been sold. The constitutional guarantee cannot be so benevolently interpreted. More realistically, there is a need to ensure increase in judicial salaries equivalent at any rate to that elsewhere in public sector. The SSRB have indeed to bear 'broad linkage' in mind.

But how much? – that is the key. There are several points to be made.

Firstly, judges cannot seriously complain that they are underpaid in absolute terms – although that has not prevented them from making serial complaints. Lord Justice Parker commented in his retirement speech in 1992: 'If you pay peanuts, you get monkeys.' While as a general proposition that may have the ring of truth, it surely does not apply to Her Majesty's judges.

Nor do the concerns which Lord Denning MR ventilated in a debate on the Lord Chancellor's salary in 1985 tug too tightly at the heartstrings. He said, 'Many of the judges were aggrieved. The younger judges were disappointed they could not provide properly for the education of their children, for their holidays and the like.', adding, 'A salary increase made them reasonably satisfied.'

Later concerns articulated were that not only could judges not pay for their holidays but might have less holidays to pay for. In a Working Party chaired by Kennedy LJ in 1995 on a proposal that the long vacation should be abbreviated, the authors wrote:

> Such a prospect would be unlikely to find much favour with the judiciary who, having recently been awarded a pay increase below the rate of inflation and far below the level recommended by the TSRB, are bound to regard the vacations as one of the few remaining attractions of the job.

David Pannick QC has wisely said, 'any judicial stress would not be caused by worries of low pay', not least because of the benefits of stability associated with the transition from barrister's chambers (or solicitor's office) to Bench. One judge, Sir Peter Bristow, candidly wrote in a memoir:

> You would fairly be said to be relieved of financial worry with your bottom placed firmly on the consolidated fund. To those who all their working lives had to pay their taxes in arrears, PAYE came as an enormous blessing.

The QC enjoys the hurly-burly of the *chaise longue*, the judge the peaceful tranquillity of the marriage bed – metaphorically speaking, of course.

Secondly it is difficult to argue that the amount paid per se can compromise their independence. Kate Malleson comments:

> The standards of justice may be poorer in terms of such matters as delay and standards of legal advice if less resources are available but that need not affect the independence of the judges. Impartial judges can dispense justice under the proverbial palm tree.

Thirdly, high salaries are surely not necessary nowadays to avoid corruption in our courts, and the original justification for paying judges has in practice evaporated. As Rodney Brazier has sensibly asked: 'If a person were susceptible to corruption would he not be so almost regardless of income?'

In the words of Lord Justice Brooke: 'And finally, we are paid large enough salaries to render us free from the sort of financial worries which might *in theory* fuel the risk of judicial corruption' – the key phrase being 'in theory'.

At a judicial accountability Commonwealth Lawyers Association conference in Kuala Lumpur in 2003, I recall the Chairman, the distinguished Australian High Court judge, Michael Kirby, looking around the table at lawyers from Malaysia, Sri Lanka, India, Scotland, England, as well as the USA – included *pro tem* for the good and sufficient reason that they were part-funding the conference – and saying that in none of our countries had the scourge of judicial corruption been erased. When I mildly inquired whether he would provide any example of corruption from England in the last 200 years, he rebuked me for being chauvinistic: Chauvinistic possibly; accurate certainly!

Fourthly, while Lord Bingham has referred to 'subtle link' based on the 'perceived relationship between what someone earns and the status and prestige which he enjoys', not even in a materialistic society can it fairly be said that the prestige of a position reflects exactly the sum paid to its occupant. Judges may occasionally – in my respectful view, unwisely – speak of footballers as role models, but do we really admire a master of the goals more than the Master of the Rolls because one earns £75,000 per week and the other closer to £7,500?

The SSRB's assessment for proper pay is based on an elusive concept of job weight, referable more to the quality of what is done than its content. Whereas in the other two groups (senior civil servants and senior officers of the armed forces) performance-related pay has infiltrated the calculation; the 1997 fundamental review roundly rejected it in these words:

> It would involve systems of management and appraisal whose authority and efficiency would be controversial and which could be seen to challenge the principle of judicial independence. The view was also expressed that performance related pay might lead to a perception that a judges actions could be influenced by considerations of personal gain and loss.

Performance-related pay was, however, the subject of internal discussion, and I betray no state secret in identifying the non-lawyers on the Body as being less hostile than the lawyers to the notion. I do not, of course, consider that assessment would be impossible. Although the quality of performance of a judge may not be as easily measured as that of a senior civil servant, the Lord Chancellor has hitherto been able to distinguish between those whose careers reach their pinnacle on the High Court Bench, those who are fit to ascend to the rarified atmosphere of the Court of Appeal, and those who can soar into the stratosphere of the House of Lords – without using such crude analytical tools as the ratio of judgments appealed and reversed to those appealed and upheld, or throughput in numbers of cases dealt with per sitting.

But in this age of transparency, who would judge the judges, and by reference to what standards? For my part I consider that even evaluation by an independent commission would not entirely dispel the impression, false though it would surely be, that judges might tailor their judgments to fatten their pay packets and might be less robustly oblivious to politician's criticisms that they manifestly are today. More important still, to distinguish in terms of pay between one High Court judge and another would lead to the conclusion that one dispensed a purer justice than the other. It may be a fiction that all judges at the same level are equal – some are clearly more equal than others; but that inequality should be reflected in their promotion, not their pay.

Mr Justice Breyer compiled a melancholy catalogue of the consequences of false economy causing 'major financial insecurity among judges', many, if not all, of which can be transposed across the Atlantic – premature resignations, diminished attraction of judicial office to well-qualified lawyers outside the judicial system, repetitive promotion from within the system with consequent risk of bureaucratisation and lower morale. Judging, he added, might become seen as a temporary assignment, a threat that the odd Fisher or Laddie apart, is less resonant in England and Wales, unless schemes are implemented to allow for judges to return to the profession.

He concluded:

> In this way the cuts contribute to diminished institutional reforms which in turn promotes public disenchantment and lack of trust in a government, less able to get the job done well and a lack of interest in participating in the work of that government. 'contending that sufficient pay 'must have and does have everything to do with the nature of the institution and the value of the strong, well functioning, truly independent judicial system for all Americans.

Nor was this a self-serving statement on the fringe of mainstream thinking. In 1989 the report of the American Commission on Executive, Legislative and Judicial Salaries, entitled 'Fairness for our Public Servants', said that reducing the real level of judicial salaries in the USA was 'threatening to diminish the quality of justice in this country'.

So we reach the heart of the matter. While Lord Bingham has modestly written 'The connection between judicial salaries and judicial independence may not be immediately obvious', he surely was stating the obvious in continuing:

> Our own tradition does depend on the willingness of the most successful practitioner at the height of their careers to accept appointment to the judicial Bench, and I gravely doubt whether that tradition can be maintained.

The real issue is surely one of recruitment and retention or staying the course, until judges become, in Lord Bridge's melancholy phrase, 'officially geriatric'. The

SSRB's own terms of reference – admittedly to be applied to various sectors of public service – specify 'the need to recruit, retain and motivate suitably able and qualified people to exercise their different responsibilities'. If the ablest eligible candidates – I put on one side the controversial claims of diversity – either refuse the invitation to the Bench or decline to apply to advertisement or, once appointed, serve only for so long as entitles them to a full judicial pension, if that, the standard of justice will inevitably, if imperceptibly, be impoverished. And in an age when the judiciary, armoured with new weapons in the form of paramount community law and the domesticated European Convention on Human Rights, and imbued with an activist spirit which has not been a constant in post-war times, play an increasingly significant role in the governance of the nation, any lowering of even high standards would be a cause for legitimate concern. To quote Holdsworth, 'a good thing is never cheap: and to pay sufficient to get a good thing is often the best economy for thereby expensive disasters are avoided'.

In England, the discrepancy between earnings at the Bar and on the Bench is notorious. It features in the biographies and memoirs of famous members of both professions. It was a reason why George Carman QC did not go to the Bench – admittedly in Hong Kong. In his autobiography Sir Neville Faulks described his options in this way: 'I wanted to be "local boy made good", but I wanted to keep my children in bread and boots for as long as I could, and the appointment would mean a substantial drop in income.' Sir Michael Kerr wrote of the agony of his decision to quit Bar for Bench: 'Above all there was the question of money. I was earning about £38,000 a year near the top of the Bar, and I think that a Judge's salary was then £11,500.'

This lawyers' dilemma is no mere contemporary phenomenon. Norman Birkett's clerk wrote: 'When Norman Birkett went to the Bench he made a very heavy financial sacrifice and so did I when I decided to go with him.' The clerk's sacrifice was appreciated by Birkett, and his own presumably tolerated.

As with Birkett, so with Atkin. Geoffrey Lewis, his biographer, wrote:

> For almost the whole of his career, Atkin was troubled by anxiety about money … By the time he was established as a leading commercial silk he was earning some £11,000 a year but this relative affluence was short lived, and, as has always been the case in England, his appointment to the High Court Bench brought with it a sharp reduction in income. He returned more than once to the idea of leaving the profession in order to earn more, first as a teacher, later for a post in the City and even when a judge, to return to the Bar.

As in the United Kingdom, so in the United States of America. As Breyer put it:

> The real pay of federal judges has diminished substantially in the past three decades. The gulf that separates judicial pay from compensation in a non-profit sector, academia, and the private sector grows larger and larger. The result, in my view, threatens irreparable harm both to the institution and in to public that it serves.

Breyer compared increases in judicial pay, which had exceeded the cost of living in Canada and the UK, with the reverse position in the United States. Interestingly, it appears that where – as in England – the order of size of income would be first practising lawyers, second judges, third law academics, in America law academics can outstrip judges – a dispiriting observation for the majority of this audience!

In Germany, by contrast, in recent times judges, previously less well paid than academics, have now overtaken them – reflecting changed perceptions of their relative contributions to the law's development.

In 1988 the TSRB themselves said (echoing Sir Peter Bristow) that drop in income could be mitigated 'in the light of the status and security of judicial office with its prospect of continuing in paid, rewarding and pensionable employment to a later age than is possible in most walks of life.'

But this sanguine statement was made before the Judicial Pensions and Retirement Act 1993 which (amending the Judicial Pensions Act 1959) raised the period of service for a full pension from 15 to 20 years, and lowered the retirement age to 70 prospectively – a double financial whammy, bearing in mind that, as the European Court of Justice has reminded us, pensions are deferred pay. The TSRB anyhow added materially: 'the discount has now become too great'.

It may well be that, as Joshua Rozenberg, has written, 'The real problem is not that judges earn too little but that lawyers earn too much'. But unless (unthinkably) there is legislation to cap counsel's private fees, the problem is a problem is a problem. In 2005, 30 barristers earned more than £1 million and a select few more than £2 million.

The recently retired Lord Chief Justice cast a wistful eye eastwards when he reflected, 'I have recently returned from Singapore and there the Chief Justice … transformed recruitment and the quality of the judiciary by obtaining a doubling of judicial salaries.' I am reliably informed that the Singaporean Judges' Remuneration (Annual Pensionable Salaries) Order 'does not deal with the bonuses, car allowances and other perks paid to them which bring the total annual emoluments of judges to 1 million Singapore dollars.' *Ex Asia semper aliquid novi!*

How real are these concerns of a diminution in the numbers of those willing to accept High Court appointments preferring city, campus or a conventional courtroom practice? Official statistics obscure rather than illuminate. As is common knowledge among the cognoscenti, they resemble in terms of accuracy – to use a modern metaphor borrowed from the Shadow Chancellor of the Exchequer – the figures for Soviet tractor production, a point appreciated by the SSRB. When High Court judges were appointed by invitation only and not through advertisement, the Lord Chancellor's Department could optimistically, but unrealistically, claim that no one counted as a loss to the Bench who had not actually declined face to face by that sometime refutation of the separation of powers.

Nonetheless, even a decade or so ago it was accepted that some asked for deferment described by Rozenberg as 'the start of an alarming trend'. And while in 1988–1991 there were no refusals, in 1991–1992 only one declined, but in 1992–1993 no less than six declined.

Similarly in April 2000–2001, 19 High Court appointments were made (seven as a result of advertisement, the others the traditional 'tap on the shoulder'). But six people refused appointment. As we put it in our Sub-Committee report in 2002:

> This significant figure, almost a third of the number of those appointed, calls into question whether there was an increasing pattern of refusals which indicates future difficulties in attracting appropriate appointees.

The full body were a trifle more cautious.

> In general, we are satisfied that there are no major problems at present in recruiting judges of the required calibre at all levels. However, we agree with the sub-committee that the refusal of a proportion of those offered appointment to the High Court gives grounds for concern. While judicial pay is only one factor, and not necessarily the predominant factor, in the refusal of appointment it must not be allowed to diverge so far from the pay of the group from which judges are mainly recruited that it deters the most able, with the result that an increasing proportion of good potential candidates will be lost to the judiciary.

And I am sceptical whether the position has truly improved even over the last three years. I could immediately name – though respect for their privacy restrains me – at least 10 senior silks who have resisted the temptations of office. In 2004 the average drop in earnings on appointment of a High Court Judge was 53 per cent. While pay is not the only factor, that militates against acceptance of such judicial appointment, the implications of these figures can be assessed by someone of lesser intellect than a senior wrangler.

Three principles of judicial pay may be said to be part of our modern constitutional settlement. It is unconstitutional to cut the salary of an individual judge of a superior court during the currency of his (or her) commission. It is unconstitutional for Parliament to reduce the judicial salary scale overall to the extent that it threatens judges' independence. And no judge can be appointed unless provision is made for his or her salary. These are guarantors of independence, but they are not, by themselves, guarantors of excellence.

In 1933 Holdsworth wrote:

> The remuneration of the judges is not sufficient to induce the ablest lawyers in the prime of life to accept judicial office. If that state of affairs is allowed to continue it must have serious effect upon the administration of the law. It will impair those intellectual standards which have made our English legal system a great legal system; it will tend to impair that law-abiding instinct which is the condition precedent for the maintenance of a high standard of civilisation, and it will weaken the chief remaining guarantee for the prosecution of the liberties of that subject.

More than seven decades on, we should still heed his warning.

# Part III

# History

# 9

# *'Sisters in Law: The Irresistible Rise of Women in Wigs'* Barnard's Inn Reading at Gresham College 2009*

IN AN UNAUTHORISED biography of Cherie Booth there appears the unmemorable line 'Michael Beloff likes women'. The author does not, I hasten to add, mean to hint that I have a reputation as a serial lover – Blackstone Chambers' answer to Silvio Berlusconi. I have been happily married for almost four decades to the same woman – as the late Sir Clement Freud would put it, to my first wife, and – as *I* would add – to my last – and even my best friends would say that I resemble Don Quixote more than Don Juan.

But, no doubt because I experienced single-sex education until the age of 18, and had no sisters, I came late in the day into regular contact with 'the females of the species'. And while a career at the Bar has left me with a capacity, not necessarily admirable, to see several sides of every question, I have never hidden my belief that women, given the chance, do most things better than men.

When up at Oxford, I successfully moved the admission of women to full membership of the Oxford Union. I was a willing participant in a successful campaign to ensure that the Reform Club opened its doors to women members – the first London club to do so. I did not have to follow the example of a distinguished colleague and old friend, who in a blaze of publicity resigned from The Garrick on the grounds that it discriminated against women, having apparently during his prolonged membership not previously noticed that it was a single-sex establishment. I wrote the first commentary on the Sex Discrimination Act 1975, and in 1991 I received the first – and as, alas, it proved the last – award made by the Women's Defence League, from the hands of Barbara Castle, for my contribution to women's rights. This was specifically for my work in the case brought by Ms Marshall in the European Court of Justice which established that it was unlawful under community law to compel women to retire earlier than men. My real triumph was to persuade the Equal Opportunities Commission to fund the litigation, that body having been earlier advised by eminent leading counsel that the claim had no reasonable prospect of success. But as I get older, I wonder against which sex the compulsory retirement rule actually discriminated!

* (2009) 123 *Graya* 33.

So when I was invited to give the Barnard's Inn reading tonight it was predictable that I would wish to reflect on a topic which was dear to my heart, not least because Gray's Inn can claim credit for electing the first woman Treasurer of any Inn of Court, the late Master Rose Heilbron, and the first woman Law Lord and member of the Supreme Court to be, Master Hale. But as I shall show, if our Inn can claim to be a late-coming pioneer, if that is not a contradiction in terms, it was not ever thus.

In 1903, Bertha Cave brought a test application on behalf of herself including, inter alias, Christabel Pankhurst, the celebrated suffragette, seeking admission to Gray's Inn. The Benchers refused to call her, so she appealed to a tribunal consisting of the Lord Chancellor, the Lord Chief Justice and five other judges. In the issue of *The New York Times* of 5 December 1903, in among a mixed bag of items, a correspondent described her efforts on appeal in the following way.

Headline:

> TOPICS OF THE WEEK IN THE BRITISH CAPITAL; Century-Old Reign of the 'Igh 'At' at Last Ended – Miss Bertha Cave's Attempt to Become a Barrister – Political Meetings the Warmest Places in London – Chamberlain Gaining Support Every Day.

Text:

> Britons are not averse to progress, provided it does not come straight at them headed by a brass band.
>
> The trouble with Miss Bertha Cave, the would-be woman barrister, was that in her campaign of progress she had to have a brass band. She could not sneak into Gray's Inn Court. If she could have slipped in through the cellar window, and little by little assumed the prerogatives attaching to a barrister, she might in course of time, say when she had reached her eightieth year, have found herself in the traditional wig, eating the traditional dinners, and smoking the traditional pipe.

*O Tempora*, I interpolate. *O Mores.*

> She had to go to work in another way and appear before the tribunal of Judges sitting in the House of Lords. Clad in a navy blue walking suit with a bolero of the same material trimmed in white, and balancing a rather piquant black hat on her head, she carried her comely self into the presence of the august Judges. She deposited a purse and a package that looked like corsets on the table, and then pleaded her case. There was no question of ability raised, it was solely a matter of sex. So she told the Judges what other countries were doing for women who desired to practice law.
>
> The Judges listened smilingly, and when Miss Cave was through promptly advised her that there was no precedent for admitting women students at any of the Inns of Court, and that they did not feel justified in creating one. 'I wish your lordships good morning.' said the little woman frigidly, and picking up her purse and her corsets she quitted the judicial presence and went out in the cold, cold world.

The issue as to whether women could be admitted to the professions as solicitors, barristers or doctors, or could enjoy the franchise or access to public office was often couched in terms of whether women were 'persons' within the relevant legislation; the cases indeed came to be called 'persons' cases. It is one of the little ironies of history that the feminists of the mid- to late-twentieth century regarded the description of women as 'persons' as being a victory for emancipation when the same nomenclature had been earlier used in the courts to deny them their natural rights. The writings of Coke were frequently prayed in aid to support rejection of the women's claims. Coke is, of course, a legendary figure in English law. His wife wrote after his death 'We shall never see his like again' – an ambiguous pronouncement clarified only by the succeeding words, 'Praise be to God.'

In Ireland an issue which arose for judicial determination was whether a woman could become a clerk to the petty sessions. Ronan LJ painstakingly listed the reasons why at common law women were previously held not qualified to perform public functions: '1. subordination of sex, 2. inferiority of body, 3. mental inferiority due to course of education and training, 4. decency and decorum'. But the court ultimately upheld the disqualification as a matter of statute, not common law, adding:

> The reason for the modern decisions disqualifying women from public office has not been inferiority of intellect or discretion, which few people would now have the likelihood to allege, it has rather rested upon considerations of decorum and upon the unfitness of certain painful and exacting duties in relation to the finer qualities of women.

It was not until 1929 in a case involving eligibility for election to the Senate in Canada that the Privy Council decided that a 'person' could include a woman.

Lord Sankey LC said, 'the exclusion of women from all public office is a relic of days more barbarous than our own …' and, casting around for a plausible explanation, delved dubiously into prehistory: 'such exclusion is probably due to the fact that the deliberative assemblies of the early tribes were attended by men under arms and women did not bear arms'.

He also said more pertinently, 'custom is apt to develop into traditions which are stronger than law and remain unaltered long after the reason for them has disappeared'.

No lesser a champion of women's rights than Master Hale has commented, 'Despite the historical learning deployed, this looks more like political than black letter reasoning'.

I agree and have nothing to add.

In consequence Master Hale teasingly suggested that the validity of her own appointment as Law Lord under section 6 of the Appellate Jurisdiction Act 1876 which refers to 'qualified persons' might be doubtful.

I disagree, and would add a great deal if the point were ever taken. Indeed a thousand swords would surely leap from their scabbards in her support.

The courts in the Empire were no more responsive to women's claims for admission to the legal profession.

In Canada, Mabel French brought two test cases. She was unsuccessful in her attempt to be admitted to legal practice in New Brunswick. Her later application to be admitted to the Bar of British Colombia also failed. The Chief Justice said

> that there may be cogent reasons for change based upon changes in the legal status of women, and the enlarged activities of modern life may be admitted, but this is a matter for the legislature, not the Court to resolve.

Judges in the Francophone regions were no more tolerant and held that, 'women could be admitted neither to the study of law nor to the legal profession in Quebec'.

In the Transvaal, a woman failed to become an attorney in a case brought before the very same Supreme Court which had been robust in overruling the Law Society's objection to admission of an Indigenous African. In the Court's view, the word 'person' included a Black man but not a white woman.

Madeline Wookey's attempt to be admitted as an articled clerk was rejected by the South African Appeal Court, Mr Justice de Villiers conceding (necessarily) that the word 'person' was, in its ordinary and natural meaning, wide enough to include women, nonetheless was not prepared to hold that the legislature intended it to be so construed. 'We cannot,' he said with a scholarly flourish, 'ignore the fact that from the time Carfania vexed the soul of some too nervous praetor with her pleading down to our own day the profession of attorney has been exercised exclusively by men, and this applied not only in Holland' – a genuflection to the Roman Dutch origins of South African law – 'but also in England.'

He conceded that restrictions based on race or religion (he mentioned Jews) or disability (he mentioned the blind) were obsolete, but denied expressly that the same applied to restrictions based on sex. The *South African Law Journal* to its credit declined to accept the logic of the difference, although its liberal record, if not its commitment to free speech, was somewhat blemished when five years later another contributor argued that, 'for women to practice law would be to revolt against nature'.

How stood matters in the New World? The mosaic constitutional pattern of the United States ensured that for aspirant women attorneys practice varied from state to state. In colonial times, for *force majeure* reasons, women were often attorneys in fact if not attorneys in law. But later there was a retreat from that position. Post-civil-war judges were astute to ban women from the legal profession, relying Scalia-like, on the originalist construction of the intentions of those who drafted the statutes for admission to the Bar, and rejecting the approach of a Steyn that statutes are always speaking.

Arabella Mansfield was the first woman to be admitted to the practice of law in the USA, in the state of Iowa, whose contemporary fame rests more upon the crucial role it plays in the selection of party presidential nominees. The Iowa Code of 1861 limited admission to the Bar to 'any white male person'. In an ingenious exercise of interpretation, the Iowa Supreme Court ruled that 'the affirmative is not any implied denial of the rights of females'. The Latin precept *inclusio unius exclusio alterius* was once described by Lord Diplock as being victim of a 'misunderstanding that is regrettably common'. Whether misunderstood or not, the precept had apparently not penetrated the jurisprudence of the Midwest at all. The Iowa State Code of 1873 blue-pencilled the potentially offending words; but it was not until the 1920s that states started routinely admitting women to the Bar, although not in great numbers – Delaware and Rhode Island being the last to capitulate – and it was not until 1957 that the Supreme Court disallowed sexist state restrictions on admissions.

In 1870 the distinctively named Lemma Barkeloo became the first woman to try a case in the American courts. She had earlier been denied entry to Columbia Law School, a member of whose Board of Trustees stated, 'I think that the clack of these possible Portias will never be heard in Dwights Moot Courts'. He was an obstacle, but not, it would seem, an oracle. Another who sought to hold back the tide, Chief Justice Ryan of the Wisconsin Supreme Court, in 1875 carried his brethren with him when regarding it as inappropriate 'that women should be permitted to mix professionally with all the nastiness of the world that finds its way into the Courts of Justice', but his triumph was only temporary. Four years later he was the sole dissenter when the earlier judgment was reversed.

In *Bradwell v Ilinois*, Myra Bradwell, successful in the Illinois Bar Exam, found herself disqualified by reason of her marriage, even though her husband was a judge. The record of proceedings mercifully does not suggest that it was because of his office.

In the Supreme Court Justice Bradley insisted that, as Blackstone had opined – I speak of the jurist, not the chambers which bears his name – women had no legal existence separate from that of their husbands. The appellant's citation of the 14th Amendment was to no avail; the privileges and immunities to which the famous equal protection clause attached did not apparently include the right to practise law. She was, paradoxically a citizen, but not a person. Her story has a happier ending. In 1892, she was admitted in practice before the Supreme Court, although she never availed herself of the right.

Even when sex was added as a prohibited ground for discrimination into the Civil Rights Act 1964, whose inspiration was the need to combat racial discrimination, it is unclear whether this was done to impede or to improve the bill.

The conclusion of Albie Sachs writing in 1978 was that, whether under a system where the judges had to respect parliamentary sovereignty or one where the judges saw themselves as guardians of a paramount constitution, 'the judges in the two countries almost invariably arrived at the same conclusions at almost precisely the same times, quite irrespective of the constitutional routes they followed'.

A variety of reasons for what, with the benefit of hindsight, seems an indefensible discrimination can be distilled from the jurisprudence.

First, the response chivalrous – that to allow women to practise law would destroy 'man's reverence for womanhood and faith in women'.

Second, the response delicate – that for women to practise law offended against decorum.

Third, the response chauvinist – that women were simply unsuited to the demands of the profession physically, intellectually and emotionally.

Fourth, the response obstinate – that the legal profession was already overcrowded.

Fifth, the response protectionist – that professional standards would be affected.

Sixth, the response pragmatic – that admission would be wasteful since women are more likely than men to withdraw from the practice.

Seventh, the response religious – that in one judge's words, 'The paramount destiny and mission of women is to fulfil the noble and benign offices of wife and mother, the law of the creator'.

Eighth, the response traditionalist – that since the profession had always been all male, so it should remain.

As the late Eric Morecambe would have put it, there's no answer to that.

It was on the basis of this last reason that it was held in 1914 that women could not be admitted by the Law Society to qualify as solicitors under the Solicitors Act 1843. Cozens Hardy MR relying on 'long uniform and uninterrupted usage' said a reform was a matter for Parliament, while he conceded that 'in point of intelligence and education and competency women … are at least the equal to a great many, and probably far better than many of the candidates who will come up for examination' especially he added, the applicant 'a distinguished Oxford student'. Swinfen Eady LJ, however, commented that the inability of married women freely to make contracts would impede them from entering into articles, musing that 'every woman can be married at some time in her life', a more cautious statement than that of Lord Birkenhead LC in the famous Viscountess Rhondda's claim, who opined, 'a female must remain a female until she dies', being oblivious to the possibilities of gender reassignment or transsexuality.

The dismantling of the barriers in Great Britain was engineered by the Sex Disqualification (Removal) Act 1919 which provided that no person should be disqualified by sex or marriage from the exercising of any public function. The prohibition allowed no scope for construing 'person' as other than applying to both sexes.

In supporting the Bill, Lord Sumner, a diehard Tory, rejected a flood-gates argument, 'that it was a stepping stone to higher things, the Bar, the vote, the Woolsack, I know not what'.

Two out of three of those events have, of course, come to pass: only the Woolsack remains unclimbed – at any rate by a Lady Lord Chancellor. Please note the gulf even in that extra-curial obiter dictum, thought then to exist between the two branches of the legal profession. Women solicitors maybe; women barristers never! But Lord Sumner was not only the sceptic of his time.

In a lecture in Cambridge in 1924, His Honour Judge Edward Parry made it clear that he considered that the key virtues of barristers were unevenly distributed between the sexes: 'Honesty and courage women have but industry crushes them; wit they admire but do not possess; eloquence they neglect; judgement they lack; fellowship is alien to them.'

And Henry Dickson KC wrote only a decade later:

> As to whether women are likely to make a real success in the profession in the future, it is rather too early to judge. I have had some experience of their worth in the Central Criminal Court of late years: but I prefer to withhold my judgment on such a very delicate question at the present time.

Yet as his reference to his experience shows, once a breach was made in the fortifications of the profession, a few female pioneers were quick to profit from it.

Margaret Henderson Kidd was the first female member of the Faculty of Advocates, although from 1923 to 1948 she remained the only female advocate. Then and till much later the ladies' robing room was situated off a lower corridor in Parliament House opposite the condemned cell, and hot water was only put in after the Second World War.

The first woman to be called to the English Bar was Ivy Williams, a Middle Templar – in 1921 – six months after Frances Kyle had been called to the Irish Bar.

The changing attitude of the legal establishment to her ascent can be illustrated by the characterisation by *The Law Journal* of her threat in 1904 to set up a third branch of the legal profession if the Law Society and Benchers did not yield in their opposition as 'a futile attempt of a persistent lady to gain admission to the Bar', while later serenading her call as 'one of the most memorable days in the annals of the English legal profession', although adding waspishly that 'the admission was never likely to be justified by any success they will achieve in the field of advocacy'. Ivy Williams herself eschewed advocacy in favour of scholarship and teaching.

Not so the silver medalist in the female race to be called, Helena Normanton, also a Middle Templar – the first woman to obtain a divorce for a client, the first to lead for the prosecution in murder, the first to plead in the High Court, the Old Bailey and the London Sessions, and in 1949 with Master Rose Heilbron the joint first English King's Counsel. By reason of the attention paid to her gender she was wrongly accused of advertising, and suspect because of her feminist activities. She argued in favour of equal pay for equal work as early as 1914 and for women to retain their individual identity after marriage. She was the first woman to be issued with a passport in her maiden name, and was an advocate of divorce law reform.

The first woman member of the Bar Council was Hannah Wright (née Cross), who died only last year.

A PPE convert, she aspired to a Chancery Practice. Her obituary in *The Times* records:

> There was no official method of getting pupillage or a seat in chambers and she had great difficulty in finding a place. She looked for an opening in a great number of

> chambers and applied for five or six, where she was given a welcoming hearing by the Head of Chambers, but was told to return next day when he would have discussed the matter with the Clerk. Then, the invariable answer was 'So sorry, but there is no lavatory for you'. Eventually she reapplied promising always to use the public lavatories in Lincoln's Inn Fields, and was accepted by the Chambers in 1 New Square. She was called to the Bar in 1931 by Lincolns Inn.
>
> Several solicitors said they would like to send her work but then added that their clients would not even consider employing a woman. One client said, 'What, are there no men at the Bar anymore?'
>
> She did not feel that judges were prejudiced against her. But in one case involving an affiliation order the magistrates took her to be the client.

Now for some statistics. In 1921 there were 20 women listed as called to the Bar; in 1929, 67; by 1955, there was a decline to 64; by 1965, the figure was 99; 1970, it was 147; 1976, it was 313. The pace of any advance was pitifully slow. It is instructive that in his 1962 Hamlyn Lecture, 'Lawyer and Litigant in England', Sir Robert Megarry had a section on 'Lawyers as professional *men*', a heading not, I think, redeemed by the benevolent precept of the Interpretation Acts that for statutory purposes men include women.

What were the causes? Let me call three witnesses for the prosecution.

First, Dame Elizabeth Lane, whose memoir, *Hear the Other Side*, provides a somewhat arch, but nonetheless revealing, account of the career of the first woman High Court judge. Her path was encumbered by hurdles both external and internal to her.

She was initially refused a place in chambers because of opposition of a senior – and traditionally Jurassic – my adjective, not hers – clerk as, I hasten to add, clerks then were! But once within the sanctum, finding herself on being briefed in an indecent assault, she burst into tears, threw the instructions in the waste paper basket, and muttered to herself that 'she would not take part in such a filthy case'.

Like Hannah Wright she encountered more prejudice among litigants than among solicitors, one calling her 'a cauliflower headed bitch'. Nonetheless her practice burgeoned. She defended, in a case arising out of a fracas between overseas soldiers stationed in this country, a private soldier who assaulted with a broom an officer whom, he believed, was making advances to his wife. She claims to have opened her defence, 'This is case of a Pole who hit a Pole with a pole', and speculates that this plea in mitigation resulted in a lower sentence than might otherwise have been the case, though *I* peevishly suggest that it might, certainly *ought* to, have resulted in a higher one.

When elevated to the Bench, she heard her clerk being congratulated by another clerk on his – not her – achievement. But even from that pinnacle she noted the prejudice against women:

> One bold female who asked whether she could not be a judge's marshal was firmly told that it was impossible because if the judges were unmarried they might feel they would be compromised and if they were married their wives would not allow it.

I turn secondly to Master Helena Kennedy and her autobiographical chapter, 'Playing Portia'. She describes both the lack of expectation in what we nowadays term euphemistically non-traditional backgrounds and the problems encountered by those who transcended such perceived limits. She records that: 'When some of my relatives were told that I had joined Grays Inn and was studying for the Bar, they imagined I had gone in for hotel management and catering,' and adds, that once admitted, 'I stepped from the equivalent of a comprehensive school in no mean city into the pages of an Evelyn Waugh novel.'

She describes in pungent detail the perils of being Master Junior, the problems with dress code, the casual sexism of the male students – all this but 30 years ago. Mercifully, *nous avons changé tout cela*, although, interestingly, the bloke-ish atmosphere of some chambers, reminiscent of that reputed to exist in Gordon Brown's inner circle, still persists.

Harry Mount's slimmest of slim volumes, *My Brief Career*, a recollection of a misspent pupillage a few years back, recalled the single female tenant as an unique figure among the members of chambers who 'had all the good manners and delivered all the pleasantries that I was used to in the outside world'. *That* observation may have the ring of truth, but otherwise the book shows that it is not only, as Shakespeare's Henry V put it, old men who forget, but young men too.

I have taken a tactical decision not to rely on my third witness, who penned reminiscences under the *nom de plume* Venisha. Her title, *Missy you've dropped your briefs*, is based on a joke whose humorous potential, never particularly impressive, was probably exhausted by five minutes after Ivy Williams' call. This justifiably little-known work can nonetheless still be found on the shelves of the Bodleian Law Library in Oxford cheek by jowl with *Chitty on Contracts* and *De Smith*'s *Judicial Review*. It is illustrated by drawings of a red-headed barrister; possibly, of the writer herself. Overall it subtracts from the sum total of human knowledge.

It is of course dangerous to generalise, but certain themes emerge from a study of such authors and the essays on those – still relatively few – women lawyers which have achieved the accolade of an entry in the *Oxford Dictionary of National Biography*; the advantage in terms of time available of singleton status or childless marriage; the interruptions caused by child-rearing; the stereotyping of women as best suited to family law.

But by the last decades of the century the rhythm of change accelerated. In 2001 the tipping point was reached: more than half of those called to the Bar were women; as at December 2008 out of a cohort of self-employed barristers numbering 12136, 30.9 per cent were women.

One reason for the great leap forward in women entering the profession in the 1970s and after was the expansion of university education in the 1960s. The Bar became a graduate profession and universities were gender-blind in their admissions processes. In the 1970s and 80s as previously all-male colleges at both the ancient universities became mixed, any Oxbridge bias at the bar profited both sexes.

Another was the impact of a progressive law. The Courts and Legal Services Act 1990 introduced an amendment section 35A, in whose drafting I played a modest – or maybe more accurately, minor – part, prohibiting discrimination on grounds of sex by barristers, barristers' clerks and those who seek to instruct the Bar.

A third was the initiative of the professional body – the Bar Council.

The 1992 Report, 'Without Prejudice', on sex equality at the bar and in the judiciary commissioned by the LCD and Bar Council by Holland and Spencer disclosed substantial inequality of treatment in the profession, especially in the early years.

This energised the commitment of the Bar Council to the cause, appointing an equal opportunity officer for women, and publishing in 1995 a code of practice, which outstripped in ambit and detail the law of the land. As a by-product, whereas Shapland and Soresby's report, 'Work and Training at the Junior Bar' in 1995 reported that no less than 40 per cent of women pupils and barristers had experienced sexual harassment and eight per cent such harassment of a serious nature; on revisiting the issue in 1997 they found the former figure had fallen to 25 per cent, and the latter by an even greater amount.

The problem mutated from one of admission to one of opportunity *to* practise, of retention *in* practice, and of promotion.

As to the opportunity to practise of the evenly balanced group called in 2000, 74 per cent of those who obtained tenancies were men and only 26 per cent women.

Master Kennedy wrote more than a decade ago 'Maternity has replaced delicacy as the major justification for keeping women out of the profession', and the observation retains at least a partial plausibility.

As to retention, the Electoral Reform Society's Survey of Barristers' Changing Practice Status, prepared for the Bar Council in November 2008, was generated by concerns about relative number of female compared with male barristers who leave the profession, and it confirmed that, of those who left the practising profession, half were women, even though women make up only a third.

The main factors were predictable; financial concerns especially in the publicly funded areas; desire – in a phrase made famous by dismissed ministers 'to spend more time with their families'; dislike of long hours and constant travel; and a small percentage because of harassment. The solutions proposed were equally conventional: more crèches, childcare facilities, flexible working arrangements; enhanced maternity and paternity leave.

As to promotion in a charming custom, inaugurated by Eleanor Platt QC, head of a specialist family law chambers, newly appointed women silks receive letters telling them of their placement in the list of those who have achieved that distinction, but the double century was only scored in 2008, and the latest reliable statistics of December 2008 show that out of 1273 QCs, 9.5 per cent were women. Only one woman is ranked by both the Legal 500 and Chambers

Directory – those dedicated followers of fashion – as in the top 50 of commercial silks – our own Master Dohmann. One young barrister (a male) in a recent book designed to strip the mystery from call to the Bar, bluntly echoed Master Helena Kennedy's explanation: 'The reason why only some 10% of women are in silk is simple; babies.'

Indeed, the Bar is not a family-friendly profession: the unpredictability of the workload in terms of volume, location, timing fits awkwardly with the equal unpredictability of parental life. The need to nurture a practice not only by talent, but by – in the modern legal culture – constant self-selling – oh for the days when one left that sort of thing to the clerks! – does not sit well with career breaks for child-rearing, although the more far-sighted chambers have progressive maternity policies.

But certainly the Bar Council ensures that no barrister, female or otherwise, is short of advice. There is 'Guidance on Career Breaks' indicating 'Things to think about', warning the reader that without what is described as nomination of a chambers buddy, 'you may come back to discover the head of chambers and senior clerk have changed and the set has moved to a new address' – an alarming prospect indeed, at any rate as far as the change in location is concerned. There is guidance on maternity, paternity and parental leave. There is even an annual returners course.

There is a Bar Nursery Association, an Equality and Diversity Committee, and Retention Sub-group, not to speak of the autonomous Association of Women Barristers as well as still more recently a United Kingdom Association of Women Judges.

All these initiatives and institutions are bound to affect the concerning statistics in the not-too-distant future. Out of those under 15 years' call in my own set – 35 in number – 16 are women, and I assure you that we have found no need to adopt policies of affirmative action to achieve that near parity between the sexes.

Interviews between the journalist son of the late George Carman QC (published in *The Times* last year) and a quartet of women who have not merely penetrated, but seemingly bypassed entirely, any glass ceiling, exude a sense of optimism that, to borrow a phrase not wholly tarnished by its association with New Labour, 'Things can only get better'. And two nights ago the Barrister of the Year Award at the annual dinner hosted by the journal *The Lawyer* – the legal equivalent of Hollywood's Oscar ceremony – went to Dinah Rose QC, a member of this Inn, the first time a woman has won it, but, I am confident, not the last.

One solution to accelerate progress may be to make judging more compatible with family life, for example by increase of the opportunities for part-time judging. Lord Falconer's proposals for judges to be able to resume their practices after retirement from the Bench, a change which he believed would encourage more applications from women has been resisted by the judiciary. We need not only more women on the Bench, but more mothers too.

A second solution – already implemented – was a departure from a system of promotions dependent on secret soundings among the senior judiciary and the Lord Chancellor's say-so, an archaic reliance on word of mouth recommendation within a small legal elite.

Beverley McLachlin, Chief Justice of Canada, has said that human beings have a tendency to see merit only in those who exhibit the same qualities as they possess. Senior lawyers, she observed, are no exception so, when they look for merit, they tend to look for someone like themselves, or, as Master Helena Kennedy put it more succinctly, there is 'the potential for cloning'.

The creation of a Judicial Appointments Commission has at least introduced a measure of transparency into the system, although it has the disadvantages, doubtless to be overcome in time, that it acts as a deterrent to the modest or indeed to those who wonder whether the protracted process without guarantee of success make it a game not worth the candle. It may not achieve all that those who inserted the obligation to promote diversity into the JAC's mission in the Constitutional Reform Act 2005 may have hoped for.

An astute observer, Kate Malleson, has written:

> Taken together the collective experience of those countries which have established commissions does suggest that their use can increase the representativeness of the bench though such effect is not automatic nor necessarily significant. An important variable would appear to be the extent to which the commission engages in active attempts to recruit under-represented groups.

Removal still would be enlargement of the pool of those eligible for appointment beyond the ranks of the practising profession.

Master Hale has written: 'We seem to be almost the only country in the world where only lawyers who are thought fit to serve in our highest courts are those who have excelled as advocates in our Courts.'

It might even be worth considering the construction of a distinct career judiciary as exists in many civilian countries.

Does all this matter? I have no hesitation in agreeing with those who say that it does.

Cogent reasons have been articulated, again by the Chief Justice of Canada, why there is need for more women on the Bench: to increase in public confidence; as a symbol of fairness which the judiciary are expected to promote; as a sound use of human resources to which Master Hale has added to promote equality of opportunity and democratic accountability. Both share the view that women on the Bench would make a difference in terms of the outcome of trials or appeals.

The scope for making that difference is surely accelerated by the change in the diet of cases in the High Court and above over the last half century. It is doubtful whether a woman would construe a charterparty in a commercial dispute differently to a man, and certain that she could not differently direct a jury as to burden and standard of proof in a criminal trial. But the salient feature of our contemporary legal system is the replacement of private law by public law as the most important dish on the judicial menu. The birth or rebirth of judicial review; the accession to the Treaty of Rome and its offspring; the incorporation of the European Convention on Human Rights by the HRA 1998 have moved the law away from the conventional areas of commerce, trusts and taxation into new realms infused with policy considerations. Whether legislative or administrative acts pass the tests of legitimate aim and proportionality allows for a variety of potential responses.

For my part, I had always recognised that in the assessment of fact, or the exercise of discretion, a judge's gender might well be influential in a decision. What I had not appreciated, until we had our first female member of our highest tribunal, is that gender could also influence the shape of legal principle and precedent.

True it is that Master Hale has written, 'the great majority of the judgments I have written could just as easily have been written or spoken by a man'. As an exception to such general rule, she instanced that 'speaking as a reasonable but comparatively weak and fearful grandmother', she would, unlike her male colleagues, have extended the defence of duress to exculpate the battered wife forced to handle stolen goods.

I venture to think that when legal historians look back at *her* career as an appellate judge they will suggest that she has brought a female prospective more frequently than she acknowledges – not least, but not only, by looking at the number of her own dissenting speeches.

Diversity of experience for appellate judges, especially when sitting as one of a group as well as for trial judges, must be prized. While the first woman on the US Supreme Court, Sandra Day O'Connor, echoed the words of Justice Jeanne Coyne, formerly of the Minnesota Supreme Court, that 'a wise old man and a wise old woman would reach the same conclusion', Judge Sotomayor, President Obama's nominee for the current Supreme Court vacancy, in a now much-quoted speech she gave in 2001, said, 'I would hope that a wise Latina woman with the richness of her experiences would more often than not reach a better conclusion than a white male who hasn't lived that life'; certainly, we should all agree, different, if not necessarily always better.

As Master Hale herself observed, 'Women lead different lives from men largely because they have visibly different bodies from men', and this must, and properly, feed into their perceptions of what is just, fair and reasonable – the primary targets of the law.

And, as she has argued, a feminist can be a judge as long as the point of view she brings 'is consistent with the fundamental principles of law one is sworn to apply and secondly that it is carefully and cautiously applied to the issues in the case'.

She can in short have an approach if not an agenda.

The US Supreme Court holding that a jury panel composed predominantly of men was not lawful perceptively said 'the truth is that the two sexes are *not* fungible'.

The possibility of different views based on gender was brought into focus in a recent case before the Supreme Court concerning the constitutionality of a strip search of a teenage girl at school on suspicion of possession of ibuprofen pills. The divergence of attitude between Judge Ruth Bader Ginsburg and her male colleagues was exposed by an unusual interview that she felt compelled to give to *USA Today* while the case was *still* pending.

And I suggest that it is not only in how cases are decided, but how cases are handled that the increase in the female judiciary will have a benign impact.

Henry Cecil wrote, 'One shouldn't be able to imagine a judge having a bath' to make the point that a judge's authority stems in part at least from being seen as a sphinx, disengaged and impartial. When he wrote it there were no women judges, but I would imagine that he would express the same sentiments in respect of them, if not only for the same reason.

But authority is not the other side of the coin of remoteness and justice can not only *be* done but can be seen to be done without macho posturing by those who dispense it.

As to how soon the changes – both work I have noted and those I have floated – will work their way through the system, there is a debate between the gradualists and the radicals.

The gradualists believe that it is only a question of time when the larger numbers of women being admitted to the Bar will be proportionately reflected in silk and judiciary, and who believe that affirmative action, designed to erase the consequences of past discrimination, will in fact reinforce rather than destroy the concept of equality. A strong candidate for the post of Lord Chief Justice during the last decade was popularly believed to have impaired his chances by his dangerous suggestion that certain women had been elevated to the Bench otherwise than on merit.

The radicals believe that whether the benign outcome envisaged by the gradualists is reality or mirage, women should not wait so long to enter into the promised land. Master Hale has said, 'most of us do not believe that sooner or later the increasing numbers of women entering the profession will trickle up to the top'.

I am neither a gradualist nor a radical, but an optimist because the upward trend is unmistakable. There is one Lord of Appeal in Ordinary, three Lady Justices of Appeal, seven women in QBD, seven in the Family Division and one in Chancery, figures originally taken from Wikipedia, but – it may be remarkably – at one with the MoJ's own list. Milestones have already been passed – in the higher judiciary. Master Ebsworth was the first woman to be appointed to the Queen's Bench Division in 1992; Dame Mary Arden was the first to the Chancery Division in 1993; Baroness Butler-Sloss, as she now is, the first woman to head a Division in 1966; Dame Elizabeth Gloster the first woman appointed to the Commercial Court in 2006; Dame Laura Cox and Elizabeth Slade are experts in employment law and sit in the Employment Appeal Tribunal; Dame Victoria Sharp, an expert in libel, will deal with the jury list; Master Dobbs is a former Chair of the Criminal Bar Association, and Dame Heather Hallet a former Chairman of the Bar Council; Dame Janet Smith is pre-eminent in personal injury litigation; Dame Rosalyn Higgins has recently retired as President of the International Court of Justice. No longer are women simply corralled into the pastures of family law; green shoots are visible outside those traditional fields. There has been a woman Attorney General, Baroness Scotland, and two woman solicitors general – the first Harriet Harman, an honorary Bencher of this Inn and aptly from the purely linguistic perspective, the first solicitor to hold that office. The somewhat patronising slogan of the cigarette manufacturers Virginia Slims in their sponsorship of the women's tennis circuit – 'You've come a long way, baby' – does not have as its compulsory corollary you've got a long way to go.

I believe the momentum for change is already irresistible and will continue to be fueled by the dramatic changes in university entry. Research by HEPI, the Higher Education Policy Institute, shows that almost 50 per cent of women now enter university compared with only 38 per cent of men; and female entrants achieve better degrees, albeit more narrowly, when they leave. During my decade as President of Trinity College Oxford we produced candidates who scored the top mark in the university in law finals in tort, administrative, company and public international law, and, the year after I left, the top candidate in law overall. The candidates had one feature in common – besides the fact that I taught none of them. They were all women, although, alas, only one has so far chosen to come to the Bar.

I see no reason why in my lifetime we should not see a woman as Lord or Lady Chief Justice to complement Beverley McLachlin in Canada, Sian Elias in New Zealand and Dorit Beinisch in Israel, or a female Master or Mistress of the Rolls.

Before reaching my conclusion, let me briefly praise some famous women, and the Inn which begat them.

Myrella Cohen, the longest serving woman circuit judge – 23 years in all – who helped to liberalise Jewish divorce laws.

Pam Barker, called at the age of 49, and rejected for a tenancy from the all-male set where she did her pupillage not just – she believed – because she was a woman, but because she was a grandmother, who returned to Hong Kong to become the pre-eminent defender of the Vietnamese boat people.

Master Angelica Mitchell – another circuit judge – cut down by cancer in the prime of whom Master Helena Kennedy wrote, 'certain upper class priorities and affiliations memorably collided with her egalitarian instincts', describing her penchant as a student for taking 'taxis to see the bank manager at Coutts about her overdraft' while being at the same 'the mistress of the well-placed four letter word'.

Jane Wynham-Kaye – General Secretary to the Health Visitors Association.

Ellice Eadie, the first woman parliamentary counsel, who drafted, among other legislation, the Matrimonial Homes Act 1967, the Divorce Reform Act 1969 and the Family Law Reform Act of the same year.

Betty Johnson, Chairman of the Girls' Public Day School Trust and Standing Counsel to the General Synod of the Church of England.

Master Marion Simmons, deputy chairman of the Competition Appeal Tribunal and pioneer in advocacy training.

For all, whether bewigged or not, Gray's Inn was their *domus* and point of departure.

Of course, the future of the headgear, the historic visible symbol of our profession, is less certain than the ascent of legal woman. My only prediction is that it will not be replaced, like the traditional judicial robes, with some pseudo-modernised equivalent, which, like the mule, has neither the pride of ancestry nor the hope of posterity. There is incidentally a feminist perspective on wigs too. Master Hale has said 'My objection to wigs is … that they humanise us as men. They deny us our femaleness, let alone our femininity.' So, in our legal culture the wigs may go, but the women will remain.

# 10

# *'FE Smith … Lessons from a Legal Life'* Birkenhead Lecture 2009*

FEW, IF ANY, lawyers have had a better known *curriculum vitae* than Frederick Edwin Smith, known throughout his lifetime by his initials 'FE'; Queen's Counsel at the age of 36 (the youngest in the country after only 8½ years at the junior bar), Attorney General at 43 – a story of continuing professional development without the acquisition of CPD points – Lord Chancellor at 46 (youngest of all time discounting Judge Jeffreys, who was not, as was once said with a degree of meiosis, 'in the line of the true apostolic succession of the Chancellors of England') and later Secretary of State for India, High Steward of Oxford University, Knight, Baron, Viscount and Earl in succession, and last, but not least, Treasurer of this Honourable Society on four separate occasions. I want in this, the third lecture in the series inaugurated during my own single Treasurership in 2008, to use his extraordinarily distinguished career as a vehicle for some reflections, his and mine, on Bar, Bench and the offices he held. The vicissitudes of his political life I acknowledge, but must pass by.

FE was not born to the purple or with a silver spoon in his mouth, although like many modern politicians, he exaggerated the lowliness of his origins. The son of Frederick Smith, Mayor of Birkenhead, himself a barrister of lesser but no little accomplishment, and one Elizabeth Taylor, daughter of a Birkenhead rate collector, he was, as his chosen motto had it, *Jaber meae fortunae*. For those who, in that delightful but archaic phrase, 'Do not have the Latin', *jaber* means workman in hard materials, more particularly Smith. I need not, I surmise, risk *meae fortunae* being 'lost in translation'.

FE went to Birkenhead School. Chancing forfeiture of a place at his local University of Liverpool, he won an open scholarship to Wadham College, Oxford coming (uncharacteristically) only fourth in the examination roll, which was topped by another legendary dark blue contemporary, CB Fry. He failed in, or did not pursue – accounts vary – a simultaneous application to Trinity

* Grays Inn. (2010) 124 *Graya* 21.

which, I may be permitted to say, was at least as much the College's loss as his own. He achieved the coveted double distinction of the Presidency of the Union and First Class Honours in law on the back of an extraordinary dedication to study, originating only six months before his finals. 'Twas ever thus! His gift for phrase-making was first revealed in his maiden paper speech at the Union when he crossed swords with the temperance proselytiser, Sir Wilfrid Lawson, who had acted honourably on his own beliefs by destruction of the entire contents of his well-stocked cellar. In a retrospective address on Milestones of his Life, FE said he would not be deterred 'from quoting the criticism' of his speech in *The Oxford Magazine* and *ISIS*, which referred to its power, conciseness, vivacity and brilliance. Would that we were all in receipt of such criticism!

Winner of the Vinerian Scholarship, defeating no less a rival than WS Holdsworth – with uncharacteristic modesty he later described himself as 'fortunate enough to defeat the learned author of the History of English Law' – he became a don at Merton for three years, writing a brief article for the *Law Quarterly Review* on the measure of damages in contract. Ignoring Dicey's sympathetic advice that he procure 'a good counsel used to criminal proceedings', he defended himself successfully before the Oxford magistrates against a charge of assault and obstruction of a police officer in the execution of his duty arising out of an incident during the visit to the University of the Prince of Wales with a pungent cross-examination of the officer in question. It is not always the case that he who is his own lawyer has a fool for a client. He was called to the Bar by this Inn in 1894, coming equal first in his Bar Finals. He was not immediately popular with the Senior Members of Hall. Asking prematurely in the time-honoured phrase, 'Mr Senior may we smoke?' he received the reply, 'No you may not'. As he explained, addressing another Mr Senior many years later, 'unaccustomed to rebuffs of that kind I rose and said "why not?" upon which your predecessor having no suitable reply ready, wisely remained silent'. He practised initially in Liverpool, where 'his father's memory still lingered'. Family connections should no longer be the *sine qua non* of success at the Bar, but, if you have them, use them!

Writing in *Graya* in 1927 on the advantages and disadvantages of the local vis a vis the London Bar, he stressed local links as essential, while adding cautiously, 'the whole truth is that no-one can generalise about the matter'.

In his first year of practice in which, as he put it, 'he was still waiting for briefs', he wrote a textbook on international law – a useful way in principle to acquire a practice, although his choice of subject was, from that perspective, somewhat arcane. Serendipitously it went into a fifth edition edited by Dr Phillipson, an authority in the area, while FE, its progenitor, was Attorney General and was puffed by the publisher on the basis that the Law Officer's 'pronouncements will be of real utility to a large class of professional men'.

He had no obvious need to prosper further by his pen for he was an early star on the Northern Circuit. At the Brewster Sessions, he was led by Marshall Hall, who said to the Attorney General on his return to London, 'I have just been leading the cleverest young fellow I have ever met in my life. His name's Smith – you ought to send him some Treasury briefs.' Taking advantage of the propensity of Liverpool solicitors to engage Liverpool counsel for London cases, he appeared for the appellant in *Wise v Dunning*, then the leading case on the right of public meeting. Although he lost the appeal, the Lord Chief Justice, Lord Alverstone wrote him a note of congratulations which he promptly framed and hung in his chambers. It said: 'you argued their case admirably. I predict for you a very brilliant future. I trust we shall often see you.' Both prediction and hope were amply fulfilled in the succeeding years. Interestingly, neither the case nor its sequel feature in Lord Alverstone's own memoirs.

He made the best of the worst material. In his first case at the Old Bailey in 1902 where Rufus Isaacs, Horace Avory and Marshall Hall were among the other advocates, he delivered an effective plea in mitigation for Goudie, whose swindle had cost the Bank of Liverpool £160,000. '[I]n the whole history of crime there is not a case in which a man has enjoyed himself so little as a result of his crime,' he perorated, 'as Goudie has.' Goudie was nonetheless sentenced to 10 years' penal servitude. Forensic sparkle may be its own reward, but it is not necessarily the client's.

Yet sometimes it is. In his first murder defence (a dock brief) of Ethel Robinson who, with a fellow servant, had suffocated their bullying mistress, FE persuaded the jury, when the facts left them no other option but conviction, to make a recommendation for mercy. The judge wrote to him from the lodgings, 'I never heard a hopeless case more brilliantly defended.'

Paying a compliment to the other side's solicitors in a county court case – a wise tactic for any ambitious barrister – he was briefed by those self-same solicitors in the Guinea Gold litigation to defend claims made by retailers for promised, but unpaid, bonuses, arising out of the US Tobacco manufacturer's purchase and subsequent winding up of the British company Ogden's. The first case went to the House of Lords; and the litigation was protracted for years. It was, in an aromatic phrase of a Liverpool silk of my youth, 'a dripping roast'. He was as much involved in criminal as well as in civil cases – an opportunity too frequently denied to the Bar in our age of increasing specialisation.

Once elected a Member of Parliament in 1906, FE moved to London. Abinger, a contemporary, wrote, 'at the Bar he dethroned in a remarkably short space of time many silks older than himself until he stood pre-eminent, clearly marked out for the great office of Lord High Chancellor of England'. Two Queen's Counsel had advised Levers, soap makers of Port Sunlight, that it would be futile to bring proceedings for defamation against the Rothermere press, which had accused them of a fraudulent sales campaign. After a night fortified by champagne and oysters – he was always *prêt à boire* as well as *prêt à manger* – FE wrote a succinct opinion: 'there is no answer to this action for libel and the damages must be enormous'. It proved indeed to be the largest ever award up to that time.

He rode the horses of politics and law, both harnessed to his ambition, aided and abetted by the long since obsolete timetable of the Commons, whose daily business began when that of the courts ended. As John Campbell, his most recent biographer put it, 'Simultaneously with his increasingly high level political career, he was continuously busy in the courts as the most casual glance as the Times Law Reports will show – divorce suits, contested wills, complicated commercial disputes, libel actions, the occasional murder.'

That simultaneity of action was displayed within his practice too. GD 'Khaki' Roberts QC recounts, 'I have never ceased to marvel at the breath-taking technique of fashionable advocates of the day – F.E. Smith for one – who managed to appear in various cases simultaneously in different courts.' This is not a methodology I would recommend to the Junior Bar.

At the end of 1910 there was a wave of elevations to the Bench from the commercial, criminal and special jury courts, and Rufus Isaacs and Simon became law officers. Marshall Hall and F.E. Smith stepped into much of the work that was released by these promotions. Sir Claude Schuster, Permanent Secretary to what was then the Lord Chancellor's Department, wrote: 'By 1914 he was in the front rank of advocates and was making an income which was, by the standards of those days, prodigious, while adding the censorious words 'He was also spending as much as he earned.'

In a defamation case, *Grand Duke Boris of Russia v Munsey's Magazine*, he received (as well as a fee) a pair of jewelled cufflinks ornamented with the Duke's initial B and the Imperial Coronet – a bonus at odds with the Bar Council's current Code of Conduct.

At the outbreak of war he served briefly in France, which required him to repay monies delivered *in advance* – oh happy days! – for briefs he had to return. There were applications to adjourn cases in which he was involved – a more compelling case of counsel's convenience than many. Mr Duke KC, explaining to Mr Justice Darling why an action could not now be heard on the day originally fixed, said, 'My friend, who was Mr F.E. Smith KC and is now Major F.E. Smith was briefed in this case', to which that judge, who never knowingly under-quipped, responded, 'I should think he's General F.E. Smith by this time.' In the event he never returned to private practice, being appointed first as Solicitor General in May 1915 and then as Attorney General. Once Attorney General, the nature of his practice was shaped by the demands of his illustrious office. He led for Crown in many cases in the prize courts. Among his leading cases in that specialist jurisdiction were *The Zamora*, and *The Ophelia* – concerned with whether a German hospital ship had been lawfully taken by forfeiting her immunity from seizure through involvement in intelligence gathering.

He prosecuted Sir Joseph Jonas under the Official Secrets Act for communicating information about British aircraft and warships to a business customer, a manufacturer of small arms for the German Government. He was called on to consider whether the ex-Kaiser should be punished for his role in the war, having noted that 'the doctrines of International Law afford abundant warrant and precedent' for punitive reparations in the preface to his re-edited work on the subject – not the aspect that a non-political academic might have chosen to stress.

His most celebrated appearance was as lead prosecutor in the trial of Roger Casement in 1916, who faced a charge of high treason as a former member of the British Consular Service who had used a German aide to promote the Irish cause against the British. In that case he appeared with Sir George Cave, Solicitor General and later Lord Chancellor, AH Bodkin, later Director of Public Prosecutions, Travers Humphreys and GAH Branson, both future judges – certainly a legal 'A' team! At a time when the Government were anxious that the United States should join in the war, so sensitive were the issues that FE's opening had to be telegraphed to the United States before even discussion with his juniors. Barely 10 pages in length, it ended vividly, 'the prisoner, blinded by hatred to this country as malignant in quality as it was sudden in origin, has played a desperate hazard. He played it and he has lost it. Today the forfeit is claimed.' But his strategy also created controversy. He showed Casement's diaries, which contained details of an unorthodox sexual life (and one which was criminal by the laws of the day) to Sergeant Sullivan, leading for the defence. The malign construction is that this was roughhouse robing room tactics designed to discomfort his opponent. The benign construction is that FE believed that it might sustain a plea of insanity, prompting Heuston in his classic *Lives of the Lord Chancellors* to observe 'his conduct in making the documents available was entirely in accordance with the high principles which govern the conduct of prosecuting counsel at the Bar'.

Casement's defence turned on a construction of the definition of treason in a statute of the reign of Edward III, as to whether being adherent to the King's enemies was an act, which, to engage guilt, had to be committed in the realm, not overseas. It did not succeed at the Old Bailey or the Court of Appeal. As Attorney General, FE had to decide whether to issue a fiat for that matter to be taken to the House of Lords – a classic example, you may think, of someone being judge in his own cause. Travers Humphreys' recollection is that FE asked the opinion of his juniors (which coincided with his own) only after he had communicated his refusal in order that he alone should answer for it in the House of Commons, and wrote 'Loyal to his juniors he was through life, loyal to his friends, a very great man.'

His last prosecution case as Attorney General was of a conspiracy by a family, the Wheeldons, (ironically) of pacifist views to murder the Prime Minister, Lloyd George, on the civil side. In the Rhodesian land case, which lasted 14 days in the Privy Council, he secured for the Crown vast tracts of the colony against the claims of the British South Africa Company, the white settlers and the indigenous population.

It is, I would suggest, a matter for regret, that the tradition that the Attorney General, as the *de jure* leader of the Bar, should be an active advocate, has been unevenly adhered to in recent years.

FE practised at the Bar for less than two decades before ascending to the Woolsack, and, he recalled, 'very largely in jury cases', before the attrition of that mode of trial in civil (and even more recently) criminal cases over the succeeding century.

Campbell asks the pertinent question, 'How high does FE really rate as a barrister?' and answered it as follows:

> As in politics so in the law a part of FE's success lay in his physical appearance, the figure he cut in court and the style which he brought to the leading role. On the platform it was the impression of vitality and physical strength; in court it was more his stillness and icy control which compelled attention. 'Somewhat qualifying that image, the young Christian Humphreys records as a bar student visiting the Old Bailey and being 'scandalised at the casual way in which the Attorney General learned back against the seat, a stance that I, in all my forty years in that court, never dared to assume.

Campbell continues, 'His second asset was his voice.'

*The Daily Telegraph*, reporting a case in 1913 which FE appeared against Sir Edward Marshall Hall, gave a fuller account of his delivery:

> He speaks deliberately with studied calmness and so low at times as to strain the ears of the more distant listeners. But when he has a point to make there is a sudden departure from this quiet conversational manner. He then lifts his voice in crescendo passages, and finishes with a blow on the table that startles the unwary. Delivered of his point he subsides at once as though nothing had happened. But the speech suggests the tide, with intermittent long separated waves, as contrasting with tumultuous current of his predecessor Marshall Hall).

The older Humphreys described him as 'that D'Artagnan of the courts' and a still more august contemporary, Winston Churchill, wrote of his 'entangling net and unexpected trident for the Courts of law'. Campbell adds, 'One of FE's greatest strengths was his power of persuasion – particularly over juries: Judges tended to be less susceptible.'

In the defence of Ethel Le Neve, Crippen's mistress, alleged to have colluded with her lover who had cut up his wife's body, buried her remains in a cellar and then fled abroad on a ship bound for Quebec with FE's client disguised as a boy, FE boldly declined to call her and won on the burden of proof. He ended:

> I do not ask for mercy I ask you only for justice and I am content you will judge her in her hour of agony with the same consideration and the same caution you would wish to be shown to a daughter of your own were she placed in such a position.

The Lord Chief Justice in summing up to the jury said that they had just listened to a very able speech on Ms Le Neve's behalf and ought to consider Mr Smith's argument very carefully indeed. The jury took 20 minutes only to acquit. Travers Humphreys who acted for the prosecution somewhat waspishly observed that, once it had been decided that there should be separate representation, 'FE not unnaturally chose for himself the much easier task of defending the lady'. Easier, but not, I would submit, easy.

Campbell concludes his analysis of FE's qualities:

> His essential attribute, however, on which his reputation really rested, was his exceptional clarity of mind and the capacity of going straight to the heart of the case. ... His extraordinary speed of assimilation did give rise to some professional jealousy as well as admiration, the suspicion that he was really a quick witted word juggler. But this overlooked the influence of his Merton years. His secret was that, more than most barristers who go immediately into practice, he had a solid foundation of academic law to which he could quickly relate whatever particular points came up.

FE himself once said in a hubristic moment, 'I never encountered a legal problem that presented the slightest difficulty to me' – although that is at odds with the recollection of Judge Hargreaves to whom FE once confessed, in a highly complex patent case, that he had failed to understand one word of it from beginning to end. But then that is an area in which a third-class chemistry degree will always outstrip a first-class degree in jurisprudence.

The oft-repeated examples of FE's wit are many. He won the glittering prizes of which he so famously spoke in later life by sharp words, not by a sharp sword. In an early case he appeared before His Honour Judge Willis QC, described in a memoir in that ambiguous way, characteristic of judicial obituaries as a 'dear gentleman, although he had rather an unfortunate habit of snubbing counsel who ventured to differ from him in Court'. FE responded to one snubbing so vehemently that everybody in court sat aghast, including Willis himself, who remained silent for the remainder of the case.

It was Willis indeed with whom he clashed most frequently. During a fierce interchange, that judge asked, 'What do you think I am on the bench for Mr Smith?', to which the response came: 'It is not for me to attempt to fathom the inscrutable workings of providence.' After yet another passage of increasingly vituperative repartee between Bar and Bench, the same judge said, 'you are an extremely offensive young man', to which FE replied, 'as a matter of fact we both are. The difference between us is that I am trying to be and you can't help it.'

When Mr Justice Ridley said to him, 'Mr Smith I have read the pleadings and I do not think much of your case', FE replied, 'Indeed I am sorry to hear that My Lord but you will find that the more you hear of it the more it will grow on you.'

And, according to a much-loved tale which is certainly Top of the FE Pops, a judge who, unlike Mr Justice Ridley, at least allowed time to pass before his intervention, 'Mr Smith I have listened to you for several hours and I am none the wiser', fared no better since FE spontaneously replied, 'No My Lord but you are considerably better informed.'

Sometimes the court reports read like a script for a comic soap opera:

> Master of the Rolls: 'Really Mr Smith, do give this Court credit for a little intelligence.'
>
> FE Smith: 'That's the mistake I made in the Court below.'
>
> FE Smith to witness: 'So you were as drunk as a judge.'
>
> Judge (interjecting): 'You mean, as drunk as a Lord.'

FE Smith: 'Yes my Lord.'

In a variant on the same theme, during the Wootton libel trial, FE cross-examined a jockey about his drunkenness. When Mr Justice Darling interposed, 'There is a maxim that drunken men tell the truth', FE retorted, 'But that is when they are drunk' and, reverting to the witness, asked 'Are you sober now?'

I suspect that, as is often the case, these anecdotes, if not apocryphal, may well be exaggerated, and I would not recommend that any members of the young Bar present in the hall tonight, seek to emulate these examples.

But FE rightly recognised that wit is no unwelcome intruder in the courtroom.

As Attorney General, in congratulating the Mr Justice Darling on his elevation to the Privy Council, he observed about Darling's reputation for judicial levity, 'The Bar has never failed to recognise that this humour never prejudices but often contributes to the elucidation of justice which has been your Lordship's passionate object during your career.'

No less celebrated is a story of FE's forensic cunning when he appeared for a bus company in a personal injury claim. A boy claimed that as a result of an injury sustained in a collision, he could not lift his arm above shoulder height. FE asked him to demonstrate this disability, which he did. FE then asked him how high he could lift it before the accident. The boy's arm shot up above his head. *Cadit quaestio*. Geoffrey Robertson QC has written, 'This reparteedious story has been endlessly repeated over the past fifty years in legal miscellanies and at legal dinners: a nursery trick played to deny compensation to the boy who was run over by a tram through no fault of his own, it remains the paradigm legal fable', a comment which appears curiously resistant to the fact that the boy's claim was a fraudulent one!

Campbell suggests:

> He was not by the highest standards a particularly subtle cross-examiner – his career boasts no outstanding interrogation to compare with Carson's in the Archer Shee case or Isaacs' examination of Sir Edward Marshall. On the contrary two of his most famous cases involved his humiliation at the hands of exceptionally difficult witnesses

adding:

> It is in fact a curious feature of FE's legal career altogether that for all his brilliant reputation and enormous earnings he was involved in no really great case – except the Casement prosecution when he was Attorney General, and controversy surrounds that. His best were early on, in his Liverpool years … As a leading silk he somehow never landed a famous case which would have enshrined him in the substantial history of the Bar as indelibly as his witty imagined rejoinders having enshrined him in its mythology.

But I consider that Campbell's verdict is too cautious. Not even the most adept cross-examiner can score a palpable hit unless to impale a witness who is actually lying. And to be instructed in a famous case is more a matter of chance than of talent: to be instructed, as FE was, consistently in high-profile litigation is less adventitious. Ten out of 23 trials in the compendium *Famous Trials of History* are cases in which he was involved as an advocate, a statistic only partly rendered suspect by the fact that he was himself the author of the book.

FE received indeed many words of praise from the public galleries, the Bar and the Bench. At the conclusion of his speech in *Wootton v Sievier* applause broke out in court. In the *Sackville Will* case, Sir Edward Carson, his opponent, referred to 'trivialities magnified by Counsel which afford so splendid an example of Mr Smith's great powers of mesmerism and fascination'. When FE led for the prosecution of TWH Crosland, a minor poet, and Lord Alfred Douglas, who were charged with falsely spreading the rumour that Robert Ross, a friend of the deceased playwright Oscar Wilde, had sexual relations with an 18-year-old boy, Mr Justice Avory said in his summing up that the jury 'are not here to convict anybody because Mr Ross has the good fortune to have secured the most eloquent counsel at the English Bar'.

Sometimes his forensic powers overreached themselves. In *Greenlands Ltd v London Association for the Protection of Trade*, a libel case, an award of damages of £1,000 was set aside by the Court of Appeal, Hamilton LJ saying:

> By no formula or manipulation can £1,000 be got at. For any damage really done, £100 was quite enough: double for the sympathy, double it again for the jury's sense of the defendant's conduct, and again for their sense of FE Smith's. The product is only £800.

On the debit side of the ledger, Campbell also noted 'The one quality that perhaps FE lacked was tact – in which Isaacs, for example, excelled. He could be impatient with witnesses, was frequently rude to judges and sometimes antagonised juries instead of charming them.' It is ironic that in his introduction to the biography of Marshall Hall, his erstwhile leader and adversary, FE could write about the latter's legendary quarrels with the Bench: 'he was often headstrong when caution would have been the wiser policy'. But by then he was himself a mere two years away from his own death: old men forget the errors of their youth.

From the start of his career the air of effortless superiority – allegedly an attribute of Balliol men alone – was in FE's case cultivated by superior effort. His plea in the Goudie case, was written out, revised and rewritten, and then committed entirely to memory. But as he grew more senior, he took more risks. When FE asked why Mr Justice Darling, who sat in the King's Bench Division over quarter of a century, had said to a friend that he would rather have FE open a complicated case than any counsel at the Bar, the friend explained that the judge had said that it was interesting to discover which of two fresh minds would grasp the facts first.

Most of all I would emphasise his extraordinary energy. Making due allowance for filial piety, his son came close to the truth:

> Every night FE Smith sat up into the small hours of the morning: in the light of day he was the most active barrister in England and was making frequent and carefully mediated contributions to the House of Commons, ranging from platform to

> platform all over the country freely using his pen and regularly riding and hunting. His stamina was almost superhuman.

He was certainly admired by his peers. '[W]ithin the last generation,' wrote Abinger,

> the Bar produced three men who can justifiably be described as great. The trio I have in mind consists of the Marquess of Reading, the Earl of Birkenhead, and Sir John Simon. They will go down to posterity as three of the most brilliant men of the twentieth century.

Another barrister, Fordham, wrote:

> Young members of the Bar now have the same admiration for Simon and F.E. Smith as I had for Hawkins and Coleridge and with a good reason. A man always looks larger when he stands on a pedestal of age and experience higher than one's own.

But the chimes of his reputation which reverberated among later generations were surely not false echoes.

His appointment as Lord Chancellor in January 1919 was, however, not universally approved, although on 9 May 1919 the Inn gave him a House dinner in which Master Mattison KC's tribute was uneasily poised on the boundary between obsequiousness and objectivity. *The Times* commented that the elevation was 'carrying a joke too far', but later repented in an obituary which said, 'His Lord Chancellorship in its legal aspect was distinguished by brilliant judgments and far reaching reforms.'

It may overstate the matter to say that, like Prince Hal, his personality changed when he ascended the legal throne, but whereas Schuster could write of FE as an advocate, 'He was regarded as a swashbuckler, wily and courageous, but headstrong and superficial, in the courts, as the man for a crushing cross-examination or a speech to the jury rather than for a serious legal argument, he wrote that as Lord Chancellor, Birkenhead,

> he soon acquired great authority among his legal colleagues. The time had come when he could bring into play the harmony which he had acquired as a teacher and a practitioner. His demeanour as a judge was dignified and impressive. He kept the Court together, and strived earnestly to do justice and to make it clear that justice was being done. His judgments were composed with great care and after close consultation with his colleagues. In style they were vigorous and often witty.

One commentator has less ambivalently observed, 'The distinction he gained as an advocate was eclipsed by his achievement as a judge'. Carson and Isaacs, his forensic peers, did not burnish their reputation on the Bench. Birkenhead, although sitting amid a cohort of ex-Lord Chancellors, certainly did so.

As Lord Chancellor, FE presided over 70 cases as well as sitting as a supplementary judge at first instance in the divorce courts on Saturday mornings to deal with a backlog of cases – an unfortunate by-product of the war. His major speeches excite admiration not only for their linguistic felicity, seasoned by the occasional apt Latin – he once referred a not exceptionally exciting statute to the Colonial Laws Validity Act 1865 as being in 'Imperial History *clarum et venerabile nomen*' – added to depth of scholarship, but also for the sense that they convey to the reader that, notwithstanding that arguments were marshalled on each side of the case, the conclusion reached seemed predestined.

While prepared to lay down general principles of law, when required, he preferred to make his judgment case-specific, not infrequently in speeches devoid of any reference to case law. He never lost sight of the essential judicial role – to decide disputes, and not to provide material for academic commentary.

In *The Volute* on the subject of contributory negligence in a maritime collision, he held, 'I think the question of contributory negligence must be dealt with somewhat broadly and upon common sense principles as a jury would deal with it.'

In *Sutton v Briggs* in deciding that a gambler might recover the money he had lost when payment was made by cheque he observed:

> The consequences of this view will no doubt be extremely inconvenient to many persons. But this is not a matter to influence the House unless in a doubtful case offering foothold for balanced speculations as to the probable intention of the legislature.

In *Fitch v Dewes*, a restraint of trade case, he said:

> The Courts have been generous in elucidating these matters by the enunciation of general principles in the course of the last few years and I am extremely anxious not to carry this process further today.

Occasionally indeed his speeches were delivered *ex tempore*.

Among his most celebrated judgments were *Bourne v Keane*, where he held that a bequest made for the purposes of masses for the dead is not void as a gift to superstitious uses, and, in overruling a long line of authority, opined, 'I cannot conceive that it is my function as a judge of the Supreme Appellate Court of this country to make error perpetual in a matter of this kind'; *McCawley v King*, a case about validity of judicial appointment which contains an interesting disquisition on the nature of constitutions; *DPP Beard*, in which he laid down the ground rules for criminal responsibility for drunkenness; and *Russell v Russell*, where (sitting as a Lord of Appeal in Ordinary) he held that a husband's evidence of lack of sexual relations with his wife was not admissible on his petition for divorce in a case in which the only evidence of adultery consisted of the birth of a child.

Sometimes his *dicta* were lapidary. In *Rutherford v Richardson*, a divorce case, he said:

> It is undoubtedly true that it is better that some slight degree of injustice should be done in an individual case than that the Courts should abandon the sure advantage of a dependable rule.

Sometimes they were light-hearted. In *Lucas Tooth*, a construction of will case, he said:

> The word 'then' is of infinite finesse, flexibility and variety. A painstaking and very elaborate analysis might no doubt exhaust the senses in which it may be employed with literary correctitude but an attempt to discern its use founded upon an examination less thorough may easily by grafting artificiality upon artificiality, undermine rules which are fundamental.

In the Introduction to his book, *Fourteen English Judges*, he wrote tantalisingly:

> If and when I find leisure to complete my work, I will, in its preface, for the benefit of anyone who attaches the slightest importance to my opinion, attempt to make plain who, and, in what order, are in my judgment the ten greatest Judges who have interpreted law in the courts of this country.

This might have illuminated his own extra-curial view of the most significant judicial qualities, but it was not to be. The ever laudatory Abinger wrote:

> His speeches as reported in the House of Lords in some of the cases that came before him were the greatest efforts ever delivered in the Upper House. He has little or no regard for precedent when he thinks the precedents are bad law, and he has swept away many cobwebbed absurdities which for centuries have bound the judges in the Courts below.

FE also showed a deft hand presiding in the Privy Council over the curious case of Archdeacon Wakeford, convicted by the Consistory Court for a night spent in a hotel in Peterborough with a woman who was not his wife. The appeal was a rehearing of the original trial, and the case for the peccant priest was advanced by Carson. The hybrid court of Law Lords and ecclesiastical assessors had to play the role of a jury and find facts, which included a need to consider the script of the hotel register book, alleged to be forged. Birkenhead was pre-disposed to disbelieve that a man of the cloth would, without resort to disguise, commit adultery in an adjacent diocese. As he phrased it epigrammatically, 'it is difficult to associate simplicity so absolute with a course so perilous', but was compelled with his colleagues to find the case made out.

In the Rhondda peerage case, as a member of the Committee of Privileges, he decided that the Sex Disqualification (Removal) Act of 1919, providing that a person shall not be disqualified by sex or marriage from the exercise of any public function, did not entitle Viscountess Rhondda to gain admission to the House of Lords. He summarised the majority judgment:

> It is sufficient to say that the legislature in dealing with this matter cannot be taken to have departed from the usage of centuries or to have employed such loose and ambiguous words to carry out so momentous a revolution in the constitution of this House.

It was not entirely surprising that he should align himself on that side of the argument: he had, after all, as a young MP, in 1910 led for the opposition on the second reading of the Parliamentary Franchise (Women's) Bill.

After disavowing any assumption of the intellectual inferiority of women, he somewhat undermined the force of his disclaimer with the words

> I venture to say that the sum total of human happiness, knowledge and achievement would have been almost unaffected if Sappho had never sung, if Joan of Arc had never fought, if Siddons had never played, and if George Eliot had never written.

He presided over the Appellate and Judicial Committee with authority but also kindness. In his memorial tribute, the then Treasurer wrote, 'He took infinite pains to show personal courtesies as well as to give professional encouragement to these advocates from overseas who appeared before the Judicial Committee.' The display of patience towards the barrister in an unfamiliar court is a sign of judicial virtue, not vice: mercifully one that the modern judiciary possesses – at any rate for the most part.

As Lord Chancellor, Birkenhead had a parallel role as legislator, and steered the Law of Property Act 1922 onto the statute book, so modernising a system of real property often encrusted by 'the barnacles of the medieval feudal system'. Benjamin Cherry, when editing a new edition of *Prideaux Forms and Precedents in Conveyancing*, dedicated it to Birkenhead – 'To whose Parliamentary genius the passing of the LPA 1922 is by general assent attributed' – adding in the text:

> But for his brilliant advocacy, backed by a command of the English language second to none, the chance of passing an omnibus Bill leading to such an epoch-making revolution in the law of property and conveyancing would have been meagre.

In his last years, in an effort to replenish his depleted coffers, FE resorted to writing legal pot boilers, whose interest lies more in their revelation of the author's cast of mind than in their content. They contain at least some *pensées* on the lawyer's role; for example:

> The broad test of the legitimacy of what I may call, in its classical sense, an offensive cross-examination, is whether that which is put to the witness is relevant to the actual, the determining issues raised by the litigation

and, 'It hardly ever pays Counsel to quarrel sharply with the Judge who is trying his clients' case.'

In an obituary referring to Marshall Hall's extraordinary enthusiasm, he wrote, 'This habit of mind, if not indispensable, is certainly useful to counsel who must continually argue difficult and doubtful cases.'

His attachment to the cab rank rule, the Bar's first commandment, was displayed in a remarkable letter he wrote to *The Times* after fellow Conservative MPs criticised his appearance for the liberal Rufus Isaacs in the Marconi case, and its sequel the Chesterton case, in which the proprietor of the journal *The New Witness* accused Rufus Isaac's brother of a range of financial vices. He reminded the readership:

> Political issues constantly present themselves for decision in the law courts. In the overwhelming majority of cases juries have done their duty indifferently between the

> parties. How long do you think this stage of affairs will endure if every conservative case is presented by conservative advocates and resisted by liberal advocates?

and referred to 'the function which every civilised country in the world has assigned to the advocate'. I agree, and on this have nothing to add.

FE appeared frequently for Horatio Bottomley, Liberal MP for South Hatton from 1906 until he was forced to withdraw as a bankrupt in 1911, MP again from 1918 until convicted of fraudulent conversion in 1922 and sentenced to seven years' imprisonment, and at the material time editor of *John Bull*, in which capacity FE had to defend many libel actions brought against the scabrous journal. Not only did FE appear frequently for him; but FE also appeared at least once against him – a good example of the same cab rank rule in action.

Simultaneously, he maintained a friendship with Bottomley, inviting him to his house at a time when he had been compelled to surrender his seat, and inviting him to lunch on his release from prison in 1927. The modern notion that barristers should maintain a detachment from their clients is not one which appealed to him, though here I would respectfully dissent.

On the Bar he wrote:

> Personally if I became involved in litigation, the consequences of which were grave to me I would infinitely rather be represented by A, a competent industrious lawyer, whom I knew would not leave the court from the moment the case began until the moment it ended; than B who would a, ten times the fee, saunter into court to cross examine a witness whose evidence in chief he had not heard, or to reply to a speech which had unfortunately been delivered in his absence

adding, 'itself no means follows that he who pays most is best served'.

Presciently discussing the possibility of direct access and partnerships at the Bar, and amalgamation of the professions, he was not adamant against fusion, although he invited its proponents to 'reflect upon the wisdom of the ancient maxim' *quieta non movere*, ie if it ain't broke don't fix it.

As to the role of Attorney General, he observed that the argument against his inclusion in Cabinet is very strong because of his judicial – more accurately, we might say 'quasi-judicial' – functions:

> It is of vital importance that he should never be influenced, or should even appear to be influenced by political colleagues in matters in relation to which he has a solemn, an individual and judicial responsibility', adding 'it must be irritating to the holder of that position to see so many men of inferior intellectual calibre enjoying the prestige of cabinet rank.

As to the role of Lord Chancellor he was hostile to the notion of a Ministry of Justice. Recognising, as he did, substance in the objection that 'any one man should unite in his own person the office both of judge and of a Minster of the Crown forming part of the executive', he considered that the then status quo had 'this great advantage that it provides a link between the two sets of institutions'. He thought that any lawyer – and he could not contemplate a non-lawyer being appointed – would be likely to be one of the second rank. He believed in organic development of the country's institutions, rooted in its own history. Who is yet in a position to say that he was wrong?

And yet he was no dyed-in-the wool conservative. He was the first Lord Chancellor to promote a county court judge to the High Court Bench, and he resisted Lloyd George's efforts more for purposes of rewarding his supporters than in pursuit of a diversity agenda to give Celtic ancestry priority over perceived merit in such elevations. He was an enthusiast for consolidation, and a cautious apostle of codification.

He presciently recognised that the growing gulf between the income of the best of the Bar and the salaries of judges might lead to problems with the filling of vacancies on the High Court Bench.

But characteristically he was not averse to blowing the nation's trumpet: 'The traditions of English Jurisprudence, the methods by which we conduct our criminal trials are the admiration of the world.'

He died when 57 – an age when many legal and certainly judicial careers have not even reached their apex – many years after he had pleaded and several years after he had judged his last case.

His coffin lay in Gray's Inn Chapel and hundreds of persons passed to pay tribute to him. He was an advocate in a golden age and blessed with the most silver of tongues. Through his life's story we can recall many features of a legal profession gone by: when the names of great silks bulked as large in the public eye as the names of star footballers do today, when forensic skills and acuity of intellect allowed advocates to be prominent in many disciplines, not focused on a few, when the relationship of Bar and solicitors was vertical, not horizontal, when the empires of law and politics had a porous boundary. Let me leave the second-last words to him, uttered at dinner in this very Hall on the occasion of his son's coming of age: 'A Gray's Inn man is better than any other man and no damned nonsense about other things being equal.' In *Domus* we can see his likeness in triplicate, but his like we shall surely not see again.

# 11

# 'Law and the Judiciary' in Blair's Britain*

TONY BLAIR WAS by profession a barrister, but his early entry to Parliament prevented him, as it prevented Mrs Thatcher, from leaving more than modest footprints in the law, or emulating Asquith, the only other twentieth-century Prime Minister with a background in the Inns of Court. He specialised in employment litigation. Between 1977 and 1983, his years of practice, 10 of the cases in which he appeared were of sufficient importance to be published in a series of law reports.

His brief life in Chambers left him with two significant legacies, one professional, one personal. He found in the Temple both his first Lord Chancellor (Alexander, familiarly Derry) Irvine, and his wife Cherie Booth. Blair, with his average second-class degree from Oxford obtained a tenancy at the expense of Cherie with her brilliant first from LSE. This episode, reflective of the male, public school ethos of the Bar at the time, did not impede her, elevated to silk in the last year of the Major Government, from enjoying a highly successful career at the Bar, but instilled in him no long-term ambition to achieve the same.

His Labour law experience was responsible for his first major front bench appointment under Neil Kinnock, shadowing Michael Howard, the Secretary of State; but later he displayed no particular appetite for engaging with legal issues, apart from voicing populist philosophy – 'the rules of the game have changed' – in the area of crime and punishment (in which he had no professional background) which appeared from time to time at odds with the public statements of his wife. When Sullivan J quashed a refusal of leave to remain in the UK an Afghan acquitted of charges of hijacking aircraft, the Prime Minister commented, 'It's not an abuse of justice for us to order their deportation, it's an abuse of commonsense frankly to be in a position where we can't do this.' The Court of Appeal subsequently commended the judge for 'an impeccable judgment'.

In his valedictory PLP brief dated May 2007, compiled to celebrate 10 years of a Labour Government, law is only mentioned in conjunction with order. The summary under the rubric of the Constitution, refers to the enactment of the Human Rights Act 1988 (HRA), but otherwise makes no reference at all of the significant changes to the judiciary and civil legal system of the same decade.

* A Seldon (ed), *Blair's Britain 1997–2007* (Cambridge University Press, 2007) ch 14.

If Blair had no particular affection for the law, he had no inbuilt animosity towards lawyers; and the legal culture of the Blair era was dominated by a web of relationships reminiscent of those charts in the late Anthony Sampson's *Anatomy of Britain* in which everyone who counted seemed to be connected to everyone else.

Lord Irvine had been his and Cherie's pupil master. Philip Sales, who served from 1997 as Junior Counsel to the Crown (Common Law) (or Treasury Devil), came from Irvine's old set at 11 King's Bench Walk, as did three High Court judges, Patrick Elias, Richard Field and Brian Keith. Irvine appointed (without advertisement) as his special adviser Garry Hart, a former partner of the prestigious city firm Herbert Smith, prompting an unsuccessful tribunal claim of sex discrimination from Jane Cohen, a legal aid lawyer.

Lord Irvine's successor was, if anything, an even closer ally of the Prime Minister.

Lord (Charles, familiarly Charlie) Falconer, who started in government service as a Solicitor General and survived responsibility for the Millennium Dome, emerged as the country's senior legal figure, when in 2003 Lord Irvine was dismissed in a manner as peremptory as that with which Harold MacMillan disposed of Lord Kilmuir 40 years before in the Night of the Long Knives. He came from the blue-chip chambers at Fountain Court, as did the Attorney General Lord (Peter) Goldsmith QC. Lord Irvine appointed another Fountain Court alumnus Lord Bingham, as Senior Law Lord, and Lord Falconer appointed his own former pupil master Lord Justice Potter, a commercial lawyer, as President of the Family Division. Shortly after Cherie Booth became a founding member of Matrix Chambers in 2000, another member, Ken Macdonald QC, became Director of Public Prosecutions.

There were further filaments of friendship in the legal web. Henry Hodge, a former solicitor, husband of Minister of State Margaret, was made Chairman of the Immigration Appeals Tribunal and a High Court Judge. The Blairs holidayed at the French *château* of David Keene, promoted to the Court of Appeal. New Labour life peers included a trio of QCs, Baroness Kennedy, Lord Grabiner (Chairman of the Board of Governors of LSE), Lord Brennan (a member of Matrix).

In no instance could even the most acerbic critic complain that the appointees lacked qualifications for their office; and in several instances the post-holder was outstandingly eligible, but there was substance to the impression that New Labour's legal establishment was an extended family.

Pivotal to the Blair administration's reform of the legal system was the replacement of Lord Irvine by Lord Falconer on the Woolsack. The precise reasons for this wholly unanticipated reshuffle have not yet been revealed. Lord Irvine was, for all the *faux pas* over Wolsey and wallpaper, still in his formidable Lord Chancellorial prime, and could reasonably have expected to remain in office until the end of Blair's second term, if not beyond. The best guess is that David Blunkett, then an influential Home Secretary, and an unrestrained critic of judges over their over-liberal (as he saw them) attitudes to crime and immigration – perennially sensitive issues for the Home Department – resented the

Lord Chancellor's constitutionally proper defence of judicial independence, and confronted the Prime Minister with an unenviable choice of which to retain in his cabinet.

The changes later embedded in the Constitution Reform Act (CRA) were a camouflage for, or at any rate a consequence, not a cause, of Lord Irvine's demise, and there is little evidence that there had been any advance thought about them.

The fact that the office of the Lord Chancellor was purportedly abolished by press release (unavailingly, given its various roots in statute) speaks volumes for the administration's assessment that (as Stalin said of the Pope) the judges' moral authority was not supported by any divisions. In looking-glass mode, consultation took place, after, not before, the event.

The CRA itself commenced (unusually) with a Statement of Values. Section 1 provided that the CRA does not adversely affect 'the existing constitutional principle of the rule of law' or 'the Lord Chancellor's existing constitutional role in relation to that principle'. The dimensions of that duty were not defined; nor was the content of the values to be protected – although during the debate between the Judiciary and the Executive over the establishment of a Ministry of Justice in the last weeks of the Blair regime, it was suggested that allegations of its breach might be deployed as 'a nuclear option'.

The major changes engineered by the CRA were:

- The abolition of the triple role of Lord Chancellor.
- The replacement of the Lord Chancellor by the Lord Chief Justice as head of the Judiciary.
- The projected detachment of the Appellate Committee of the House of Lords from Parliament and its reconstitution as a Supreme Court in name (as it had for some while been, in fact) so reflecting a continental concept of separation of powers.
- The creation of a Judicial Appointments Commission (JAC) (coupled, inevitably, with a Judicial Appointments and Conduct Ombudsman).

In anticipation, a revivified Judges Council approved the terms of a concordat reached between the Lord Chief Justice and the Lord Chancellor, as to who had responsibility for what. Its negotiation survived Lord Woolf's public description of Lord Falconer as 'a cheerful chappy' – an observation not designed to cause offence, but one which clearly did so.

The functions of the Lord Chancellor, developed over a millennium, spanned at the commencement of the first Blair administration, the legislative executive and judicial spheres of Government. He was a member of the Upper House and its Speaker, a Senior Cabinet Minister, and presided over the Appellate Committee of the House of Lords. He had responsibilities for overseeing court administration, making appointments to the Bench at all levels (including the lay magistracy) and of Queen's Counsel, and overseeing the funding of legal services. To this, during Lord Irvine's tenure was added implementation of the HRA and in 2001 responsibility for constitutional affairs (previously within the Home Office fiefdom).

The single most significant feature of Lord Falconer's time as Lord Chancellor was his (staged) abdication of the very powers to which Lord Irvine had so tenaciously clung. The title of Lord Chancellor lingered on, symbolic not substantial, the consequences of a minor revolt in the House of Lords; but the smile on the face of the Cheshire Cat had more connection with the animal itself than the titular Lord Chancellor has with the traditional holder of the office.

Lord Irvine sat only rarely as presiding judge in the House of Lords or Privy Council. Lord Falconer never did and he (and his successor) since April 2006 has been debarred from doing so. Power to appoint judges was surrendered to a Judicial Appointments Commission JAC; and, to appoint Queen's Counsel to an equivalent body. The new and more significant title as Secretary of State for Constitutional Affairs (replaced on 9 May 2007 by Secretary of State for Justice) indicated that for the future the role was political. While mandated by the CRA to defend judicial independence and by the Courts Act 2003 to maintain an efficient court system, the incumbent may do so, without any experience of the legal system as a practitioner or any knowledge of it as an academic, since the future qualification for the office will merely be the possession of such experience as the Prime Minister considers appropriate.

The Lord Chief Justice assumed the title of President of the Court of England and Wales with the statutory duty of representing the judiciary's views to Parliament and Government, for overseeing the deployment of individual judges, for allocation of work within the courts, and for ensuring that appropriate structures are in place for the training and support of judges.

The removal of the Lord Chancellor from the summit apart, there were no major changes in the hierarchy – Lords of Appeal in Ordinary, Lords and Lady Justices in the Court of Appeal, High Court judges, Circuit Judges (and Recorders), District Judges and Deputy District Judges. The surrender by the Lord Chancellor of his judicial functions, led to the Vice Chancellor in the Chancery Division becoming the Chancellor. The Courts Act 2003 introduced new post-holders, the Head and Deputy Head of Civil Justice. The CRA did the same for Criminal Justice and Family Justice. The Official Referee's Court was rebranded the Technology and Construction Court and the Crown Office list the Administrative Court.

The Supreme Court will consist of 12 judges. The current Lords of Appeal will become the first members of the new court and will thereupon cease to be entitled to sit in Parliament. They will be called Justices of the Supreme Court and the senior members will be President and Deputy President. They will inherit the jurisdiction of the House of Lords and of the Privy Council in devolution matters. Reflecting yet again the impact that architecture has on the legal system, the Court will not come until being until it can be properly housed – the preferred (by the Government) venue for the new Court is Middlesex Guildhall.

Not all Law Lords supported their detachment from Parliament or even their physical relocation; some did, others hedged their bets: 'There can be no doubt,' wrote the Senior Law Lord, 'that since June 2003 the mountains have laboured mightily: it remains to be seen whether they have brought forth a mouse, or a valuable measure of overdue reform or a monster.'

Lord Bingham of Cornhill was the first judge since Lord Alverstone to bring off the career coup of becoming both Master of the Rolls and Lord Chief Justice. Both his successors in charge first of civil, then of criminal justice, Lord Woolf of Barnes and Lord Phillips of Worth Matravers did the same. This double, once as rare as the cup and league double in football, rapidly achieved the status of a norm – and in the same era.

Lord Bingham, however, went further, and procured a treble, becoming Senior Law Lord in 2000. This position was thus given new status. Previously, it was allotted on the principle of Buggins' turn.

Other personal (as distinct from institutional) innovations during the Blair era included the first woman Law Lord, Lady Baroness Hale of Richmond, in 2004. In 1997 there was only one female Lord Justice (Butler-Sloss), but she was followed by Mary Arden, Brenda Hale, Janet Smith and Heather Hallett (the Crown Court Act 2003, section 63 belatedly introduced the title 'Lady Justice'). However, there were, neither at start nor finish of the Blair years, any ethnic minority representatives in posts above the circuit bench save for Mrs Justice Dobbs. Lawrence Collins became the first solicitor to be appointed directly to the High Court 2006 and then to the Court of Appeal in 2006. Sir Jack Beatson was the second High Court Judge (after Lady Hale) to have been appointed whose primary previous occupation was as an academic, latterly as Rouse Ball Professor of English Law at Cambridge.

In 1998 High Court appointments were for the first time advertised. In 1999 in the wake of Sir Leonard Peach's report, an Advisory Commission for Judicial Appointments was established. An audit carried out by that body chaired by Sir Colin Campbell in 2003 found the present system 'seriously lacking in transparency or accountability'.

As a result of this critique, as well as for reasons of constitutional propriety, the JAC was set up with effect from April 2006 to select candidates for judicial office in England and Wales across all areas of the judiciary, from High Court judges to non-legal tribunals, and to recommend one candidate for each vacancy. The new rules gave the Lord Chancellor a right of single rejection for which he must provide reasons: he cannot select an alternative candidate. The JAC consists of 15 persons, a judge, a solicitor, barrister, tribunal member and justice of the peace with a lay majority. The lay chairman Baroness Prashar was the former Civil Service Commissioner.

The JAC set itself three objectives: to define merit; to identify fair and effective assessment methods; and to encourage a wider range of applicants. The definition of merit comprises five core qualities and abilities with 17 supportive behaviours. Intelligence, integrity, scholarship, analytical skills and judgment, authority, and articulateness are naturally paramount, but mandatory criteria skills such as patience, courtesy and sensitivity to the other cultures and gender might well have excluded many celebrated judicial figures in even the recent past.

The system represents a sea-change from that which prevailed in May 1997 when the Lord Chancellor, after what, in another context, were famously called 'the customary processes of consultation' among the senior judiciary, picked, chose and invited himself. A wholly closed system has been replaced by a more open one. However, there is no doubt that the unduly modest (and indeed the unduly arrogant) will be deterred by the very need to apply for fear that any rejection may somehow become public and others, suffering from neither of these qualities, by the sheer complexity of the system (supported, as it is, by a huge bureaucracy). It remains to be seen how much the constituency of these (especially at the High Court level and above) will differ from the beneficiaries of the abandoned methodology and, in particular, whether that constituency more accurately reflects the national demographic, and, to the extent that it does so, does not concurrently compromise what its Chairman has described as 'the outstanding reputation of our existing office holders'.

The new arrangements for appointment do not in any way qualify either judicial security of tenure or the principle that judges' pay cannot be diminished during their term of office, legacies of The Act of Settlement 1701. For the future under the new constitutional arrangements, the amount of salary 'is to be determined by the Lord Chancellor with the agreement of the Treasury', the one with responsibility for the rule of law, the other for the wealth of the nation.

As a matter of practice, the Senior Salaries Review Body (SSRB) with its Judicial Sub-committee makes recommendations to the Lord Chancellor, usually if not always accepted. In the other two groups within the SSRB's remit (senior civil servants and senior officers of the armed forces) there was a move towards performance-related pay, but it was rejected for the judiciary for fear of compromising judicial independence.

Those who had taken the Queen's shilling did not during the Irvine/Falconer years in fact express major worries with their pay packet. Only in 2005 was there a minor (at any rate compared with *les événements* of 1931) crisis when the judges sought exemption from legislation in force from April 2006 which imposed a lifetime limit on tax relief allowed on pension benefits. This was said to breach their legitimate expectations on appointment, but was assuaged by Lord Falconer's stealthy and well-spun announcement, in an act of political *legerdemain*, that he would spend an extra £9 million a year on judges' pay and pensions.

However, as the gap between the earnings of top practitioners, the pool of recruits and judges widened, there was a perceptible trend, already apparent at the start of the 1990s of those invited to take up High Court appointments declining to do so – something almost unthinkable even 30 years ago. In 2001–02, 19 High Court judges were appointed, but six refused. As the Sub-committee reported in 2002:

> This significant figure – almost a third of the number of those appointed – calls into question whether there was an increasing pattern of refusals which indicates future difficulties in attracting appropriate appointees.

The decline in numbers of practising barristers who were concurrently MPs (a phenomenon the explanation for which lies beyond the scope of this chapter, but whose heyday was in the Edwardian era almost a century ago) meant that the tradition that the law officers were in the Commons was for the first time broken. John Morris MP QC, a Secretary of State for Wales in the last Labour administration, was succeeded as Attorney General by Lord Williams of Mostyn QC, and, when he became Leader of the House of Lords, by Lord Goldsmith QC. Lord Falconer QC was the first Solicitor General and was succeeded by Harriet Harman, a solicitor (so, paradoxically, aligning title with title holder) then made a QC and Mike O'Brien likewise.

Before 1997 the Solicitor General used to act as the Attorney General's deputy and carried out functions delegated by the latter. Since the Law Officers Act 1997, which made the roles interchangeable, the two ministers could divide the duties between themselves as they saw fit, but custom, if nothing else, preserved a vertical rather than a horizontal relationship. They have achieved functional but not political parity.

The Attorney General continued to appoint the Director of Public Prosecutions, oversee the work of the Serious Fraud Office and the Treasury Solicitor's Office, and represent the Crown Court in major international litigation, and in trials of the constitutional dimension. Lord Goldsmith, an accomplished advocate, was particularly engaged by this aspect of his role.

But it was during his tenure that the position of Attorney General as a member of the Government, yet simultaneously its independent legal advisor, came increasingly under scrutiny. His advice, allegedly in contradiction to his first impression, that the invasion of Iraq in 2003 would be lawful, his role in halting the enquiry into corruption linked to the sale of BAE systems to Saudi Arabia, and his assertion in 2007 that he retained a necessary part in any decision as to whether or not Blair allies could be charged in relation to the receipt by the Labour Party of undisclosed loans by putative peers, prompted suggestions that his office should be decoupled from government altogether. The seed planted in the dying months of the Blair administration may flower in the post-Blair era.

During the period under consideration both criminal and civil court structures and systems were subject to intense scrutiny.

A review of the Criminal Courts of England and Wales (2001) was carried out by Lord Justice Auld and many of its recommendations were implemented in the Courts Act 2003. A key proposal – that crown courts and magistrates courts should be amalgamated to a single court – was, however, rejected: moving together was preferred to merger. The Criminal Justice Act 2003 made practical provisions for ensuring that fewer cases went to the Crown Court.

A single Commission of Peace for England and Wales was created to give justices of the peace a national jurisdiction, though in practice they will continue to sit in local justice areas. Concurrently 98 local courts closed, and increasing numbers of legally qualified district judges (previously stipendiary magistrates) sat together with or in place of lay justices, and the transfer of authority in many areas with implications for delivery of justice from the justices to their clerks. There was in consequence a growing sense that, notwithstanding repeated statements by Lord Chancellors to contrary effect, there was a hidden agenda to abolish the very system of lay justice.

Juries, however, remained talismanic. The Home Office consultation paper of July 1998 considered unavailingly the abolition of right to jury trial in respect of a range of offences including grievous bodily harm and theft. Provisions of the Criminal Justice Act 2003 which allow a trial by judge alone where there is a 'real and present danger' of jury tampering: or in complex fraud cases where the interests of justice were thought to require it, are yet to be brought into effect. Concern continued to be expressed as to whether juries – another amateur institution in a professional world – were the best instrument of justice, barely mitigated by the abolition of various immunities for jury service including those of barristers and judges (in the Criminal Justice Act 2003).

One major fraud trial ('the Jubilee trial') collapsed under its own weight in 2006 at a cost to the public purse of £60 million, and the prospect of a system straining under the burden of an ever-increasing number of lengthy terrorist trials (for which a special panel of 21 judges was created) prompted further anxiety. But the civil liberties lobby in Parliament retained the upper hand (especially in the Upper House) to defeat or compel withdrawal of tentative government efforts at diminishing juries' role.

The subject of crime and penal policy, the fruit of the criminal justice system, is dealt with elsewhere in this volume. From the perspective of the judiciary, 'the torrent of criminal legislation' posed problems in practice as well as of principle – as successive Home Office ministers struggled to give useful meaning to the first Blair mantra, 'tough on crime'. Lord Justice Rose spoke for many when in the course of one of his judgments he described the provisions of the Criminal Justice Act as 'labyrinthine' and 'astonishingly complex', adding for good measure in another case that they were 'deeply confusing', and concluding

> we find little comfort or assistance in the customary canons of construction for determining the will of Parliament which were fashioned in a more leisurely age and at a time when elegance and clarity of thought and language were to be found in legislation as a matter of course rather than exception.

Judges remained concerned at the end as at the outset of the Blair administration that their purpose to make the punishment fit the crime was being impaired by legislative incoherence, political pressure, and lack of prison space.

Auld followed Woolf. The Civil Procedure Act 1997, providing a statutory foundation for the Report of Lord Woolf into 'Access to Justice' received Royal Assent in February 1997 just before the demise of the Major administration. It was enacted against a background of continuous change in civil justice: judicial case management, alternative dispute resolution (ADR), conditional fees for personal injury and insolvency cases were already part of the legal landscape.

But if the Conservative Government was the midwife, the Blair Government was the nurse of the new civil procedure rules (CPR) which came into effect on 26 April 1999 and were described as 'a new product code with the overriding objective of enabling the Courts to deal with cases justly'. They were infused with the concepts of proportionality – the devotion of time and money not in excess of that required by the issues at stake – and equality of arms – that, so far as practicable, parties should be on an equal footing, as well as being designed to eliminate delay expense and complexity. There were provisions to promote settlement and to mitigate the traditional adversarial culture. Judges were to manage cases both pre-trial and at the trial, and no longer to allow parties (and their lawyers) to dictate the pace of legislation. Under the rules there were developments of group litigation orders and the representative action, stopping short, however of full-blown class actions, US-style. Archaic phrases were removed from the vocabulary of the rules although not all such changes clarified, and traditionalists regretted the replacement of pithy Latinisms with more ponderous Anglo-Saxon prose.

Before 1997 appeals in civil cases from county court and high court were generally heard by the Court of Appeal. Sir Jeffery Bowman identified the workload of that Court as excessive. Part IV of the Access to Justice 1999 Act (AJA 1999) reformed the system. In civil and family cases permission is normally required to appeal any first instance decision and more appeals are dealt with at a lower level than before. The Courts Act 2003 requires the Lord Chancellor to appoint a Head of Civil Justice (with a deputy if need be) to assist in the smooth running of the system.

The consistent themes in the reorganisation of court business in the civil and criminal fields during the Blair years were flexibility in deployment of judicial resources, the allocation of cases to lowest appropriate level, and the increasing involvement of judges in administration at the expense of judging.

Beneath the surface of formal adjudication by judges then developed an emphasis on ADR, encouraged by the Lord Chancellor's Department – subsequently renamed Department of Constitutional Affairs and latterly the Department of Justice – and indeed blessed by the courts themselves, not only arbitration but mediation, conciliation and negotiation.

Only coroners courts survived the tide of the reform, and a bill is proposed for the next session of Parliament to modernise the last relic of a medieval legal system, whose peculiarities were exposed in contentious litigation over the format of the inquest into the death of Diana, Princess of Wales.

The AJA 1999 provided for two new schemes to replace the existing legal aid scheme whose origins lay, like the National Health Service, in the post war Attlee administration and which was similarly subject to increasing strains as demand outweighed resources. A Legal Services Commission was established to create and maintain and develop a Community Legal Service, for civil and family cases. It has a duty to use its resources, which reflected the priorities set by the Lord Chancellor to secure the best possible money value and to liaise with other funders of legal services. The Commission was also to be responsible for a Criminal Defence Service (for the first time in England) providing a Public Defender Service.

Public-funded legal services could only be provided by those who held Legal Service Commission contracts (building on a franchising system in place since 1994) to those who survived both merits and means tests. Previously lawyers were paid after the event, calculated by reference to time expended on the case; thenceforth they were to be paid by block contracts with prices for lawyers fixed in advance. But the contract system necessarily limited suppliers and inevitably imposed regulatory and administrative burdens on solicitors.

From 1 April 2005 there was a mandatory system of fixed fees covering all types of controlled civil work, except immigration. When graduated fixed fees were introduced for family and criminal work, barristers took the view that they were being denied 'proper remuneration' and voted to abandon the cab rank rule for cases subject to the system. There was even a brief strike.

A letter to *The Times* on 30 November 2006 from a Law Society Council (LSC) member suggested that the rise in legal aid spending was not the result of professional inefficiency but of

> bureaucracy imposed upon solicitors by the Legal Services Commission; more and more legislation, policies and initiatives; sloth and incompetence in the manner that cases are investigated and considered for charge; poor listing practices in the Magistrates Courts and the Crown Courts; incompetent management of the Courts along with too many managers and not enough people processing the work.

Fixed fees, it was suggested, led to fixed amounts of time and effort devoted to the work.

Whatever its cause, the fact of the rise was undisputed and in July 2006 Lord Carter presented a Review of Legal Aid Programme at the invitation of Lord Chancellor, which made 62 recommendations for a move to market-based approach – a characteristic Blairite concept. Among the key ones were: best-value tendering for legal aid contracts based on quality, capacity and price from 2009; new responsibilities for the Law Society and Bar Council to enhance quality of legal aid supplier market; fixed fees for solicitors carrying out legal aid work in police stations to encourage more efficient practices, including cutting costs related to waiting and travelling times; revised graduated fees for Crown Court advocates and a new graduated fee scheme for Crown Court litigators to reward earlier preparation and resolution of cases; tighter control of very-high-cost criminal legal aid cases; standard fees for civil and family legal help; and new graduated fees for solicitors in private law family and childcare proceedings.

The Law Society criticised the complexity of the LSC's draft contract terms. The Bar applauded the criminal raised advocacy graduated fee scheme in place in April 2007, which ended a decade of diminution (in real terms) of the value of fees for defence work, and a redistribution from long cases (which enabled a few barristers to earn enviable sums from the public purse) to 1–10-day cases, but objected to proposed rates for long complex cases, and price competitive tendering. Both branches of the profession were united in their concerns about the future of publicly funded legal provision. 'We are facing,' the President of the Law Society recently wrote, 'the long-term under-funding of an impoverished legal aid system and the additional threats posed by the government's foolhardy timetable for changes in the legal system.'

Both the professions anchored their criticism in the needs for the vulnerable, those accused of crimes, in family disputes, or seeking welfare benefits, to be properly represented. The Government, while careful not to suggest that the criticism was fuelled by professional self-interest, contended that the ever-growing demands for the legal services were putting intense pressures on the national economy, but like Harpagon in Molière's *L'Avare*, who aspired to a better table at a lower cost, claimed less convincingly that better justice could be provided at less expense. A variety of judicial review challenges claiming in particular that the reforms will put small firms servicing minority communications out of business are in the pipeline.

The AJA 1999 also affected reforms in relation to the private funding of litigation. Conditional fee agreements were extended in 1999 to all civil cases except family cases. Both the uplift payable for successful cases and litigation insurance premiums could be recovered in costs from the other side. Third parties became entitled to establish funds to support litigation also on a conditional basis. While supporters of the measures argued that such measures increased access to justice from those too rich to qualify for public funds, but not rich enough to pay for lawyers, critics warned against the spur to 'ambulance chasers' and the potential for conflict of interest between client and lawyer.

The Report of Sir Andrew Leggatt, former Lord Justice of Appeal – the first serious review since the Franks Report 1957 – identified a system of adjudication, outside the boundaries of ordinary court system, which had grown like topsy, and was in consequence topsy-turvy. Leggatt recommended a common administrative service; of grouping of existing tribunals and to nine divisions, with each related to a single subject area, each with its Appellate tier, and appeals on points of law (and thereafter the Court of Appeal). As was usual with reports of this period, not all his recommendations were accepted, but a new tribunal service accountable to the Department for Constitutional Affairs was launched in April 2006 without the need for legislation, and a Tribunals Courts and Enforcement Bill has been introduced into Parliament.

The Bill reflects many of the principles applied elsewhere to reforms of the court system, importantly, involvement of the JAC in the appointments process; interchangeability of roles (for example circuit judges will be automatically tribunal members); a duty on the Lord Chancellor to provide administrative support; carefully limited two-tier appeal rights; and, less importantly, the redesignation of legally qualified members as tribunal judges.

Some tribunals will share a common administration, and the leadership of the Senior President of Tribunals, but their jurisdictions will remain autonomous: the employment tribunals (and the Employment Appeal Tribunal) because of the nature of the cases that come before them, involving one party against another, unlike most other tribunals which hear appeals from citizens against decisions of the state; the Asylum Immigration Tribunal (AIT) because (unlike the other tribunals) they have a single tier appeal only.

The Government had originally intended to immunise the AIT's decisions from judicial review, but retreated in the face of massive opposition from all sides of the political spectrum.

The Blair years saw a series of controversial inquiries of different origins. Lord Hutton's into the death of Dr David Kelly was non-statutory; the Bloody Sunday Inquiry chaired by Lord Saville was set up under the Tribunals of Inquiry (Evidence) Act 1952. But the lack of coherence prompted the Inquiries Act 2005 to provide a new framework by which a minister can establish an enquiry into events that have caused public concern, endowed with appropriate coercive powers to commandeer documents and to summon witnesses. Inquiries will generally sit in public, but (controversially) there is a discretion to hold them in private; however, the issue of diverting judges from their judicial function was not addressed in the Act directly, and the provision requiring a minister to consult the Lord Chief Justice about such appointments may put a brake on, but will not bring a stop to the practice. Lawyers as a class may (like politicians) be unpopular: judges retain substantial respect, but it is doubtful if it is enhanced by their deployment in such extra-curricular exercises.

The AJA 1999 accelerated the thrust of the Courts and Legal Services Act 1990 and enshrined the principle that lawyers with appropriate qualifications and subject to appropriate rules of conduct should be able to exercise full rights of audience in all proceedings. It provided for the Lord Chancellor to authorise bodies other than the Law Society to grant rights of audience and to authorise their members to conduct litigation, including the Chartered Institute of Patent Agents, the Institute of Trade Mark Attorneys and the Institute of Legal Executives. This did not, however, affect overmuch the Bar's dominance in advocacy and they countered the challenge by changing their rules so as to accept instructions direct from clients rather than through solicitors.

In 2003 Lord Irvine dramatically suspended the system by which he had annually selected (on the Queen's behalf) successful applicants for the rank of

Queen's Counsel in the wake of a critical report by Sir Colin Campbell. However, despite fears in the profession that the status would be forever abolished, in 2006 it was reinstated by Lord Falconer but with the Lord Chancellor excluded from the selection process, now handed over to an independent panel. A fee of £2,500 is now required for an application, but this did not appear to deter ambitious applicants, and in 2006 of 175 successful applicants there were 33 women and 10 from ethnic minorities. Honorary silk was bestowed more frequently than before on senior solicitors and academics.

The professions were not immune to the modernising spirit of the age. Already by 1997 the traditional position at the Bar whereby pupils (apprentice barristers) paid their pupil masters had been reversed. Now scholarships of ever-increasing size were offered by sets of chambers to counter the attractions of the substantial salaries paid by blue chip city firms to new qualified solicitors. The Bar indeed adopted a rule which prohibited unfunded pupillages – although, as an example of the law of unintended consequences in action, it may have worked against those from non-traditional constituencies. School placement programmes to promote the Bar as a career to new constituencies and a Bar Vocational Course loan scheme negotiated with major banks are part of the current Bar Council agenda. A committee chaired by Lord Neuberger is examining the virtue of further reforms. Whether outreach programmes, any more than those of the ancient universities, will dispel perception of a closed professional shop, engendered by anachronistic media representation and concerns of law lecturers in the newer universities, has yet to be seen.

To negotiate the shoals of anti-discrimination law, chambers adopted far more rigorous systems of assessments for aspirant pupils and tenants, and, for the most part, recognised the guidance of the Pupils Applications Clearing House and its descendant (OLPAS) designed to introduce some order and equity into what had previously been an anarchic system in which chambers competed methodically against each other for the best and brightest recruits like football club managers seeking out teenage players.

For barristers and solicitors alike, continuing professional education became mandatory – swelling the ranks of conference organisers, complementing an increasing emphasis on practical training before and at the stage of pupillage at the Bar or articles as solicitors. *Pro bono* work became fashionable.

Transfers between the two branches of the profession increased – Herbert Smith & Co became the first City firm to employ two QCs while traffic in the reverse direction was still more common. Relations between the professions improved even if the Bar insisted that its code of conduct including the cab rank rule ought to be applied to all advocates, while in major firms' Chinese walls had to be constructed so as to avoid conflicts of interest. Responding to globalisation, there were mergers between City firms, and between them and many US (or continental) equivalents. Clifford Chance's merger with the US firm Rogers & Wells created the world's first billion-dollar practice.

Despite all these internal modernising initiatives, in July 2003 the DCA concluded that the regulatory framework in England and Wales was 'outdated, inflexible, over-complex and insufficiently accountable or transparent' and commissioned Sir David Clementi to investigate.

He duly proposed an independent officer for legal complaints and a legal standards board to oversee the profession; permission for barristers to enter into partnerships with solicitors; permission for non-lawyers to manage and own legal practices – the last of these, a Heineken approach designed to allow the legal services to reach hitherto unreached parts seemed destined to result in a Tesco law. While he recommended that in any such new style law company alternative business structures qualified lawyers should be in the majority, the Government has opted for unlimited external ownership and investment, taking, in the view of some critics, the lawyers out of the law. Bridget Prentice, the Minister for Constitutional Affairs, notoriously equated the purchase of legal services with the purchase of baked beans.

The Legal Services Bill currently before Parliament sets out proposals for a new regulatory framework – the Legal Services Board (LSB), which will authorise frontline regulators, Bar Council, and Law Society, to carry out day-to-day regulation, provided they meet LSB standards. In tandem there will be a new Office for Legal Complaints to handle complaints for the whole legal profession. Given the fact that the professions had already sought to separate their representative from the regulatory rules, this excited the concern that the Falconer legacy to the legal profession would be regulation, regulation, regulation.

None of this impeded an inexorable upward trend in qualified lawyers. In July 2004 there were 121,165 qualified solicitors – a growth of 50 per cent in the decade: women constituted 39,199 – an increase of 120 per cent, ethnic minorities 8.031–2.2 per cent up to nine per cent. At the same time there were 11,564 barristers in independent practice of whom 8,153 were men and 3,411 were women; these included 1,078 QCs, of whom 991 were men and 87 were women.

While changes in the legal system and its institutions are matters for the political arms of government, changes in the law itself are shared with the judicial arm. In this context the conventional view relegates the judiciary to a minor role. The legislature can affect changes in areas previously controlled by the common law. The judiciary, by contrast, cannot affect changes in legislation. The sovereignty of Parliament is said to be a constitutional fundamental.

This picture requires continued modification for three main reasons.

Firstly, the impact of the UK's accession to the Treaty of Rome involved the traversing of a legal rubicon: thenceforth the laws of the UK were subordinate to a higher norm. This development preceded the Blair administration by quarter of a century; but, despite the rhetorical rejections of a European superstate from many of its prominent figures, the Prime Minister included, leaving the European Union was never an option on the table, and Luxembourg (the European Court of Justice) as well as Brussels (the European Commission) impinged ever further on the national substantive law in a host of areas ever more loosely connected with a common market.

Secondly, the domestication of ECHR by the Human Rights Act 1998 (HRA) with effect from 2 October 2000, gave judges the novel power to declare that duly enacted legislation itself was incompatible with convention rights, or else face defeat at the hands of the European Court of Human Rights in Strasbourg. The power was rarely used, but partly because the HRA simultaneously imposed on the judges the duty to interpret legislation so as to make it compatible with Convention rights, 'so far as possible' reading words into or out of a statutory scheme, and on some occasions effectively undermined the very thrust of the legislation itself, for example reinstating the right of persons accused of rape to cross-examine the alleged victim on her previous sexual experience. The HRA, by annexing most convention rights, involved the Court in deciding such open-textured and politically freighted questions as to what inference with them was 'necessary in a democratic society', stimulating a debate as to if (and when) the judiciary should show deference to executive or legislative choice.

HRA has thus substantially added to the weapons at the disposal of an already activist judiciary extending of the control of executive action by means of the machinery of judicial review which corralled and sometimes frustrated the wishes of the Government. Because the courts are also identified by the HRA as a public authority, it also invigorated the development of the common law.

In many areas, judges' use of the HRA has been relatively uncontroversial. Sidling in where Parliament has feared to tread, the courts have effectively created a right of privacy in cases involving persons ranging from the model Naomi Campbell to the Prince of Wales, while simultaneously extending the boundaries of freedom of expression – especially where political speech is involved.

More controversially, and spurred on by decisions from Strasbourg, the courts have abrogated the Home Secretary's role in determining for how long prisoners sentenced to life imprisonment should serve. They have modified the interpretation of various statutes to protect the rights to a fair trial and the presumption of innocence. They have launched a series of torpedoes at the Government's desire for stricter control of immigration and restrictions on asylum-seekers. David Blunkett counter-attacked 'I am personally fed up with having to deal with a situation where Parliament debates the issues and then the Judges then overturn them.'

In *A v Secretary of State for the Home Department* the House of Lords determined that detention without trial of suspected foreign terrorists was incompatible with the HRA: disproportionate and discriminatory. Lord Bingham of Cornhill explained how the balance of constitutional power was struck:

> It is also of course true, that Parliament, the executive and the courts have different functions. But the function of independent judges charged to interpret and apply the law is universally recognised as a cardinal feature of the modern democratic state, a

> cornerstone of the rule of law itself. The Attorney General is fully entitled to insist on the proper limits of judicial authority, but he is wrong to stigmatise judicial decision-making as in some way undemocratic.

On 25 July 2006, the Prime Minister commissioned a review of the HRA – although, as with not a few Blairite initiatives, words do not appear to have been followed by prompt action.

Thirdly, in the course of rejecting a challenge based on the nuances of the Parliament Acts of 1911 and 1949 to legislation banning hunting with hounds, two of the Law Lords hinted that in extreme circumstances they would refuse to give effect to legislation which offended in their view basic constitutional values, reflecting a philosophy of judicial authority last articulated by Sir Edward Coke in the seventeenth century.

Lord Steyn said:

> The supremacy of Parliament is still the general principle of our constitution. It is a construct of the common law. The judges created this principle. If that is so, it is not unthinkable that circumstances could arise where the courts may have to qualify a principle established on a different hypothesis of constitutionalism. In exceptional circumstances involving an attempt to abolish judicial review or the ordinary role of the courts, the Appellate Committee of the House of Lords or a new Supreme Court may have to consider whether this is constitutional fundamental which even a sovereign Parliament acting at the behest of a complaisant House of Commons cannot abolish.

These dicta represented a high water mark of the development of judicial review prompted by a variety of factors, but, most relevantly, for present purposes, by a reaction against an ever-more intrusive state and an imbalance of political forces where (as during the Thatcher era) one party enjoyed such numerical supremacy in the House of Commons as to render MPs effectively unable to provide redress for citizens' grievances. The judiciary at the same time revivified the ancient tort of misfeasance in public office; developed the concept of exemplary damages for abuse of public power; formulated a principle of legality holding that not only ambiguous but general words were incompetent to infringe an existing constitutional principle, while beating a measured retreat from the rule in *Pepper v Hart* which had allowed them to use, in strictly limited circumstances, ministerial statements as an aid to construction of statutory provisions but had involved indirectly, an albeit modest, qualification of their independent role as interpreters. Lord Irvine had indeed anticipated the possibility that the judges might seek to subvert the Blair agenda. In a lecture given in 1996 he inveighed against judicial supremacism, but without noticeable impact.

The law also developed in a subterranean way, uninfluenced by the political agenda. The judges continued, indeed completed the journey away from a purposive and contextual construction of contracts and statutes; they conceived the technique prospective overruling of earlier decisions); they eroded the boundaries between domestic law and international law. They expanded the boundaries of negligence to embrace the performance of public authorities of statutory functions and revoked the immunity of advocates from suits for negligence. They promoted equality of sexes in distribution of assets on divorce.

In one sphere they could indeed claim to have prompted legislative reform. In denying redress to a young man who, in defiance of a council warning notice, dived into a shallow lake and broke his neck, Lord Hobhouse of Woodborough uttered some trenchant words which found echoes in the Government's subsequent Compensation Act 2006, mandating courts to take account of the possible deterrent effect of imposing liability for negligence, and which itself spawned in 2007 rules for compulsory registration of claims-handling companies.

In a final effort to embed his legacy the Prime Minister announced that a Ministry of Justice was to be established on 9 May 2007 to bring together Her Majesty's Courts Service, the Tribunals Service and the current responsibilities of the DCA with the National Offender Management Service – including criminal law and sentencing policy. The Office of Criminal Justice Reform (OCJR) and the Ministry of Justice will have complete departmental oversight of civil and family justice as well as key elements of constitutional and rights-based policy such as data protection and the HRA.

A simultaneous circular letter from the Lord Chancellor stated that the Ministry of Justice would strengthen further the already strong judicial–Executive relationship set out in the concordat.

But despite the New Labour new speak with which this initiative was proclaimed, senior judges who, once more, were not consulted in advance, were concerned that safeguards to ensure that independence were required under the proposed regime. They feared that unless the budget for the courts was ring-fenced, it would be consumed by the demands of the prisons and probation service; that they would be forced to tailor sentences according available prison space; and that the Minister of Justice, the Lord Chancellor, would face judicial review proceedings before the very judges whose budget he controls, creating an unseemly picture of conflict of interest.

Ad hoc as many of changes in the architecture of the law during the period appeared to be, there was an underlying rationale, reflected in Lord Hewart's oft misguided dictum 'justice must not only be done but must manifestly and undoubtedly be seen to be done', evinced an increased sensitivity to the appearance, as well as the actuality of justice. This underlay the demise of the Lord Chancellor as judge, the projected demise of the Law Lords, and the threat to the traditional role of the Attorney General, as well as the insistence that the professions if not, in Adam Smith's phrase, conspiracies against the laity, not their natural servants, could not independently police their own.

The editors of the 9th edition of *Walker and Walker's English Legal System* wrote, 'The last 7 years since the 8th edition of this book have been wholesale changes and reform in virtually every aspect of the Legal System.' The 10th edition will be able to identify yet further change. Whether the changes are improvements, time alone and as always will tell.

For at the end of the three Blair administrations the same issues dominated the legal agenda as at the start, with the same inherent tensions of continuity against modernisation, merit against diversity, justice against economy. Triangulation has provided no final answers.

The changes made to the system during the Blair era are not likely to be reversed. Powers separated will not be conjoined. While the litigation culture still remains essentially adversarial with outcomes, dependent upon the dedication of resources and the forensic performance of counsel, there will continue to be a move away from a court-based system of dispute resolution and the traditional emphasis on oral advocacy. New forms of dispute resolution will increasingly supplant it, whether it be via new administrative tribunals, proliferating Ombudsman (in both public and private sector) or mediation and its cousins. The Civil Service will continue to encroach upon judicial territory. It may be that a lighter touch of regulation will find favour with a Conservative administration; but the laicisation of administration of the law will prove to be an irreversible trend.

As Mr Blair departs the scene with a controversial Ministry of Justice in its first weeks of operation, a Legal Services Bill still to reach the statute book, and from their respective perspectives, judges, barristers and solicitors up in arms about both, he may console himself that no one could accuse him of undue favouritism to the profession of which he remains a member.

# 12

# *Oxford Dictionary of National Biography*

## 12.1. GEORGE ALFRED CARMAN

CARMAN, GEORGE ALFRED (1929–2001), barrister, was born at 20 Breck Road, Blackpool, on 6 October 1929, the son of Alfred George Carman (*d.* 1988), an auctioneer of furniture, and his wife, Evelyn *née* Moylan (*d.* 1954), a seamstress. At eight, he was sent to board at St Joseph's College, Blackpool, where he was taught by Irish Christian brothers under a spartan regime. On Sundays he served as an altar boy. Aged fourteen he transferred to an equally severe Roman Catholic seminary at Upholland in Lancashire, where he spent only two years but became a prefect, head boy, editor of the school magazine, and, according to his headmaster, Brother Woodhouse, 'one of the most useful members of the School XV'. It was Woodhouse who set Carman's sights on Balliol College, Oxford. There, in 1947, on the basis of his performance in the modern subjects scholarship, he won a place as a commoner to read jurisprudence after an interview with the law fellow Theo Tylor. Tylor advised him, prematurely, that as he had no family or friends in the law he ought to become a solicitor.

After national service, where he became a captain in the Royal Army Education Corps, Carman went up to Oxford in 1949 (Balliol having successfully applied for his early release). He graduated in 1952 with what Tylor described as 'a cracking good first' – a feat equalled in that year only by Nicolas Browne-Wilkinson, later senior law lord. Awarded the Paton memorial studentship and the Younger prize, he was also president of the Younger Society, Balliol's law society.

Two other Oxford events transformed Carman's career. He lost his north-country accent and he gained a friend in Jeremy Thorpe, with whom he traded law essays for Oxford Union speeches. After being called to the bar by Lincoln's Inn in 1953 as a King George V coronation scholar with the certificate of honour in bar finals, he did a pupillage in the chambers of Neil Lawson at 1 Harcourt Buildings.

Without either money or London connections, Carman decided to practise in Manchester at chambers in 60 King Street whose head, Geoffrey Heilpern, laboured under the false impression that he was Jewish. In 1957 he contemplated becoming a Conservative MP, and received a glowing reference from Sir David Lindsay Keir, the master of Balliol: 'He would be adopted as a man of intelligence, character and a sense of responsibility which he certainly has.' There is no evidence that he took any further steps down the political path. After practice on the northern circuit which was characteristically varied, he took silk in 1971, joining Byrom Street chambers in Manchester. In accordance with the convention of the time he also acquired a seat in an associated London chambers at 5 Essex Court, The Temple. He became a recorder in 1972 and appeared destined for a lucrative, but unmemorable, career at the provincial bar.

Success as a barrister demands a coincidence of luck and talent. Carman's fortunes waxed when in 1973 he defended the manager of the big dipper at the Battersea fairground on a charge of manslaughter. This brought him to the attention of David Napley, a leading solicitor specializing in criminal law, who was representing another defendant. As a result Carman was instructed by Napley to defend Jeremy Thorpe against a charge of conspiracy to murder his former lover Norman Scott. These proceedings, which concluded in June 1979, were a strong contender for the title political trial of the twentieth century: Carman's successful defence of Thorpe made him a household name. The trial also gave impetus to the career of Gareth Williams, a young silk from Wales, who became one of Carman's most redoubtable adversaries in the courts before switching to politics and becoming Attorney General and leader of the House of Lords.

Carman's subsequent roster of clients in criminal trials attracted media attention. In 1981 he acted for Leonard Arthur, a doctor accused of murdering a baby with Down's syndrome; in 1983 for the *Coronation Street* star Peter Adamson, accused of indecently assaulting two young girls at a swimming bath; and in 1989 for Ken Dodd, the comedian, accused of tax evasion. In all these cases he achieved acquittals. Among other cases, he appeared in 1980 for Lord Kagan, the Gannex raincoat tycoon who was charged with failing to pay customs duty; in 1982 for Geoffrey Prime, the so-called GCHQ traitor; and in 1983 for the family of Robert Calvi, the banker found hanged by Blackfriars Bridge.

Carman then moved into libel law, colonizing the last area where the tribunal of fact was conventionally a jury. He acted for, among others, George Best, Richard Branson, Imran Khan, and Elton John, as well as for a wide range of broadsheet and tabloid newspapers, whose first choice as a leader he almost invariably became. An advocate, not a lawyers' lawyer, he was always happiest addressing the twelve men and women of a jury. Despite his early academic distinction, in his mature years he left jurisprudence to his juniors, and was uncomfortable in any situation where facts took second place to legal principle. He wore his learning so lightly that it became almost invisible. But with a jury he was without equal. Standing only 5 feet 3 inches tall, he showed that it was possible to have presence without height. He deployed a peculiar combination of vulgar imagery and traditional syntax. Of the former cabinet minister David Mellor, he said that if a politician 'behaves like an ostrich and puts his head in the sand, thereby exposing his thinking parts, it may be that a newspaper is entitled to say so'; of Sonia Sutcliffe, wife of the Yorkshire Ripper, that 'She danced on the graves of her husband's victims … The truth and Sonia do not make good bedfellows'; of Neil Hamilton, a former member of parliament, that he was 'On the make and on the take' and 'a man with no honour left'; of Ken Dodd: 'Some accountants are comedians, but comedians are never accountants'. In the Jeremy Thorpe case, he suggested to the prosecution witness, Peter Bessell: 'You see the Ten Commandments as akin to an examination question, with only seven of ten to be attempted'. He quickly attracted sobriquets: Gorgeous George, Giorgio Carmani, the Silver Fox, the Great Defender, the King of Libel.

Carman had too a habit of producing, at a late stage in a trial like a conjuror, new material which changed the whole course of the hearing. Gillian Taylforth, a star of the television soap opera *Eastenders*, was accused by *The Sun* of engaging in oral sex with her fiancé in a lay-by. She sued for libel, in proceedings that were heard in 1994. After she had already left the witness box relatively unscathed, Carman applied for her recall so as to cross-examine her – decisively – on a video taken at a private party (allegedly supplied by an anonymous friend) which showed her making indecent gestures with a sausage. Carman repeated that tactic in 1999, in a claim brought by the MP Neil Hamilton, who complained that Mohamed Al-Fayed, proprietor of Harrods, had falsely suggested that he (Hamilton) had accepted bribes to represent his (Al Fayed's) commercial interests in parliamentary debates. Carman made successful play with a lately disclosed document which implied that Hamilton had previously asked for a reward for lobbying for a tax law change to favour an oil company. Perhaps the most notable example of Carman's technique occurred in 1997, in a case involving a former cabinet minister, Jonathan Aitken, who was withstanding all Carman's efforts to impale him on the charge of enjoying, while a minister of the crown, private hospitality at the Ritz Hotel in Paris from an Arab businessman. Aitken had to withdraw his claim peremptorily when Carman flourished a receipt whose date showed that Aitken's wife (who, Aitken asserted, had discharged the controversial Ritz bill) had been in another country at the material time. This technique of delayed surprise became known in legal circles as 'doing a Carman'. Since to have concealed disclosable documents from the other party to the litigation would have been a breach of civil procedure rules, it must be assumed that it was the product of good luck rather than of improper management.

Carman had, too, the facility of appearing to be both referee and pugilist in the same proceedings. In his final submissions he gave the jury judicial-type directions at the same time as undermining what remained of his opponent's case. Yet, ambitious as he was to be a judge, it is doubtful that the judge's robes would have become him so well as did the advocate's. In 1981 he accepted a High Court judicial appointment in Hong Kong, but then rejected it to look after his sick wife. Instead he transferred his professional base from the provinces to the metropolis, moving in 1982 from 5 Essex Court to New Court chambers, of which he later became head, although in a more ornamental than executive role. On its dissolution in 2000 he joined the chambers of Elizabeth Appleby QC and Michael Beloff QC at 4–5 Gray's Inn Square.

Carman's family life was complex. Soon after settling in Manchester he married, on 16 July 1955, Ursula Patience Peer Groves (*b.* 1930/31), of Lymm, Cheshire, the daughter of a wealthy local grandee, James William Peer Groves, a Salford brewer. They separated in 1958 and were divorced in 1960, Carman expunging reference to the marriage from his entry in *Who's Who*. On 9 July 1960 he married Cecilia Catherine Mary Sparrow (*b.* 1937/8) of Hornsey, London, a singer; she was the daughter of Albert George Sparrow, a pianoforte factory manager. In 1976 this marriage was also dissolved, following their separation in 1972. On 6 March 1976 he married Frances Elizabeth Venning (*b.* 1950/51), a chef; she was the daughter of Thomas Colyer Venning, a highway engineer. They separated in 1983 and were divorced in the following year. His wives' ages at the time of their marriages were between twenty-two and twenty-five: his own progressively older. He had one son, Dominic, from his second marriage. Dominic's biography of Carman, published after the latter's death, applied the precept 'warts and all' to an advanced degree: Carman was depicted as a heavy drinker, a gambler, a wife-beater, a repressed homosexual, and an enjoyer of louche company. Carman's last fifteen years were spent in the company of a fellow barrister, Karen Phillips.

Born a Catholic, Carman died an agnostic, on 2 January 2001, at his home, 8 Prospect Place, Copse Hill, Wimbledon, London, from prostate cancer, after three years of well-concealed treatment. He had been forced to retire only months earlier. His funeral service took place at Westminster Cathedral and there was a memorial service at St Clement Danes. The obituaries were eulogistic, as newspapers honoured one who had been either a valued ally or a feared opponent. In death, as in life, Carman continued to hit the headlines.

## 12.2. GORDON SLYNN, BARON SLYNN OF HADLEY

**Slynn, Gordon, Baron Slynn of Hadley** (1930–2009), judge, was born on 17 February 1930 at 3 Lancaster Gardens, Halton, Runcorn, Cheshire, the elder son of John Slynn (1900–1971), police constable, and his wife, Edith, *née* Phillips (1904–1983). He was educated at Sandbach, a grammar school in Alsager, where his forensic talent first emerged in the school debating society. At Goldsmiths College, University of London, he took a degree in English history and French and acquired a teaching qualification, as well as becoming president of the student union. In 1951, while on a short-service commission in the educational branch of the RAF (winning the sword of honour), he joined Gray's Inn to keep open his career options. Accepting the advice of the then under-treasurer he was admitted to Trinity College, Cambridge, as a pensioner in 1954 and took a first class in part two of the law tripos in 1955 and the LLB course in 1956, as well as becoming president of the University Law Society. Top in his bar finals, and in receipt of a clutch of scholarships and awards on which he relied heavily, he was called to the bar in 1956 and joined the chambers at 1 Hare Court as a pupil of Roger Parker. A handsome man, with classical good looks, he was an admirer of physical beauty in others. On 9 June 1962 he married Odile Marie Henriette Boutin (*b*. 1936). The daughter of Pierre Lucien Boutin, she was a vivacious and educated Frenchwoman who had nursed him in hospital when he suffered a haemorrhage after a tonsillectomy. She was later founder and first chairman of the British branch of Child In Need India, and chairman of the Society of the Protection of Animals Abroad. There were no children of the marriage.

In the decade between 1957 and 1967 Slynn developed a commercial practice and an income commensurate with it. Following his marriage he purchased Egginton House, a William and Mary edifice in Bedfordshire, and told his former pupil master, 'I am going to be a great man and it will be a suitable house for me then'. His rise up the legal ladder was swift. Appointed junior counsel to the minister of labour in 1967, in 1968 he was promoted to junior counsel (common law), the so-called 'Treasury devil', chief assistant to three successive attorneys-general. One of them, Peter Rawlinson, wrote, 'whenever I had to appear in any case, at home or overseas, I always insisted that Gordon should also be briefed … he was very able'. In that role he helped to fashion modern administrative law, and in Strasbourg defended the government (not always successfully) before the European Court of Human Rights, in such seminal cases as *Golder v United Kingdom* (1975), which laid down that the right to a fair trial impliedly guaranteed a right of access to a court, and *Sunday Times v United Kingdom* (1979), which led to the relaxation of the national law on contempt of court. Lord Denning, master of the rolls, wrote of one of Slynn's appearances as Treasury devil, 'Mr Gordon Slynn was outstanding. The best I have ever known. He will go far.' That prediction was amply fulfilled.

In 1974, instead of becoming a high court judge, a position of which the Treasury devil then had a legitimate expectation, Slynn took silk but retained his Treasury practice, in part due to financial need – a novel course of action which caused some resentment among the more ambitious members of the junior bar. However, it proved difficult to combine his Treasury practice with private law work while the government had prior claim on his professional services. He also said that he had been happy while on government service to receive a third of the fee received by the other side's leading counsel, but he objected to receiving less than one third of the fee of the junior. After this experimental journey down a diversionary path, he reverted to the main legal highway, becoming in 1976 a judge in the Queen's Bench division (being knighted the same year), and then president of the Employment Appeal Tribunal (1978–81), where he sat with representatives of both labour and industry – a system for which he became a proselytizer.

In 1981 Slynn struck out again in a new direction, as an advocate-general in the European Court of Justice – a hybrid status, part judge and part advocate. From 1988 to 1992 he was a member of the full court itself. During his time in Luxembourg, he sought to infuse substantive community law with common law principles of fairness, and the procedural law of the European Court of Justice with the virtues of oral advocacy.

The first part of Slynn's sojourn abroad was more fruitful than the second. As advocate-general he was able to express his own thoughts on issues at length. In *Commission of the European Communities v Federal Republic of Germany* (1987) he rejected on grounds of proportionality the German argument that only pure beer could be marketed as beer because additives would put the health of alcoholics at risk, saying succinctly, 'accepting that such a person may need protection, there are other ways of achieving it: medical advice as to quantum and self restraint to name only two'. As a member of the full court, however, he had to merge his often strong views with those of his colleagues, some of whom came from an academic background and lacked his judicial experience, in order to achieve the short judgments characteristic of that court and often, since dissenting opinions were not allowed, reflective of compromises. Nonetheless he acquired the admiring description, 'juriste de grande vitesse'.

By the early 1990s Slynn was anxious to return to the United Kingdom and let his interest be known to (some said lobbied) Lord Mackay of Clashfern, the lord chancellor. In 1992 he duly became a lord of appeal in ordinary (taking the title Baron Slynn of Hadley). As a law lord his knowledge of European Union law was invaluable. He was not merely professionally involved in European law, but in philosophy a committed European as, illustrated by in particular, his Hamlyn lectures (1992) and his Romanes lectures at Oxford (1994). Once challenged by a critic that he had collaborated in a judgment of the European court adverse to the interests of the United Kingdom, he retorted that he had been appointed as a judge not as a Briton.

As a law lord, Slynn's contributions were not merely Eurocentric. In *R v Brown* (1994) he dissented from the majority who held that sado-masochists who inflicted injury upon each other for pleasure were guilty of a criminal offence. In *Fitzpatrick v Sterling Housing Association Ltd* (1999) in equally liberal vein he upheld the rights of same-sex partners to enjoy the benefits of protected tenants as family members. In the Privy Council in *Pratt and Morgan v attorney-general of Jamaica* (1993) he held that fourteen years on death row constituted cruel and unusual punishment contrary to the Jamaican constitution – a decision which excited controversy among Caribbean jurisdictions which retained the death penalty. In *Lewis v attorney-general of Jamaica* (2001) he held that where a state, again Jamaica, had acceded to a human rights treaty no execution could be carried out until the prisoner had availed himself of the opportunity for redress.

In other areas Slynn upheld what he perceived to be established principle. In the Pinochet case (*R v Bow Street metropolitan stipendiary magistrate, ex parte Pinochet Ugarte*, 1998) he decided (in a minority) that extradition to Spain of the former Chilean dictator, who faced criminal charges there for crimes committed in office, even including torture, would be contrary to international law on state immunity. It was because of the non-disclosure by Lord Hoffmann, another member of the same appellate committee, of his links with Amnesty

International, an intervenor in the case, that the matter had to be argued a second time, in 1999. It was then decided that Pinochet was not entitled to state immunity, but also that he could be prosecuted only for crimes committed after 1988, the date the United Kingdom incorporated into domestic law the United Nations Convention against Torture. (Pinochet was in fact subsequently allowed to return to Chile, on medical grounds.) Slynn, presiding in the first case, was thought – unfairly – to bear some responsibility for this unedifying episode. In 2000, by then the longest serving law lord, he should by convention have become the senior law lord but was passed over in favour of Lord Bingham of Cornhill, a rare disappointment in a career of almost unbroken success.

In 2002 Slynn retired from judicial service in the United Kingdom and promptly became an arbitrator and accredited mediator as well as president of the Court of Appeal of the Solomon Islands. He had been treasurer of Gray's Inn in 1988, while still commuting from Luxembourg. In that office he gave expression to his love of theatre and music, instituting an annual miscellany of performances by members of the inn, as well as inaugurating the Friday evening concerts. Characteristically he gave freely of his advice to the young.

Slynn was a clubbable and convivial man, a connoisseur of wine and a lover of dogs. He would never willingly pass over an opportunity to attend a party or to give a lecture, especially abroad, even at the risk of occasional over-commitment. He received more than twenty honorary degrees and many other awards and distinctions, and delighted in the ornate robes which often accompanied them. He was life president of the Lord Slynn of Hadley European Law Foundation, founded by George Dobry in 1998 to develop links between United Kingdom law (and its basic principles of judicial independence and support for human rights) and the legal professionals of central and eastern Europe. The foundation survived him and constituted his major legacy. His last crusade was in support of the People's Mujahideen of Iran, which he successfully campaigned to have removed from the British and European Union lists of prohibited terrorist organizations.

Slynn's last years were overshadowed by illness, cancer having been first diagnosed in 1997. He bore the disease with fortitude, giving up few, if any, of his many activities. He died on 7 April 2009 at the Cromwell Hospital, Kensington, London. His funeral was held at St Margaret's, Westminster, on 20 April, and a celebration of his life was held at Gray's Inn on 2 December. He was survived by his wife, Odile. Never wholly satisfied with what he had achieved, he had nonetheless achieved much.

## 12.3. DONALD JAMES NICHOLLS, BARON NICHOLLS OF BIRKENHEAD

**Nicholls, Donald James, Baron Nicholls of Birkenhead** (1933–2019), judge, was born on 25 January 1933 at 5 Tilstock Avenue, Bebington, in the Wirral, the younger son of William Greenhow Nicholls (1902–1993), a Lloyds Bank clerk, and his wife, Eleanor Jane, *née* Looney (1895–1939), a teacher who died of bronchial pneumonia when Donald was only six years old. His father sought to encourage Donald and his elder brother, Clifford (1931–2011), to consider his second wife – Winifred Agnes Blackwood (1909–2007), whom he married in December 1939, and with whom he had two daughters, Marjorie (*b.* 1948) and Joyce (*b.* 1949) – as their mother by eliminating traces of his first. This gave rise to an arresting opening line in Nicholls' s memoir, which title also served as the motto on his coat of arms: 'I was almost 60 years old when I first saw a photograph of my mother'.

Brought up as a member of the Plymouth Brethren, his father's faith, Nicholls won a scholarship to Birkenhead School, which he entered in 1943 aged ten years and seven months, setting a trend in his career of outstripping his coevals: he was twice fast-tracked at school. He took his higher school certificate examinations before he left the school in 1949 still aged only sixteen and a half – though, anomalously, he had failed the Latin component of his school certificate. The school magazines otherwise disclose no written trace of any extracurricular activities cultural or sporting. His memoir states sparely, 'I enjoyed my time'.

To his headmaster's disappointment, though potentially an Oxbridge scholarship candidate, Nicholls left school not for purposes of further education but to seek employment. He was rejected by Lloyds Bank, despite the paternal connection, and became a junior clerk in the registrar's department at Port Sunlight, the modern village created by the Lever brothers. He next studied for the Chartered Institute of Secretaries examination, which serendipitously included a section on the law of contract. He wrote in his memoir that 'I was fascinated. This introduction to the world of legal principles whetted my appetite for more'. He satisfied it by reading copies of the *All England Law Reports* in his boss's office.

Conscription interrupted Nicholls's civilian career. Between 1951 and 1953 he did his national service with the Royal Army Pay Corps, where he was commissioned a second lieutenant by a sympathetic lieutenant-general. Between 1953 and 1956, his parents having reconsidered their earlier opposition to his attending university, he read for an intermediate LLB degree at Liverpool University, where the faculty was led by Seaborne Davies. He still lived at home and supported himself with a variety of vacation jobs. A multiple prize- and scholarship-winner, he graduated with first-class honours. In 1987 he received an honorary doctorate from the same institution.

Encouraged by Davies to pursue his legal studies in Cambridge, Nicholls was admitted to Trinity Hall. The college wrote that his record at Liverpool University 'has been so outstanding in Law that we found a place for him, after interview, in spite of a badly overcrowded list'. He was ineligible for the college's award, but, with its support, won a state scholarship. Again a multiple prize-winner, he gained a starred first in 1957 in part two of the law tripos and a further starred first in his LLB in 1958. While still an undergraduate he gave supervisions to Girton student Rosalyn Cohen (later, as Rosalyn Higgins, president of the International Court of Justice). He was devoted to Trinity Hall, of which he became an honorary fellow in 1987: both his sons and his grandson studied there.

Unable to afford the substantial premium then needed to obtain articles to a solicitor, Nicholls had already decided to become a barrister, maintaining a preference for the hazards of professional life at the bar to the relative certainty of an academic career and declining Trinity Hall's offer of a law fellowship. The recipient in 1955 of a Middle Temple entrance scholarship, he was called to the bar by the inn in 1958 with its top Harmsworth scholarship and the certificate of honour for the highest mark in bar finals, for which he made use of his future wife's lecture notes. He became a Bencher of the inn in 1981 and its treasurer in 1997. In that role he initiated a series of discussions entitled 'The inns in a changing world', in which he described them as 'an asset which the profession squanders at its peril'.

Nicholls joined the chambers of Harold Christie at 13 Old Square, Lincoln's Inn. His pupil master was Peter Oliver, also an alumnus of Trinity Hall and later a law lord as Lord Oliver of Aylmerton (whose entry for the *Oxford DNB* Nicholls later wrote). Like Oliver, who, in an unusual role reversal, devilled the tyro barrister's first set of instructions, Nicholls developed a chancery practice that included landlord and tenant, wardship, and conveyancing cases. He was given a red bag in which to carry wig and gown, the traditional sign of appreciation by a leader for a junior, by John Brightman, another future law lord.

In 1974 Nicholls took silk after, surprisingly, a first failure, His mainstream instructions broadened into commercial, intellectual property, and tax areas, with a minor sporting penumbra. For Manchester United he resisted an unwelcome take-over bid. He acted for the Marylebone Cricket Club in its dispute with the rebel tourists to South Africa and for Yorkshire County Cricket Club at odds with England opening batsman, Geoffrey Boycott. With less profile but more profit, in his last two years at the bar he represented British Leyland who were seeking to stop other companies making exhaust pipes to fit Morris Minor cars.

In 1983 Nicholls was appointed a High Court judge in the Chancery Division. In that capacity he fined the National Union of Mineworkers and its leader Arthur Scargill for defying his order that a strike in its Yorkshire branch should not be described as 'official'. The fine broke the strike. He resolved the competing claims of the wife and last mistress of comedian Dick Emery, and Terry Venables' suit brought after his sacking as manager of Tottenham Hotspur by the club's chairman, Alan Sugar.

In 1986 Nicholls was elevated to the Court of Appeal. In 1991 he was appointed vice-chancellor, head of the Chancery Division, and in 1994 a lord of appeal in ordinary – a triple fast track. He served in the last office until 2007, from 2002 as second senior law lord. He reached the statutory retiring age before the opening of the Supreme Court, whose institution he opposed. Speaking in the

House of Lords, he said, 'on this I am an unrepentant pragmatist. The present system works and everyone accepts that', also pointing out that 'suitable ivory towers do not come cheaply'. From 1988 to 2004 he was a non-permanent judge of the Hong Kong court of final appeal, one of the first two English judges. He also served as chair of the lord chancellor's advisory committee on legal education and conduct from 1990 to 1997 and from 1997 to 1999 as chair of the committee on parliamentary privilege, which involved greater intrusion on his judicial work than he welcomed.

Nicholls' considerable contribution to jurisprudence was influenced, but unconstrained, by his chancery background. In *Royal Brunei Airlines Sdn Bhd v Tan* (1995) he clarified the confused law on constructive trusts. In *Attorney-General v Blake and Another* (2000) he ordered an account of profits at the suit of the crown where the convicted spy George Blake published in his autobiography information acquired in his capacity as a member of the Secret Intelligence Service in violation of *the Official Secrets Act*. In *Reynolds v Times Newspapers Ltd* (1999) he held that the defence of qualified privilege in defamation claims should embrace publication of political information, not as a separate category, but subject to satisfaction of criteria that gave appropriate weight to the media's freedom of expression on all matters of public concern. *The Defamation Act*, 2013, built on his analysis by creating a statutory defence of 'publication on a matter of public interest'. Another defence, incarnated in the same statute, of 'honest opinion', reflected Nicholls's revision in a case in the Hong Kong court of final appeal, *Tse Wai Chun Paul v Albert Cheng* (2000), of the common law defence of 'fair comment'.

In *White v White* (2000) Nicholls held that, while there was no presumption of equality in division of assets in a divorce, departure from it required good reason. In *Campbell v Mirror Group Newspapers Ltd* (2004), in a claim brought by the 'supermodel' Naomi Campbell, he recognised, against the backcloth of the incorporation of the *European Convention on Human Rights* into British law, a novel right of privacy. *Ghaidan v Godin Mendoza* (2004), against the same backcloth, enlarged the traditional concept of husband and wife in the rent acts. In that case Nicholls held that co-habiting homosexual couples should be treated the same as heterosexual couples for the purposes of succession as a statutory tenant.

Nicholls' judicial speeches were notable for their foundation in first principles, and the succinctness and clarity of their articulation. In espousing an exception to the former in *Fairchild v Glenhaven Funeral Services Ltd* (2002), where the House of Lords held that successive employers in breach of a duty of care to employees to protect them against asbestos dust all should be held liable even though the plaintiff employee could not prove whose particular breach caused the damage, he emphasised the rarity of such situations and the need for compelling justification. But in *Re Spectrum Plus Ltd* (2005) he countenanced the introduction into English law of the device of prospective overruling. While for Nicholls the law had to be coherent as well as fair, a legal system had also to enjoy 'necessary elasticity'. In his memoir he explains his occasional dissents as 'a useful pointer to a better outcome'.

Nicholls' judicial language was all the more effective for its restraint, but he could, in appropriate circumstances, give vent to powerful expressions. In *R. v Bow Street Metropolitan Stipendiary Magistrate, ex parte Pinochet Ugarte (No. 1)* (1998), about whether the Chilean dictator Augusto Pinochet could be extradited to Spain to face trial for human rights violations, he rejected the submission that Pinochet was immune from prosecution and arrest for his acts as head of state, observing that the acceptance of that principle would have meant that British law would have protected Adolf Hitler, emphasizing, 'The contrary conclusion would have made a mockery of international law'. He once described a silk's submissions as 'repellent'.

In many of his cases Nicholls gave important guidance on how domestic legislation should be construed in the light of the interpretative mandate of the *Human Rights Act* of 1998 to bring all legislation into line with *European Convention* rights 'so far as it is possible to do so'. In a significant lecture published in 2005 ('My kingdom for a horse: the meaning of words'), he said, somewhat acerbically, 'It is a little ironical that a provision in the Human Rights Act should in this respect fit uneasily beside the principle of legal certainty which is one of the principles underlying the European Convention on Human Rights'. In the same lecture he planted some radical seeds, still not fructified, for modification of the principles of contractual interpretation by extending the ways in which both pre-contractual negotiations and post-contractual conduct could be taken into account.

Nicholls was always concerned that access to justice should be protected. In his maiden speech in the House of Lords he supported the controversial introduction of conditional fees, saying, 'I am concerned that financial might should not oust legal right', 1 November 1994). For similar reasons he once said that his primary wish was that the *Supreme Court Practice*, colloquially the 'white book', the guide to civil procedure in the higher courts, should be replaced by something written in plain English.

On 27 August 1960, in Ashton under Lyne, Lancashire, Nicholls married fellow barrister Jennifer Mary Thomas (1935–2021), younger daughter of William Ewart Chambers Thomas, physician and surgeon, and his wife, Enid. She had been a law undergraduate at Girton but they first met when eating their requisite dinners at the Middle Temple. They had three children, John (*b.* 1963), later a barrister and QC, Gill (*b.* 1965), later a solicitor, and Christopher (*b.* 1971), later a chartered accountant with Deloitte. While the law always had first claim, family apart, on his time, Nicholls had gentle interests both indoor and outdoor, including opera and playing the piano, gardening, and long walks. He lived latterly on Leigh Hill Road, Cobham, Surrey, and died at St Peter's Hospital, Chertsey, on 25 September 2019 following a stroke.

In his memoir Nicholls wrote, 'It is sad when people look back and wish their principal occupation had been different. I have no such regret. No doubt in part, perhaps in large part, this is because I was successful in my chosen profession. That always helps.' It was a characteristically wry observation but there could be no disputing his own success. He provided a paradigm example of the fact that the law has always been a career open to the talents.

## 12.4. SIR JOHN GRANT McKENZIE LAWS

**Laws, Sir John Grant McKenzie** (1945–2020), judge and jurist, was born at St Mary's nursing home, Raleigh Street, Nottingham on 10 May 1945, the only son and elder child of Frederic Laws (1917–1961) and his wife Margaret Ross, *née* McKenzie (1913–2010), both doctors who served in the Royal Army Medical Corps during the Second World War. The family was then living at Oakdene, 6 Southey Street, Nottingham. His maternal grandfather was John Grant McKenzie, Congregational minister, psychologist, and for thirty years professor of sociology and psychology at Paton Congregational College in Nottingham. Growing up in Easington in co. Durham, Laws was educated at Durham Cathedral Choir School and as a king's scholar at Durham School, where he was a serial prize-winner for languages, both classical and modern, and divinity, president of the debating society, but deliberately resistant to all forms of sport. He won a senior open classical scholarship to Exeter College, Oxford (of which he became an honorary fellow in 2000), and obtained first-class honours in both classical moderations and *literae humaniores*, graduating in 1967. It was his study of moral and political philosophy, as he later acknowledged, that shaped his approach to the law.

It was not nominative determinism which led Laws to a legal career. His reading as a teenager of a biography of F. E. Smith, Lord Birkenhead, persuaded him to become an advocate, in his own words 'a very romantic profession with a lot of contest in it'. In 1970 he was called to the bar by the Inner Temple, of which he became a Bencher in 1985 and treasurer in 2010. He was a member of chambers at 2 Garden Court (later 39 Essex Street), where his pupil master was William (Bill) Macpherson, later a high court judge.

Laws' abilities as a junior attracted the attention of his chambers colleague Simon Brown, later a law lord and supreme court justice, then first junior Treasury counsel (common law), the overflow of whose case load Laws increasingly shouldered, and to whose role in 1984 he succeeded. In recognition of the traditional name for the office, the Treasury 'devil', he had devils embroidered into his socks. He represented the government primarily, but not exclusively, in the burgeoning field of judicial review. Most notably he appeared on behalf of the secretary of state for transport in *Factortame*, where the House of Lords disapplied provisions of the *Merchant Shipping Act 1988* which imposed restrictions on Spanish fishing vessels, holding that the *1972 European Communities Act* established the supremacy of European Community law over even a British statute.

Laws carried out his duties abroad as well as at home. He appeared not only in the European Court of Justice and the European Court of Human Rights but also travelled to the Falkland Islands as counsel to a commission of inquiry into the fire at the King Edward Memorial Hospital in Port Stanley in 1984, to Australia in 1987 in an unsuccessful attempt to prevent the publication there of *Spycatcher* by former MI5 officer Peter Wright, and to Gibraltar in 1988 for the inquest into the killings of three IRA members there.

Helped rather than held back by a slight squint, behind thickly rimmed spectacles, Laws was an advocate of conspicuous lucidity and charm with a rich voice. His eloquent and erudite arguments were adorned by idiosyncratic signature words such as 'deploy' and 'august' or phrases such as 'in the interstices of'. He jotted down such of his opponents' submissions as he considered demanded a response with an ever-stubbier pencil. He bore lightly the heavy responsibilities of his office with a combination of midnight oil and scotch whisky. One of his regular opponents, Stephen Sedley (later a Court of Appeal judge), said that Laws sometimes refrained from taking an arguable point to win a case for fear of its leading to distortion of orderly development of the law. He prioritized strategy above tactics.

Laws became a recorder in 1985 and a high court judge in 1992, in which role he sometimes played gamekeeper turned poacher, ruling against the government, his former client. In a significant judgment in 1997, he held the lord chancellor's substantial increase in court fees to be invalid, reasoning that 'it prevented some people from litigating at all in areas where there was no legal aid … It effectively prevented access to a constitutional right, namely access to the Queen's Court' (*R. v Lord Chancellor, ex parte Witham*, 1998). This concept, of a constitutional right of a superior order to other rights, he developed both inside and outside court. In a lecture delivered in 1995 on 'Law and Democracy' he suggested that even parliament could not legislate to 'abolish fundamental freedoms', incurring a reproach from Lord Irvine, the shadow lord chancellor, that this smacked of 'judicial supremacism'.

Nonetheless in 1999 Laws was promoted by Lord Irvine, by then ensconced on the woolsack, to the Court of Appeal, where he served until 2016, becoming its senior judge, and where he gave many important, if sometimes controversial, judgments, always delivered in elegant prose. He sat also in the privy council and as an ad hoc judge in the European Court of Human Rights.

In 2002 Laws denied Sunderland market trader Steven Thorburn, the so called 'metric martyr', the right to sell fruit and vegetables in pounds not kilograms, holding that the *1972 European Communities Act*, whose impact he had debated from the bar in *Factortame*, was a constitutional statute, which could only be repealed by express legislation and not merely impliedly by a measure such as the *1985 Weights and Measures Act*, on which Mr Thorburn relied. Laws later outlined the components of his constitutional principles in a letter to

*The Times* (17 September 2019) as 'reason, fairness and the presumption of liberty', to which he gave an enhanced status beyond their conventional use as the orthodox tools of the supervisory jurisdiction.

In 2010 Laws held that Gary McFarlane, a relationship counsellor, had been rightly dismissed by his employer Relate for refusing to give advice to same-sex couples. He rejected the argument in evidence from Lord Carey, the former archbishop of Canterbury, that Christians should be given special protection under equality legislation for reasons of conscience, holding that 'The promulgation of law for the protection of a position held purely on religious grounds is irrational preferring the subjective over the objective, but it is also divisive, capricious and arbitrary' (*McFarlane v Relate Avon*, EWCA Civ 880). Although a committed Anglican, if, paradoxically, unpersuaded of the existence of God, Laws believed firmly in the separation of church and state.

Because of his warmth of personality, courtesy, and wit, Laws was as popular with his judicial colleagues as he was with the advocates who appeared before him – and his many friends both within and outwith the law. He was a member of the Garrick Club, whose tie sometime clashed with the flowery shirts which he habitually wore on informal occasions.

Laws was disappointed in his ambition to be appointed to the supreme court, which most in the legal profession had assumed was his natural destination. Lord Neuberger, a former president, said in a memorial address that he had never heard a satisfactory answer to the question as to why Laws was denied that accolade. Instead Laws became in 2016–17 the Arthur Goodhart visiting professor in legal science at Cambridge, where he developed further his thinking on the relationship of ruler and ruled, articulated in his 2013 Hamlyn lectures, 'The Common Law Constitution'. His Cambridge lectures, edited by Nigel Pleming and David Feldman, were posthumously published under the title *The Constitutional Balance* (2021), with a foreword by Lord Neuberger.

Laws' wide-ranging interests in judicial review, advocacy, classics, philosophy, and theology had made him a prolific author and lecturer; and brought him as well a number of varied appointments. He was an honorary vice-president of the Constitutional and Administrative Bar Association; the judicial visitor of University College, London; the visitor of Cumberland Lodge, used by the inns of court for the training of young barristers; from 1992 an honorary fellow of Robinson College, Cambridge; and between 2011 and 2014 visiting professor at Northumbria University. He was aptly described by Feldman as 'an academic by inclination' but he was an academic who loved to teach.

Most conspicuously, from 1994 Laws was president of the Bar European Group. At its annual conference each year throughout his 25-year presidency, held always in a different European location, he made a speech illuminated by the contribution of his 'historical researcher', in which guise he referred to his wife. On 9 June 1973, at Eastergate Church, he had married Sophie Susan Sydenham Cole Marshall (1944–2017), a theologian and lecturer in *New Testament* studies at King's College, London (subsequently professor of humanities and dean of

Regent's American College, London), whom he had met at Oxford, and wooed in an unorthodox exercise of the *ars amatoria* by reciting in full Macaulay's epic poem 'Horatius at the Bridge' as well as learning to punt. She was a fellow ailurophiliac and Hellenophile. In 1986 they purchased a house on the island of Andros overlooking the Aegean Sea, where Laws would read philosophy during the day, before repairing to a local bar or taverna to drink retsina at night and to exploit his knowledge of both ancient and modern Greek.

Laws, who lived latterly on Warwick Way, Pimlico, was a devoted family man. Their adopted daughter Margaret Grace, who worked in public relations, had two children. In substitution for the Greek myths which he once read to his daughter, Laws taught his grandson James some rude words which prompted the child, misunderstanding the full import of the lesson, to conclude that John's own name was 'bum', a soubriquet Laws then adopted in family e-mails.

Sophie died in 2017. The combination of two blows, professional and personal, in quick succession, left marks on Laws from which he never fully recovered. He himself died on 5 April 2020 of Covid-19 at the Chelsea and Westminster Hospital, where he was being treated for sepsis. Like appellate judges Sir Thomas Scrutton in the United Kingdom and Learned Hand in the USA, while Laws never ascended to the apex court in the jurisdiction in which he plied his profession, like them he left a far larger footprint than many who did.

# Part IV

# Sport

# 13

# 'Pitch, Pool, Rink ... Court? Judicial Review in the World of Sport'*

WAS ZOLA JUSTLY accused? Why was it wrong for Gatting to bowl a maiden over? Should Royal Gait have been deprived of Royal Ascot triumph?

An athlete is suspended from international competition on the charge that she had 'taken part' in a meeting in South Africa in which she had not actually run. England's cricket captain is demoted for having a drink in his hotel room with a barmaid. The horse which had passed the post first in the Ascot Gold Cup is placed last because it had interfered with another horse which was never in real contention for a prize. All these incidents in the scope of a single sporting summer triggered allegations of injustice. In each instance there were serious suggestions – ultimately not implemented – that the decisions *might* be challenged in the courts. Gone is the era when the jurisdiction of sporting bodies was, to borrow Lord Atkin's phrase, 'a domain into which the King's writ does not seek to run and to which his officers do not seek to be admitted'. On the contrary, as Parker LJ observed in 1987, the law involved is 'a developing field', though some limit to that development was set when I appeared before the late Walton J, then the duty judge, in his drawing room in Wimbledon on a Saturday afternoon in an unsuccessful effort to persuade him that a light heavyweight boxing contest due to take place in Monte Carlo on the next day, while recognised internationally in the sport as for the championship of the world, should not be so recognised in the Chancery Division!

In this article I wish to explore the basis upon which the courts can control the exercise of powers, in particular disciplinary powers, by sporting bodies, and to examine the peculiar problems of substantive and adjectival law which arise in this area. I shall deal with judicial review both in its wider sense – the exertion of a supervisory jurisdiction – and, more speculatively, in its narrow sense, proceedings brought under RSC Order 53. It would be churlish for me not to acknowledge at the outset the pioneering work in this field of Edward Grayson, whose *Sport and the Law* (1988), provides a quarry of material which anyone interested in the subject may profitably mine.

I do not pretend that the area is self-contained, that there is a body of law applicable solely or almost solely to the activities of sports authorities. On

* [1989] *Public Law* 95.

the contrary, it is the uncertain boundaries of the area as well as the variety of the problems that it throws up in practice that lend fascination to the subject. Those boundaries, and the terrain that lies within them, I shall now attempt to chart.

Traditionally and typically, bodies controlling sport on a national or international basis, such as the Test and County Cricket Board, the International Amateur Athletic Federation, or the International Federation of Football Associations, are unincorporated associations. Such bodies, not being the creatures of statute, derive their powers from contract. The contract is contained in the association's rules, which govern the relationship of the body with its members. Even where, less usually, the bodies such as the Football Association or the British Amateur Athletics Board are incorporated – by guarantee in most instances – nonetheless the articles of association, and the regulations promulgated by the body, create a framework of contract.

It is for the courts to interpret such rules. In *Williams v Reason*, in which the celebrated Welsh full-back sued in respect of an allegation that he had infringed the regulations of the International Rugby Football Board by writing a book for reward, Stephenson LJ said:

> The first issue in the case, the construction of the Board's rules and regulations was indisputably a matter for the Judge. The law is stated as follows in Halsbury's Laws of England, 4th ed., vol. 12 (1975), p.594, para. 1461: 'Functions of judge and jury. The interpretation of a written document is, generally speaking, a matter of law for the Court.'

The exercise may be a difficult one because, as the case law suggests, the drafting is often imperfect and the process of addition and amendment has been carried out without reference to the structure as a whole; so that, as with a building converted over the decades in different styles, all unity is lost. In *Reel v Holder*, Lord Denning MR said with reference to the rules of the International Amateur Athletic Federation:

> One can argue to and fro on the interpretation of these rules. The people who drew them up would not possibly have envisaged all the problems which would have to be coped with in the future in regard to them. The Courts have to reconcile all the various differences as best they can.

The methods of interpretation of such rules are not necessarily those applicable to Acts of Parliament or commercial documents. A more relaxed approach to construction is required as with the rule books of trade unions. In *Cowley v Heatley*, a South African-born swimmer claimed that the Commonwealth Games Federation had misconstrued the word 'domicil' in their regulations and had unlawfully banned her from competing in the Commonwealth Games in Edinburgh. Sir Nicholas Browne-Wilkinson V-C said:

> One had to look for the meaning of the word in that context; to inquire beyond the language and see what the circumstances were with reference to which the words

> were used, and the object appearing from those circumstances which the person using them had in view.

Judge-proofing is impossible; the courts will ignore efforts to exclude their role as interpreters of law. With reference to rules of the British Amateur Weight-Lifting Association, Lynskey J said:

> The parties can, of course, make a tribunal or council the final arbiter on quotations of fact. They can leave questions of law to the decision of a Tribunal, but they cannot make it the final arbiter on question of law.

A provision such as that in the rules of the International Amateur Athletic Federation (rule 11.12), which seeks to make resort to the courts itself a breach of the rules attracting a penalty, is undoubtedly invalid.

Furthermore, if an issue of construction is raised both in the domestic forum and in the High Court, the High Court proceedings will be accorded precedence. Thus John Conteh, the boxer, was granted an injunction to restrain the British Boxing Board of Control from holding a meeting to determine whether he had been guilty of misconduct in failing to carry out a contract to train for a particular fight when he had issued a writ for a declaration that the contract was itself invalid. It proved an expensive victory. He wrote in his autobiography, 'I was soon to discover that legal advisers' percentages don't come any lower than managers' or promoters.' My clerk was evidently 'getting a result', or even 'doing the business'!

What are the grounds upon which the decisions of sports authorities may be challenged in the courts? First, if the rules, properly construed prohibit the conduct complained of, the aggrieved party has a simple claim. It is not unusual to find a sports authority apparently ignoring the constraints of its own constitution. In *Davis v Carew-Pole*, Pilcher J held that the stewards of the National Hunt Committee had committed a triple error: (1) they had disqualified and warned off a livery stable keeper for 'training and running' a horse under their jurisdiction which the plaintiff had undoubtedly trained but did not run; (2) their indefinite disqualification breached their own rule requiring a specified time scale; and (3) the actual offences alleged were not subject to regulations relied upon. Likewise, the World Professional Billiards and Snooker Association wrongly banned Cliff Thorburn from taking part in the world championship after he had been positively tested for drugs in another competition, although their rules did not provide for such a ban.

Secondly, rules which on their face permit a particular course of conduct may themselves be invalid and ineffective because they are contrary to (or outside) either the specified objects of the body in question or to general principles of law or it may be that though the rules themselves are valid, and the course of conduct is apparently within a discretion conferred by them, the exercise of the discretion can itself be attacked as invalid on analogous grounds.

Thirdly, any rule or action which offends against public policy, either of the common law or as enshrined in some statute, can be struck down. The aspects of public policy which are most relevant are the principles relating to restraint of trade, to discrimination on various grounds, and to natural justice.

Rules or decisions in this area cannot operate in unreasonable restraint of trade. At a time when the rewards for professional sportsmen are increasing, and the boundaries between professional and amateur sport become blurred, the principle is an important one.

In *Eastham v Newcastle United Football Club Ltd*, the defendant club employed the plaintiff as a professional footballer subject to the 'retain and transfer' system. Under that system a player who was retained by one club could not be employed by another; nor could he be transferred to another club without the consent of both. Wilberforce J ruled that the system went further than was 'reasonably necessary to protect ... legitimate interests', and rejected an argument that the length of time during which the system had operated, showed that it was necessarily 'in the general interest of the game'.

What was good for football was good for cricket. In *Greig v Insole*, the Test and County Cricket Board was held to lack power to alter its rules so as to disqualify from Test cricket persons who played in the outlawed Packer World Series. 'A professional cricketer,' said Slade J, 'needs to make his living as much as any other professional man'; and he concluded, 'The defendants acted in good faith and in what they considered to be the best interests of cricket. That, however, is not enough to justify in law the course which they have taken.'

Both the Sex Discrimination Act 1975 and the Race Relations Act 1976 have provisions which affect sporting bodies, since they forbid discrimination in the conferment of authorisations which are needed for or facilitate engagement in any occupation, including sport. Not that discrimination is always easy to prove: witness the case of *Saunders v Richmond-upon-Thames Borough Council*, where the applicant failed in her claim that she had been refused a job as a golf professional on the grounds of her sex, although the letter acknowledging her application was addressed 'Dear Sir' and seven out of 19 questions at her interview related to her sex (for example, 'Do you think men respond as well to a woman golf professional as to a man?'). Doubtless her failure can be attributed to the advocacy of the writer, who was said to have made 'numerous submissions, mainly of a trifling character'.

The Sex Discrimination Act, however, makes a significant exception:

> Nothing in Parts II to IV shall, in relation to any sport, game or other activity of a competitive nature where the physical strength, stamina or physique of the average woman puts her at a disadvantage to the average man, render unlawful any act related to the participation of a person as a competitor in events involving that activity which are confined to competitors of one sex.

This section has been considered on three occasions by superior courts. In *Bennett v Football Association Ltd*, it was held to justify the refusal of the Football Association to allow a female (in that case a 12-year-old girl) to play football with boys. In *GLC v Farrar* it was held, obiter, to have no application to deal with a situation where the sexes wanted to play with themselves – so to speak – and not with each other. But in *British Judo Association v Petty* it was held not to permit discrimination against a woman as a referee.

Discrimination on grounds of race has not yet, to my knowledge, stimulated litigation at High Court level. In an era when so much British sporting success depends upon the achievements of black immigrants or their descendants, Linford, Colin, Fatima and the like, it would be counterproductive as well as immoral if crude racial bars operated in the sporting field. But the legislation prohibits discrimination on grounds of nationality or national origins as well as of race or colour. Indirect discrimination, the application of ostensibly neutral criteria that have, without justification, disproportionately adverse impact on members of a minority group, is also contrary to the Act. So, it is not inconceivable that any sporting body that operated a nationality bar or even a residence qualification might fall foul of the law at the suit of a foreign-born sportsman whose earning potential was damaged by its application to him.

In *Nagle v Feilden*, where the refusal of the Jockey Club to issue a licence to a female trainer was held to be prima facie invalid, there are, in some of the dicta, the germ of a principle that *any* unjustifiable interference with the right to work might be vulnerable, even if any discrimination was outside the two areas now covered by statute, or if indeed there was no discrimination at all, but merely a capricious or arbitrary ban.

Natural justice, and its twin pillars, the rule against bias, actual or apparent, and the right to be heard, certainly apply to the proceedings of sporting bodies. Indeed, the wealth of case law suggests that fair play, the principle said to epitomise the best values of sport, is often conspicuously absent from the procedures of its governing authorities.

It was in the context of an action for libel for publication of the Jockey Club's decision to withdraw a racing trainer's licence because a drug had been administered to a horse trained by him, that Tucker LJ remarked that what was required by the rules of natural justice depended 'on the circumstances of the case, the nature of the inquiry, the rules under which the tribunal is acting, the subject-matter that is being dealt with, and so forth'. Horses for courses, indeed. But Denning LJ identified a touchstone which has made some form of hearing a pre-requisite of a decision of this kind: 'common justice requires that before any man is found guilty of an offence carrying *such consequences*, (sc. financial) there should be an enquiry at which he has the opportunity of being heard.'

And although in *McInnes v Onslow Fane* (a boxing case), it was held that an applicant for a licence (unless he had a legitimate expectation of it) may not be entitled to a hearing whereas someone threatened with *removal* of a licence will, that restraint on the scope of the principle may not survive scrutiny by a higher court.

The second main rule of natural justice came into play when Cantley J held that the banning by a Football Association tribunal of Don Revie, the ex-England football manager, for 10 years was invalid when the tribunal was staffed by officers of the association whose previously published remarks about Revie showed an unacceptable level of prejudice and prejudgment.

Some general limit to the court's powers of interference was set in *Currie v Barton*. The committee of a county tennis association was held not to be in breach of natural justice in deciding to ban a player from an amateur county team without first inviting him to appear before the committee to put his side of the story in person. Nicholls LJ did not think that 'the rules of natural justice could apply to a position where a monopoly power over a sporting activity made decisions about team selection, provided the decision did not affect a person's ability to earn a living'. But this limit too may prove temporary. Not only is today's amateur often tomorrow's professional, so that his purse may be in the long term affected by decisions of such bodies but, as the law of defamation shows in particular, reputation is an interest traditionally protected by the law.

One aspect of natural justice requires special consideration before an audience of lawyers: can an aggrieved party claim to be represented at any hearing of a sporting authority? In *Pett v Greyhound Racing Association Ltd*, the Court of Appeal, Lord Denning presiding, held at an interlocutory stage that a trainer was prima facie entitled to an oral hearing at an inquiry by the defendants' stewards into alleged doping, and, though the rules of the club were silent, entitled to be represented by counsel and solicitors, since the matter was of serious importance to him affecting 'his reputation and his livelihood'. However, in the full hearing, Lyell J decided that the prima facie views of the Court of Appeal were not warranted, and that legal representation before the local stewards was not 'an elementary feature of the fair dispensation of justice'. Since the case was settled before any further appeal took place, Lord Denning was temporarily denied the last word on this piece of judicial independence. But a year later he enjoyed it in another case saying 'Lyell J. thought we were wrong … But I think we were right.' Interestingly, however, in *that* case, Lord Denning held that a rule prohibiting legal representation before a Football Association tribunal was valid:

> The club is at liberty to bring these points before the courts at once and have them decided with the aid of skilled advocates. If they choose not to bring them before the court, but prefer to put them before a lay tribunal, they must put up with the imperfections of that tribunal and must abide by their ruling that there be no legal representation.

Conformably with the generally flexible approval which obtains in the whole area of natural justice, the courts have shrunk from imposing a straitjacket of legalism on the proceedings of sports associations. In *Calvin v Carr*, the Privy Council held that procedural defects in a stewards' inquiry could be cured by the decision of the Appeal Committee of the Australian Jockey Club. Lord Wilberforce referred to 'an essentially domestic proceeding in which the standards are those which have come to be accepted over the history of this sporting activity'. Similarly, in *Machin v The Football Association*, a High Court ruling against a referee's report allegedly incorrectly recording a foul tackle was overruled by the Court of Appeal, who upheld the finality of his finding, despite video evidence which undermined the referee's verdict. It would clearly be undesirable if the authority of the referee could be undermined by court proceedings.

The European Court of Justice has had to consider discrimination on grounds of nationality in the world of professional sport in two cases, *Walrave v Association Union Cycliste Internationale* and *Dona v Mantera*. The former concerned world championship rules for motor-paced bicycle racing: the latter concerned the rules of the Italian Football Federation. The following principles have emerged:

1. The practice of sport is subject to Community law only in so far as it constitutes an economic activity within the meaning of Article 2, EEC.
2. The activities of professional or semi-professional sports players which are in the nature of gainful employment or remunerated service are such economic activities.
3. The prohibition of discrimination on grounds of nationality under Articles 48, 52 and 59 EEC not only applies to the action of public authorities but also extends to rules of any other nature aimed at collectively regulating gainful employment and services, and thus to the rules of a sporting organisation.
4. Where the sporting organisation is international, the non-discrimination rule will apply to all its legal relationships in so far as they can be located within the territory of the EEC by reason either of the place where they are entered into or of the place where they take effect.
5. The relevant provisions create individual rights which national courts must protect.

This has (and has had) clear consequences in relation to the employment of overseas stars in the Football League. What the county cricket clubs have done by choice, the Football League clubs may soon do with the backing of law.

But are the weapons available to the litigant to be gleaned from private law only, as supplemented by the developing law against discrimination? Or is there scope for the play of principles of public law, that is, of principles applied by the courts in exercising the power of judicial review?

In *Breen v AEU*, Lord Denning MR again pointed the way forward:

> It is now well settled that a statutory body, which is entrusted by statute with a discretion, must act fairly. ... The discretion of a statutory body is never unfettered. It is a discretion which is to be exercised according to law. That means at least this: the statutory body must be guided by relevant considerations and not be irrelevant. If its decision is influenced by extraneous considerations which it ought not to have taken into account, then the decision cannot stand. No matter that the statutory body may have acted in good faith: nevertheless, the decision will be set aside.

> Does all this apply also to a domestic body? I think it does, at any rate when it is a body set up by one of the powerful associations which we see nowadays. Instances are readily to be found in the books, notably the Stock Exchange, the Jockey Club, the Football Association, and innumerable trade unions. All these delegate power to committees. These committees are domestic bodies which control the destinies of thousands. They have quite as much power as the statutory bodies of which I have been speaking. They can make or mar a man by their decisions. Not only by expelling him from membership, but also by refusing to admit him as a member: or, it may be, by a refusal to grant a licence or to give their approval. Often their rules are framed so as to give them a discretion. They then claim that it is an unfettered discretion with which the courts have no right to interfere. They go too far. They claim too much. … Their rules are said to be a contract between the members and the unions. So be it. If they are a contract, then it is an implied term that the discretion should be exercised fairly. But the rules are in reality more than a contract. They are a legislative code laid down … to be obeyed by the members. This code should be subject to control by the courts just as much as a code laid down by Parliament itself. If the rules set up a domestic body and give it a discretion, it is to be implied that the body must exercise its discretion fairly. Even though its functions are not judicial or quasi-judicial, but only administrative, still it must act fairly. Should it not do so, the courts can review its decision, just as [they] can review the decision of a statutory body. The courts cannot grant the prerogative writs such as certiorari and mandamus against domestic bodies, but they can grant declarations and injunctions which are the modern machinery for enforcing administrative law.

If this be right, the court can exercise a more vigorous scrutiny. It may not substitute its own views for that of the body concerned, but it can overturn decisions infected by immaterial considerations, or even review a decision which contravenes the principle of proportionality: for example, a grossly excessive penalty, say a lifetime ban, on an athlete doped, without his knowledge, by his doctor or trainer, or, perhaps, the £12,000 fine imposed on Steve Davis by the World Professional Billiards and Snooker Association for breach of a rule of the Association which required attendance of competitors at press conferences.

But what then are *immaterial* considerations? If the body is incorporated, the objects set out in its memorandum provide a touchstone of materiality. Even if the association is unincorporated, its rules usually contain a statement of objects or principles by which its decisions can be judged. So in *Baker v Jones & Ors*, it was held that the application of the funds of the British Amateur Weightlifters' Association to meet legal costs of certain officers in their individual capacities was ultra vires its objects, since the association as an unincorporated body could not be liable for the tortious acts either of its officials or its council members. Likewise, conditions attached to permission by the British Boxing Board of Control for John Conteh to fight in the United States, namely that he deposit part of his purse to abide the outcome of a dispute with his manager and Mickey Duff, were struck down. It was held that, though the regulations empowered the imposition of conditions, they must relate to the fight itself and not to extraneous matters.

So were a sporting body to take action for political reasons and not sporting ones – were, say, the Test and County Cricket Board at the behest of the Government to ban from test cricket anyone who had played in South Africa, might a court not interfere, following the precedent of *Goring v British Actors Equity Association* where instructions of Equity, the actors' union, to its members to decline professional engagements in South Africa were held invalid as their purpose was 'to promote a general cultural boycott of South Africa (a sectarian purpose), not for the purpose of promoting the professional interest of its members'? Similarly, if an international sporting authority sought to ban from a championship a national team because of the activities of another team from the same nation in a different sport, could not a court say, as did the House of Lords in *Wheeler v Leicester City Council*, that to punish someone for the alleged misconduct of another was unreasonable and unfair? The question is not hypothetical. There was an attempt to prevent the English athletes from competing in the 1982 Commonwealth Games because of the British Lions tour of South Africa. Could it even be said – at any rate with the benefit of hindsight – to have been *Wednesbury* unreasonable not to select Sebastian Coe for the 800 metres in Seoul? Be that as it may, the prospect of public law principles being applied in this field makes it worthwhile to examine some particular problems that might arise.

If a person has a contract with a sporting body, he can, on the right facts, bring proceedings for breach of contract. But if there is no contract, what is the basis upon which relief can be claimed? In *Cowley v Heatley*, Sir Nicholas Browne-Wilkinson V-C doubted the existence of the jurisdiction, although he found it unnecessary to rule on the point. Those doubts were, in my view, ill-founded. The courts have extensive powers under statute and the rules of court to grant injunctions and declarations, and the cases show that the power *is* deployed. In *Eastham*, the plaintiff was granted a declaration not only against his own club but against the Football Association and League, 'whether or not (he had) a legal cause of action against the defendants'. In *Nagle v Feilden*, the Court of Appeal said that a person denied the right to work, and not merely one deprived of it, had a remedy in law.

The issue of whether the aggrieved party has a contractual relationship with the defendant authority goes to the question not of '*Is* there a remedy at all?', but of '*What* remedy is there?', because it is probably only where a breach of contract or a tort can be established, that damages, as distinct from a declaration or an injunction, can be obtained.

But whatever remedy may be available, does an applicant aggrieved by the actions of a sporting body go by way of writ or originating summons, or can he, indeed must he, institute the procedures of RSC Order 53? Until recently the matter appeared beyond doubt. In *Law v National Greyhound Racing Club Ltd*, the plaintiff greyhound trainer sought a declaration that a suspension by the defendant company's stewards of his licence breached the rules of racing. The Court of Appeal rejected the defendants' submission that the claim was misconceived and that the plaintiff should have sought judicial review. It observed that the authority to suspend the plaintiff's licence was derived wholly from a contract between him and the defendants, and the status of the stewards was that of a domestic tribunal. As Fox LJ stated, 'What the defendants do in relation to the control of greyhound racing may affect the public, or a section of it, but the defendants' power in relation to the matters with which this case is concerned are contractual.'

But in *Finnigan v New Zealand Rugby Football Union Inc*, a somewhat different approach was taken by the New Zealand Court of Appeal. *Ex Antipodibus semper aliquid novum?* In 1985 the council of the New Zealand Rugby Football Union decided to accept the invitation of the South African Rugby Board for a New Zealand representative rugby football team to tour South Africa. Members of certain rugby clubs commenced an action in the High Court challenging the council's decision. They claimed that the decision failed to comply with the object stated in the Union's rules of promoting, fostering and developing amateur rugby union football throughout New Zealand. The Court of Appeal rejected a challenge to the plaintiffs' standing. The judges reasoned that, while technically a private and voluntary sporting association, the New Zealand Union was, in the New Zealand context and in relation to this decision, in a position of major national importance. The plaintiffs could not be dismissed as mere busybodies. Unless such persons *were* accorded standing, it might well be that in reality there was no effective way of establishing whether or not the New Zealand Union was acting within its lawful powers. In a key dictum, the court observed:

> In this particular case, therefore, we are not willing to apply to the question of standing the narrowest of criteria that might be drawn from private law fields. In truth the case has some analogy with public law issues. … [It] falls into a special area where, in the New Zealand context, a sharp boundary between public and private law cannot realistically be drawn.

And if, (i) in the post-*Datafin* era the test for liability to judicial review becomes one of substance, not form, dependent upon the nature of the powers exercised and not their source, (ii) as Lord Denning suggested, the principles which are to be applied to the determinations of sporting bodies include public law principles, and (iii) the test of standing to challenge their decisions is sufficiency of interest as defined by Order 53, then it may be that, at any rate where the body has monopolistic or near monopolistic powers over the sport in question, judicial review will become the appropriate, and hence the necessary procedure.

One reason for welcoming such a development is that the virtues of the judicial review procedure, economy and expedition, are superior to that of a full-blown trial, at any rate where there are no primary issues of fact to be resolved.

So where do we go from here? No less than three vice-chancellors of different generations and jurisdictions have taken the view that the courts should abstain where possible from interfering with the decisions of bodies controlling sporting spheres. Megarry V-C spoke of 'activities which those bodies are far better fitted to judge than the Courts'. Browne-Wilkinson V-C added, 'Sport would be better served if there was not running litigation at repeated intervals by people seeking to challenge the decisions of the regulating bodies.' And in *Gasser v Stinson* Scott J expressly applied the earlier dictum in refusing to hold in restraint of trade the International Amateur Athletic Federation's rules suspending from competition athletes found to have taken prohibited drugs, a decision of which Ben Johnson's legal advisers may not be oblivious.

But is this policy of judicial self-restraint warranted? As Megarry V-C conceded, these bodies 'are concerned with the means of livelihood of those who take part in the activities'. The 'right to work' is protected in appropriate circumstances in private and public law; it can, in the modern era of commercialised sport, embrace the right to play. Would similar arguments in favour of lowering the standards of fairness and reasonableness, of according a wider margin of appreciation to those who construe the limits of their own powers, or denying on generalised discretionary grounds relief where breach of laws is established, command any support if the injured plaintiff had been wrongly denied the right to ply for hire in a taxi-cab or even to sell alcoholic beverages? As for the argument that the sports bodies know best, experience may perpetuate, not eliminate error; and Wilberforce J indicated in *Eastham* that the rules of sporting bodies cannot be treated as the Mosaic or Medan law.

It is, I suspect, the floodgates argument that is the unspoken premise of the Vice-Chancellarial observations, the fear that limited court time will be absorbed by a new and elastic category of case with much scope for abusive or captious litigation. It is an argument which intellectually has little to commend it and pragmatically is usually shown to be ill-founded. For it is often the case that, once the courts have shown the willingness to intervene, the standards of the bodies at risk of their intervention tend to improve. The threat of litigation averts its actuality.

There is therefore no reason why the field of sport cannot define law's new, or at any rate next, frontier; and if Britain can no longer head the world in sport itself, perhaps it can do so in sporting litigation. Members of the bar, on your marks!

# 14

# *'The Specificity of Sport: Rhetoric or Reality?'* Edward Grayson Memorial Lecture 2012*

EDWARD GRAYSON, IN whose memory this annual lecture, sponsored by BASL, is named, has been aptly described as the founding father of sports law. Whatever may be the achievements of those who have later frolicked in this legal field, whether as academics, advocates or arbitrators, Edward has one claim to fame that can never be surpassed. He was there first.

I have many fond memories of Edward, a man as lovable as he was unorthodox. We once travelled together to a sports law conference in Potsdam – our journeys coinciding only because Edward had not uncharacteristically missed his earlier flight. As we shared a taxi from Berlin airport to the hotel, Edward took it upon himself to ask our driver what he had done during the war, a question which might have been tactless had it not also been superfluous since the driver could scarcely have been born before the swinging sixties. But throughout the balance of our stay Edward played the role of the elderly Englishman abroad to perfection, attracting the solicitous attentions of a cavalcade of beautiful *frauleins*, while I found myself assisted only by women of a certain – a euphemism for uncertain – age. I was pleased to be able to persuade the editors of the *Oxford Dictionary of National Biography* to include in this year's supplement an essay on Edward – a privilege usually only accorded to deceased holders of the highest judicial office – and to pen it myself; and we are delighted that Edward's wife Wendy and son Harry are here tonight.

Edward himself might have taken vocal issue with my perspective because, paradoxically, although sports law's only begetter, he firmly denied that there was any corpus of jurisprudence recognisable as sports law. He wrote of the debates about whether or not sports law exists as 'arcane, arid and artificial' – he had a good ear for alliteration – and continued 'as a tabloid headline or sound

* (2011) 19 *British Journal of Sport and Law* 88.

bite the shorthand version serves a convenient, practical and populist purpose. As a judicial concept, it never has and never will exist'.

A modern follower in Edward's footsteps, Dr Jack Anderson of Queen's University, Belfast, noted in a recent textbook:

> There is no equivalent of the IOC within the common law whereby an area of law can lobby for official recognition or even associated status, though it is of interest to note that sport is not one of the 150 or so sub-headings within Halsbury's laws of England which includes well-thumbed sections of the law relating to 'Library and other Scientific and Cultural Institutions' and the Law of Weights and Measures.

Pausing only to reflect on the lack of identity of the source of Dr Anderson's assertion that the sections are well thumbed, and on the limited lifestyle opportunities of a person whose thumbs are so frequently engaged in so mundane an activity, I note that his observation is obsolescent. Butterworth's is soon to publish in Halsbury a title on sports law, preceding stamp duty and statutes for alphabetical rather than associational reasons, of which I am the general editor, and two of whose contributors are respectively my son and my niece, showing that the age of nepotism is not entirely dead. I do not, however, intend simply to reprise that endless argument as to whether sports law does or does not exist. I intend rather to approach the issue crabwise, and ask what is, but also what might intelligibly be meant, by the much-used phrase 'the specificity of sport'.

The origins of that phrase are obscure, but, like so much contemporary jargon, it is, I surmise, Brussels-born Euro speak. Certainly, by the time the European Commission published its seminal White Paper on Sport on 2007 it could speak of the phrase as something 'often referred to'. That paper identified it as a concept to be approached through two prisms.

I shall mention the second first because it seems to me to be the less interesting of the two; that is:

> The specificity of the sport structure, notably the autonomy and diversity of sports organisations, a pyramid structure of competitions from grass roots to elite level and organised solidarity mechanisms between the different levels and operators, the organisation of sport on a national basis, and the principle of a single federation per sport.

None of these factors seem to me of themselves to differentiate sport in any important sense from other areas of human activity, and all are subject to exceptions. Retailing encompasses autonomous and diverse entities ranging from Tesco to the neighbourhood corner shop; debating, music and politically non-correct beauty contests have a pyramid structure – as indeed does 'Britain's Got Talent' – of which I would merely comment that the title's proposition is too frequently disproved in the performance. I am touching later on what is, I think, meant by an 'organised solidarity mechanism' but suspect that whatever it is, it is not unique to sport. Income tax itself is an organised solidarity mechanism of a kind. Have not our Government after all assured us that we are all in this together?

Sport is, moreover, organised not only on a national, but also on an international basis, a point noted in the monumental judgment *In Re Televising Premier League Football Matches* which was concerned with whether agreements between the PL and Sky and BBC were contrary to the public interest tests under the now repealed Restrictive Practices Act 1976; and the notion that a single federation per sport is intrinsic to its activity is belied by recurrent discussion as to whether men and women of goodwill should set up a rival to FIFA or indeed the FIA, purged of the less savoury features of those two monopolies, and by the actuality of the alphabet soup of boxing organisations, balkanising the title of world champion, even if at present the seven *soi-disant* world heavyweight championships are shared between two Ukrainian brothers. True it is that certainly in the liberal western world the administration of sport is regarded as better left to self-governing organisations, but it is idle to pretend that the state, conscious of the contribution of sport to the national economy, the national health and, not least national prestige, does not in all countries in differing degrees, involve itself directly or indirectly in regulating sport, sometimes, as in France by overarching legislation, and even more recently in England, where the Government have nudged the Football Association into reformist mode. Sport, like the professions, law or medicine, is now part private, part servant of public policy.

However, the first of the Euro-apothegms cuts closer to the heart of the matter in its reference to:

> The specificity of sporting activities and of sporting rules, such as separate competitions for men and women, limitations on the number of participants in competitions, the need to ensure uncertainty concerning outcomes and competitions and to preserve a competitive balance between clubs taking part if the same competitions.

If I had to identify the features essential to sport – *sine quibus non* – they would be these first that sport, like sex, requires not only the participation of at least two persons, but that, unlike most sex, the participation consists of a contest. Second – and by now the sexual analogy has truly all but exhausted itself – that contest should have an uncertain outcome. And third, that there must be a measure of relative equality between the contestants. Ordinarily competition in a pure capitalist model is intended to result in the elimination of the inefficient company or firm. But in the world of sport there must not only be plural competitors to guarantee competition, but also competitors, who are at least sufficiently viable and effective to ensure interest in the competition to the non-participant who wants to watch, listen to commentary on, or simply read about results in the newspapers. There is indeed a mutual interdependence of participants in sport. In the case already mentioned the Restrictive Practices Court stated that it was 'manifest' that competitive balance is something which makes a football competition more attractive – a concept the court earlier described as embracing the 'unpredictability of the outcome of a high proportion of the matches played within the competition and thus uncertainty about which club will win the championship' – even if nowadays the only uncertainty is which of the two Manchester clubs will win it.

As Sir Alex Ferguson, with his gift for the pithy vernacular, would say, 'Football – bloody hell'. The only certainty in football is that sometime in the season Joey Barton will be sent off – at least once.

The transatlantic decision in *US v NF League* distinguished between the desirability for professional teams to compete as hard as possible on the playing field but the undesirability of their so doing in a business context. It is, of course, the uncertainty of outcome that has made sport the most powerful magnet for the gambling industry – a parasite on sports' body – with too often insalubrious consequences when participants and their puppet masters seek means of circumscribing the area of uncertainty, as in the notorious case of the three Pakistani cricketers at the Lords Test in 2011.

The particular features of sport have led many prominent sports administrators to make a plea that sport be entirely excluded from the reach of EU law including Dr Jacques Rogge, the President of the IOC. But such was always a vain hope. As Professor Stephen Weatherill has pithily put it, 'Sport cannot have it both ways. It cannot scoop up the fruits of commercialization yet aspire to keep community law entirely at bay.' Jacques Rogge was the modern equivalent of King Canute, but with this difference: the legal waves had already submerged him before he even sought to exercise his influence to repel them.

So, the question became not whether, but to what extent, community law would affect sports rules and governance. Sport did not feature in any treaty provision until the Lisbon Treaty, where it was identified as one of the competences of the European Union, but that did not dissuade the Luxembourg judiciary from earlier intervention in the field.

Because sport is all about competition, it might have imagined that it would have been in the area of competition law that the sport first felt the law's pinch. It was not in fact so. As Lewis and Taylor observe, 'The competition rules of the EC Treaty were drafted with more orthodox industries in mind than sport. Concepts such as 'undertakings, cartels and the single market do not translate easily when applied to the sports sector.' In the *Bosman* case (1995), to which I shall inevitably return, it was only the Advocate General Lenz, and not the ECJ, who formulated its conclusions by reference to competition considerations; and it was not until *Meca Medina* a decade later (2006) that the Court said unequivocally that 'the mere fact that a rule is purely sporting in nature does not have the effect of removing from the Treaty the person engaged in the activity governed by that rule or the body which has laid it down'. And the Court made it clear too that just because rules of a purely sporting and non-economic nature might not fall within the scope of the free movement principle, *non sequitur* that they fell outside the scope of competition law too, but held, on the facts, that anti-doping regulations were, as long as the sanction was not extravagant, a proportionate response in pursuit of a legitimate objective. I should add by way of footnote to that case that the defence of the long-distance swimmers, held guilty of a doping offence in that case, was that they had ingested what Dr Anderson somewhat squeamishly refers to as a stew made of boar's meat.

More specifically, it was in fact a stew made of boar's testicles. There was actually no evidence before the CAS Panel which I chaired that the dish was on the menu the night before the competition. The defence was indeed balls.

So, what else – to revert to more decorous subjects – can justify what would otherwise be unlawful anti-competitive behaviour? There are many statements by the Commission that the benefit of solidarity through cross-subsidisation of funds from richer to poorer is a legitimate factor to take into account in a competition analysis. In the *UEFA Broadcasting Regulations* case, which concerned the acquisition of broadcasting rights to football events – broadcasting being the good parasites on sports body of sport, just as gambling is its opposite – the ECJ noted:

> The Commission recognises that a cross-subsidisation of funds from richer to poorer may help achieve this. The Commission is therefore in favour of the financial solidarity principle, which was also endorsed by the European Council declaration on sport in Nice in December 2000.

In the Commission's 'orientation document' on broadcasting rights it was expressly explained:

> Such restrictive agreements must meet the four criteria for exemption of [what is now Article 101(3) TFES]. The fulfilment of these criteria should not be based on purely commercial considerations. The special characteristics of the sport in question have to be taken into account. These could include, for example, the need to ensure 'solidarity' between weaker and stronger participants or the training of young players, which could only be achieved through redistribution of revenue from the sale of broadcasting rights

And the Commission Working Paper which accompanied the White Paper 2007, itself in an Annex, cast the net still more widely:

> When considering the criteria for possible exemption [for collective selling of rights], the characteristics of the sport must also be taken into consideration. It is often argued that it is important to take account the solidarity between the stronger and weaker economic actors or between the professional and amateur sides of the sport or that a sport is played by young people. It must also be considered how far the collective selling of rights by a sports association, when combined with a balanced distribution of the resulting revenue, can be seen as justified to promote sporting activities within the population, as well as providing for interesting sporting competitions.

In pursuit of the same sport-specific objectives in 2009, UEFA unanimously approved a financial fair play concept as part of its club licensing and financial fair play regulations, requiring football clubs to break even over a period of three years before they can, as from 2014, be granted a licence to compete in the Champions League. The European Commission has endorsed the regulation. Observing that the licensing system should respect the internal market and competition rules, they referred again to the specificity of sport in the application of EU law. The problems potentially posed to Mr Abramovich and the ruling family of Abu Dhabi need no elaboration.

Salary caps are current in rugby leagues, rugby union and basketball in England – and a contractual feature of the quartet of major professional sports in the USA – but as is notorious and obvious, not – or not yet – in professional football. They are clearly anti-competitive in that they restrict the ability of clubs to compete with each other for the best player – whether actually so like Cristiano Ronaldo or Wayne Rooney – or those optimistically thought to be so – like Alan Sugar's comic caricature overseas import Carlos Kickaball. But a plausible argument can be founded in their favour on the specificity of sport, namely that they are necessary to preserve at any rate a measure of competition balance between clubs. Money does not necessarily guarantee success in football competitions, but equally, success cannot be achieved without it: a glance at the Premier League hierarchy over the seasons of the first decade of the new century tells the tale. Until UEFA grasp the nettle, it is not a case of the Euro jury being out, as of there being no summons to jury service.

To give one last example, in *AEK Athens and SK Slavia Prague v UEFA* a challenge was made by ENIC, an investment vehicle which had stakes in a number of well-known football clubs and challenged a rule prohibiting club and a common control from playing in the same UEFA club competition, I represented ENIC. Not only for that reason, ENIC lost the case. CAS held that the rule 'appears to have the effect of preserving competitions between club owners and between football clubs rather than appreciably restricting competition of the relevant market or on other football markets'. The Commission later took the same view.

But it is not only competition law in which sport is governed by rules with a different subjacent philosophy to that which obtains in other walks of life. Employment law provides further examples and has been the soil from which many of the most famous sports law cases have sprung. In a normal industry an employee whose contract has expired is usually free, subject to any justifiable restrictive covenants to find new work with another employer. But the contradictory concept of a player as a form of chattel was deeply embedded in the field of football despite the efforts of one Herbert Kingaby to free himself in 1911 from his contract with Aston Villa. In *Eastham v Newcastle Football Club* the England inside forward – the very description is redolent of an age gone by – successfully challenged the then 'retain and transfer' system in professional football by which the rules of the then Football League permitted a club to retain a player's registration at the end of each season or otherwise seek a transfer fee for that player from another club.

The principles in *Eastham* were transplanted from football field to cricket pitch in *Greig v Insole* on an analogous but not identical context in which the South African-born England player – by no means the last of that particular genre – challenged, again successfully, the ICC/TCCB rule that any player who made himself available for Kerry Packer's World Series Cricket would be on consequence ineligible for test cricket.

The litigation spotlight switched from England to Europe in *Bosman*. This footballer, whose actual sporting achievements provided scant copy for the back pages, guaranteed himself a Pele- or Messi-type immortality by challenging the transfer rule operating in Belgium under which a player whose contract had expired with Club A, but who wished to play for Club B, could not do so unless Club B paid a transfer fee as a *sine qua non* of the player's receipt of a registration certificate to play for it. Bosman himself wanted to move from FC Liege in Belgium to FC Dunkerque in France, neither team being exactly Champions League material. UEFA, a party to the proceedings, submitted that in any application of fundamental free movement principles to professional football, a degree of flexibility would be essential because of the particular nature of the sport, in particular that sporting equilibrium would be undermined if clubs who trained and developed players could not be compensated when they moved elsewhere. The ECJ accepted the legitimacy of the objective of maintaining a competitive balance 'by preserving a certain degree of equality and uncertainty as to results', but held that the transfer regime then in place did not on the evidence promote such objective. As Dr Anderson graphically noted, Herbert Kingaby scratched at it; George Eastham cracked it; but Jean-Marc Bosman well and truly smashed the glass ceiling that restricted the employment mobility of professional football players.

I would add that Jean Louis DuPont, the players' legal representative, also acquired a quantum leap in reputation and income, enjoying as a result of his success the sobriquet 'the Bosman lawyer', rather like the James Stewart character, the brave but not sharp-shooting sheriff, acquired in the eponymous film, through a different stroke of good fortune, the description 'The Man who shot Liberty Valance'.

One consequence of *Bosman* was the production by FIFA of the Regulations on the Status and Transfer of Players. The basic position articulated in Article 13 is that the relationship of player and club is dictated by the contract between them; and while reflecting the desideratum of contractual stability in providing that no contract can be terminated during the course of a season (Article 16) otherwise permits such termination for 'just cause' (Article 14) and, more relevant, for 'sporting just cause' where an established player has appeared in fewer than a tenth of the matches in which his club has been involved during such season (Article 15).

'Sporting just cause' is not defined otherwise than by reference to the need to determine it on a case-by-case basis taking into account the player's personal circumstances. It has been held that a player has no right to be selected for a club's first team and that a player must at least indicate discontent with the lack of playing opportunities before he can rely on the defence. But while it is reasonably clear as to what sporting just cause *is not*, it is wholly obscure as to what it *is*. No player has to date succeeded in relying on it, and despite sundry rumours, that Carlos Tevez – to modernise a hoary quip, a man with more clubs than Rory McIlroy – has not yet sought to do so. In neither instance are sporting sanctions – another self-evidently sports specific concept – effectively ineligibility for matches, applied, but in the latter compensation may be payable to the affected club. Training compensation is itself a feature of football law, alien to other business spheres. As Marie Demetriou writes in her chapter in the second edition of Beloff, Kerr, Demetriou and Beloff on *Sports Law*, due out in autumn of this year, and long awaited, at any rate by the publishers, 'it is difficult to think of another context in which prospective employers are subject to financial disincentives to recruitment'. If Sainsbury's attract a trainee from Tesco (without any inducement of breach of contract being involved) it will not be expected to compensate Tesco for the education provided to that trainee.

It is in the CAS case law on Article 17, which provides for the consequences of termination without just cause, that the ghost of the argument as to whether a footballer is a chattel or a person lingers on. Article 17 bears all the hallmarks of a compromise between the two irreconcilable objectives of contractual stability and freedom of employment. Indeed, the draftsman who appeared before me in a CAS case as an advocate, by then in private practice, candidly admitted as much in response to my question. It has been said that a camel is a horse designed by a committee. Article 17 resembles nothing other than Dr Doolittle's Pushmi-Pullyu pulling simultaneously in two different directions …

I shall not recite all the factors listed as constituting the basis for calculation, but note only for present purposes that there is express reference to 'the specificity of sport'. The first of the cases which sought to construe it involved Andy Webster, a Scottish international, who broke his contract with Heart of Midlothian to move to Wigan FC. Hearts claimed a sum of four and a half million pounds, said to represent his market value. A CAS panel, of which I was a member, awarded only £150,000, representing the residual remuneration value of his contract. I betray no confidences in admitting what is apparent on the face of the record, that the Panel's perspective was that there was no justification in treating a footballer differently from another employee, or indirectly sterilising his ability to switch clubs by attaching too high a price tag to such a move.

At a later BASL conference at the Emirates, I was congratulated by Gordon Taylor of the PFA but berated by Maurice Watkins of Manchester United for the award. The *Webster* decision was also roundly criticised as 'very damaging for football and a Phyrric victory for those players and their agents who toy with the idea of rescinding contracts before they have been fulfilled. CAS did not properly take into consideration the specificity of sport' – a criticism which might have been more painful to the panel, had it not fallen from the lips of none other than Sepp Blatter. Nonetheless, subsequent CAS panels have effectively overruled, with courtesy if not comity, the *Webster* case; and in *Matuzelem* – in broad terms – adopted a market value test.

Sport is of course on the radar of European law only to the extent that it is an economic activity: so that as early as *Walrave-Koch v UCI* it was recognised that there was an extension to the principle of free movement in matters such as 'the composition of sports teams, in particular national teams, the formation of which is a question of purely sporting interest, and as such has nothing to do with economic activity'. It would evidently make no sense for a match to be billed as between France and England if all the players playing for France were English and vice-versa.

But at a level below that it is less obvious why there should be any quota of home-grown players for clubs in a particular national league; and none such presently exist. Arsenal have, from time to time, fielded teams without a single English player, let alone one from Highbury or Islington. *Bosman* itself rejected UEFA's contrary arguments based on such factors as the need to enhance the pool for national teams: and the various formulae of 3 + 2 (UEFA) or 6 + 5 (FIFA), which are different in a way which it does not need a Stephen Hawking to unravel, are seeking to bypass the principle that there can be no discrimination of grounds on nationality, direct or indirect. The Commission has so far accepted the more nuanced UEFA rule that clubs participating in their competition must have a minimum of home-grown players in their squad; but the Commission's indulgence is not the law. *La luta continua*.

Both the criminal law and the law of tort illustrate the exceptionality of sport. The general rule is that a person can consent to common assault, where no injury has been caused, but not to the application of the force which causes him actual bodily harm or worse. If such a rule were applied to sport, much sport would not exist. So, the rule is necessarily modified so as to avoid that unthinkable conclusion. A doctrine of implied sporting consent was introduced in a trilogy of late Victorian cases.

But how far does consent go?

In *R v Barnes* the question was whether a footballer should be convicted under section 20 of the OAPA for a tackle causing senior injury to an opponent's leg and ankle. The Court of Appeal identified a number of factors which determined, within the sporting context, the acceptability or otherwise of a player's conduct, which would have no purchase in off-field deliberate aggressive bodily contact: 'The type of sport, the level at which it is played, the nature of the act, the degree of force used, the extent of the injury, the state of mind of the defendant.'

Still more remarkable is the immunity of professional boxing from the scope of the criminal law since that sport is defined by the deliberate infliction of injury (*pace* the Queensberry rules) on another. Small wonder that a judge of the intellectual distinction of Lord Mustill was reduced to saying of an Australian judgment:

> The heroic efforts of that learned judge to arrive at an intellectually satisfying account of the apparent immunity of professional boxing from the criminal process have convinced me that the task is impossible. It is in my judgment best to regard this as another special situation which, for the time being, stands outside the ordinary law of violence.

The fact that the appeal was concerned with sado-masochistic activities of a kind too exotic to detail gratuitously in a public lecture, and so Lord Mustill's observations were strictly obiter, does not detract from their acuity.

The special relationship of sport and the criminal law was excellently summarised in a Canadian case:

> The playing field is not a criminal law free zone. The laws of the land apply in the same way as they do elsewhere. The legal analysis of whether a crime has been committed on the playing field is the same as it is on the street, though contact sport presents a unique factual context of that analysis.

Edward's ghost would applaud the first part of that analysis. He wrote eloquently of the 'corruption inherent in the bastard expression "professional foul"' and noted correctly that 'what has been called a professional foul in the past is in reality an actionable criminal and civil assault'.

The civil imitates in this sphere the criminal law. The case law when a participant in a sport owes or breaches a duty of care to another (and who that other is) is not entirely coherent – and this is not the time or place to attempt a reconciliation – but a common thread, uniting all the major judgments, is that the sporting context (and the dangers inherent in it) mean that the threshold for liability is higher that it would be off pitch or off piste. As Judge LJ (as he then was) put it in *Caldwell v Maguire* – a case in which our National Hunt Jockey claimed damages for injury sustained as a result of alleged careless riding:

> In the context of sporting contests, it is also right to emphasise the distinction to be drawn between conduct which is properly to be characterised as negligent, and thus sounding in damages, and errors of judgment, oversights or lapses of attention of which any reasonable jockey may be guilty in the hurly burly of a race.

So it's a case of legal horses for courses.

Sex discrimination provides a further illustration of sports specificity, here not only carving out an exception to general rules of law but subverting them entirely. It is axiomatic that the underlying principle of modern anti-discrimination legislation is equality of treatment between the sexes. Yet the Equality Act 2010, section 195, building on section 44 of the Sex Discrimination Act 1975, institutionalises such discrimination in competitive sport, making only modification of the earlier law by subsection 5, which states that whether a sport is a gender affected activity – the touchstone of segregation – 'it is appropriate to take into account of the age and stage of development of children who are likely to be competitors'. Lord Denning, once in a case concerning a claim for equal pay with her male equivalent brought by a woman counter-hand in a betting shop in a rough area, pointed out that certain physical and mental qualities are not merely the prerogative of one sex or another: 'He may have been a small, nervous man who could not say "boo" to a goose. She may have been as fierce and formidable as a battle axe.'

In the sphere of equal pay, what was sauce for the gander proved also to be sauce for the goose. But if a woman cannot play in a man's team, the question of equal pay will not arise. Matthew Syed, an acute commentator on matters sporting, recently observed that, so deeply ingrained is sex discrimination in sport that separate competitions continue to be organised for men and women, even in table sports such as snooker or billiards, where there is no obvious basis for suggesting that it would be unfair, because of physiology, to unite them.

The importance attached to separate competitions for men and women in sports, which, unlike equestrianism, the activity is 'gender affected' is exemplified by the sad case of Caster Semenya, winner of the gold medal for the 800m in the World Athletics Championships in Berlin in 2009. She was said to have characteristics more masculine than feminine – to be in short, an 'intersex' person. In consequence, the IAAF has adopted sophisticated rules, to which I gave input at a conference held in Vidy in 2010, to identify those eligible to compete in women-only competitions based on their quantum of hyper-androgens – an improvement on the sex tests of decades gone by where aspirants to women's competition when gender was in doubt had their unclothed bodies subjected to a visual examination – something that may have been appropriate for putative stars of pornographic movies, but not for elite sportspersons.

The law against disability discrimination has equally to take account of sport's specificity.

The definition of disability under the Equality Act 2010 is that an individual has a physical or mental impairment that has a substantial and long-term adverse effect on the individual's ability to carry out normal day-to-day activities.

It is self-evident that, save exceptionally, such impairment will affect the individual's capacity. The escape hatch for employees of sportsmen and women, or those who provide sporting facilities, lies in the restricted definition of 'normal day-to-day activities' which the government guidance suggests does not include playing sport – a somewhat dispiriting approach for those who consider that sport is – or should be – a part of everyday life.

Of course, in the same way as there are women-only competitions, so too are there competitions for the physically or mentally impaired – of which the Paralympics are the pinnacle. And the question whether it ought to be possible for a disabled sportsperson to cross the boundary to participate in open competition has been given focus by the case of Oscar Pistorius – the blade runner – who compensated for his disability by artificial limbs. Ordinarily there is no problem: the use of prosthetics (or wheelchairs) is the very badge of Paralympic sport.

The controversy over whether this gave him an advantage over able-bodied competition or merely reduced his disadvantage was laid to rest in his case by the CAS decision which, however, the panel stressed was based on the then available evidence.

On any view Mr Pistorius is a remarkable athlete and I suspect that no rival, domestic or international, would be minded to renew the challenge to his participation in the Olympics, which is not to say that such a challenge, if brought, might not, on the basis of the most recent research, succeed.

No less complexity attends the relationship of sport and age discrimination. Under the Equality Act 2010 direct discrimination occurs (section 13(1) where a person (A) discriminates against another (B)) if, because of a protected characteristic, A treats B less favourably than A treats or would treat others.

But where the protected characteristic *is* age, A does not discriminate against another (B) in circumstances within the scope of the Act if A can show A's treatment of B to be a proportionate means of achieving a legitimate aim (section 13(2)).

Two sections of the Act (employment) potentially bear on sport and issues such as team selection. Under section 29 of the 2010 Act a service provider (A) (which includes a provider of facilities – section 31(2)) must not discriminate against a person (B) as to the terms on which A provides a service to B, or by subjecting B to any other detriment.

Under Part 7 of the Act concerned with associations (which would cover clubs or regulators), an association must not discriminate against a member, potential member or associate in the way it affords him access to a benefit or facility or subjects him to any other detriment (section 101(3)(a) and (d)).

Neither section 29 nor section 101 have yet to be fully bought into effect in respect of age discrimination. In the Consultation Paper preceding the Act, the Government explained:

> Age limits or age bands are currently used in sporting events where it is necessary to secure fair competition, or the safety of competitors. We proposed to include an exception to ensure this practice can continue. The benefits of allowing an exception for age-restricted sports competitions are as follows:
>
> - It enshrines the principles of fair competition – for many sports, success in competition is dependent upon the size, weight, strength, flexibility, dexterity, stamina or experience of the competitor. Taking account of a person's age is important therefore in ensuring that a player does not gain an unfair advantage, as this would contradict the ethics of sport and fair play.
> - It promotes safe competition – there are notable links between injury rates and the age of competitors. In response to this, some sports impose minimum age requirements to protect young athletes. For example, gymnastics,[89] weightlifting and contact sports competitions.
> - The approach is in line with international practice – taking account of the age of a competitor is often necessary in order to comply with rules determined at an international level or by international sports governing bodies. For example, there are many different age requirements for sport at international level, such as under 21 football tournaments.

How this exception will be formulated is for the future.

Sports regulation has itself other notable distinctive features. The concept of sporting nationality is distinct from that of nationality in the legal sense, a topic of increasing importance as sporting mercenaries sell their talents to the highest bidder. And sporting bodies and sporting competitions do not align themselves with conventional political or geographical boundaries: words which bear one meaning in ordinary legal instruments may bear another in instruments governing sport. Israel is a member of UEFA for the purposes of its transfer regulations. Similarly, FC Monaco is treated as if it were a French club. Taiwan, as Lord Denning decided in *Reel v Holder*, was a separate country for the purposes of the IAAF rules, a decision which prompted Primo Nebiolo, the President, to move the domicile of the Federation from England to Monte Carlo, where the legal (not to speak of the meteorological) climate was more benign. And, at odds with its usual desire to multiply its membership, the IOC changed its criteria for becoming an NOC with the apparent objective of ensuring that the Gibraltar NOC (GOC) was ineligible, a change whose retrospective application is currently being challenged by the GOC in the Swiss courts.

One feature which certainly differentiates sport from other industries is its developed pattern of global regulation with bodies such as FIFA, the IAAF, FINA and FIA exercising worldwide control over their particular sports, as well as the IOC whose control, because of the intermittent nature of its quadrennial competition, enjoys less width because of the Olympics' special nature, but greater depth. WADA recently and successfully, praying in aid advice I gave them, locked horns with the BOA over the latter's lifetime ban on Olympic participation for so-called drugs cheats. The very issue at stake was not whether the WADA rule was an adequate response to doping offences on which, with all due respect to Lord Moynihan, views may legitimately differ, but whether a harmonised code allowed of any exceptions for the state signatories. The CAS held that it did not.

The case is only one of many which reminds us that sport has too, what is in nature, if not in name, in CAS a world court with a jurisdiction more far-reaching in its areas than the ICJ or ICC, with new outposts in Shanghai, Kuala Lumpur, Cairo and Abu Dhabi supplementing those already established in Sydney and New York.

CAS has created and developed a number of specialist doctrines and principles which can have application only in a sporting context – the so-called *lex sportiva* – or for classical purists *lex ludica*:

- The field of play doctrine which seeks to limit interference with an official's decisions.
- The concept of comfortable satisfaction as the standard of proof for sporting disciplinary offences.
- The strict liability rule in relation to doping violations.
- The bias towards eligibility.

The essence of the field of play doctrine is that it is for sporting bodies, via their appropriate officials, to take decisions relevant to the conduct of particular events. They only lose their immunity from review by CAS in circumstances of arbitrariness and bad faith (meaning fraud, corruption or malice), or some equivalent vice.

The doctrine protects even the technology whose use to determine whether a ball was in or out in tennis, a batsman was or was not out LBW, whether a try has or has not been scored is a notable ingredient in modern professional sport, building on the more conventional use of photographic evidence to determine who – human or horse – crossed the line first. And it is necessary there, as well, for though the camera may not lie, it can be economical with the truth.

But the principled as distinct from the pragmatic basis for the doctrine is by no means clear.

In *Yang Tae-young*, in the men's all-round gymnastics final – the blue ribbon of the sport – the official admittedly undermarked the Korean's performance on the fourth apparatus out of view, which relegated him at the end of the competition to the silver medal position. The panel, which I chaired, determined that the complaint of mismarking should have been taken to the jury of appeal and said that it would not itself interfere with an official's decision just because he had made a mistake.

We reasoned:

> While in this instance we are being asked not to second guess an official but rather to consider the consequences of an admitted error by an official so that the 'field of play' jurisprudence is not directly engaged, we consider that we should nonetheless abstain from correcting the results by reliance of an admitted error. An error identified with the benefit of hindsight, whether admitted or not, cannot be a ground by reversing a result of a competition. We can all recall occasions where a video replay of a football match, studied at leisure, can show that a goal was given, when it should have been disallowed (the Germans may still hold that view about England's critical third goal in the World Cup Final in 1966), or vice versa or where in a tennis match a critical line was mistaken. However, quite apart from the consideration, which we develop below, that no one can be certain how the competition in question would have turned out had the official's decision been different, for a Court to change the result would on this basis still involve interfering with a field of play decision. Each sport would on this basis involve interfering with a field of play decision. Each sport may have within it a mechanism for utilising modern technology to ensure a correct decision is made in the first place (e.g. cricket with run-outs) or for immediately subjecting a controversial decision to a process of review (e.g. gymnastics); but the solution for error, either way, lies within the framework of the sport's own rules; it does not licence judicial or arbitral interference thereafter. If this represents an extension of the field of play doctrine, we tolerate it with equanimity. *Finality is in the area all important; rough justice may be all that sport can tolerate.*

The common law recognises only two standards of proof beyond reasonable doubt for criminal cases, and balance of probabilities for civil cases. The elusive notion that there was a sliding standard depending upon the nature of the issue had been discarded. It was said by no lesser a jurist than Lord Hoffmann that when the test of balance of probabilities is engaged, it may be more difficult to establish that the animal seen in the park was a lion than a dog, but does not mean that the test itself is different. However CAS has indeed invented a third concept – that of comfortable satisfaction – which lies at some point between the two conventional standards and, in my view, aptly reflects the fact that disciplinary proceedings also occupy different legal territory to criminal proceedings on the one hand, and civil proceedings on the other; they are less serious than the former, but more serious than the latter.

Fundamental to the idea of fairness to sportsmen and honesty of results is the strict liability rule in doping offences, in which even inadvertent absorption of banned substances is penalised. It is no defence to an athlete to claim that he was the victim of mislabelling, contaminated stock or faulty advice.

As was said in *Quigley v UIT* (a case about a disqualified marksman):

> The vicissitudes of competition, like those of life generally, may create many types of unfairnesses, whether by accident or the negligence of unaccountable persons, which the law cannot repair ... It appears to be a laudable policy objective not to repair an accidental unfairness to an individual by creating an intentional unfairness to the whole body of other competitors.

In this instance, the interests of the many have to be preferred to the interests of the one.

There are further purely practical considerations. To prove guilty intent would be difficult when all the key facts were known to the athlete only. To prove actual enhancement of performance would necessitate of expert evidence. Litigation in which *mens rea* or efficacy was an issue would be damaging to finality of results and destructive of the budgets of many sports bodies.

Principled objections founded on such positive concepts as the presumption of innocence, natural justice and right to work, and such negative ones such as restraint of trade or anti-competitive practice, have proved insufficient to undermine the rule.

But the rigours of the strict rule are tempered by a number of considerations.

First CAS, has demanded that a strict liability standard must be clearly articulated. In *Quigley* CAS said:

> The fight against doping is arduous and it may require strict rules. But the rule makes, and rule appliers must begin by being strict with themselves. Regulations that may affect the careers of dedicated athletes must be predictable. They must emanate from duly authorised bodies. They must be adopted in constitutionally proper ways. They should not be the product of an obscure process of accreditation. Athletes and officials should not be confronted with a thicket of mutually qualifying or even contradictory rules that can be understood only on the basis of de facto practice over the course of many years of a small group of insiders.

Second, a bright line has been drawn between the sanctions relevant to the competition in which the athlete is proved to have had the presumed benefit of drugs and those relevant to the athlete's long-term future. In respect of the latter, all circumstances may be taken into account, and here the degree of fault, if any, of the athletes, comes into critical focus.

A highly controversial disqualification at the Sydney Olympics was that of the teenage Romanian gymnast Răducan, who underwent a doping test after the event on 21 September 2000, which revealed the presence of pseudoephedrine. The IOC Executive Board decided to disqualify her from the women's individual all-round event and to withdraw her gold medal.

The panel said:

> The anti-doping code considers doping as a strict liability offence. This means that no intentional element is required to establish a doping offence. The mere presence of the forbidden substance in the urine sample is sufficient.
>
> It supports the strict consequence of an automatic disqualification – severe as it may be in that it affects the gold medal winner – in a matter of fairness to all other athletes.
>
> This is why factors such as the athlete's age (she was 17 on September 30), her weight, the need for medication (there were other medicines available, as well as procedures to be followed, where medication with a banned substance is required for health reasons), the fact the drug may not have enhanced the performance, and the gymnast's reliance on the team's doctor were all held irrelevant. *Such matters were, however, taken into account in not imposing a sanction beyond disqualification.*

A constant theme of CAS decisions is that, whenever possible, rules should be interpreted in a way which enables athletes to compete. In a recent appeal before the SDRP in which I represented the British women rhythmic gymnastics team and persuaded the arbitrator that British Gymnastics had wrongly interpreted their selection policy to bar the team from participating in London 2012, I was able to pray in aid certain basic principles of CAS case law:

- First, an athlete has the right to know the criteria which he or she must meet in order to qualify for the Olympic Games.
- Second, selection criteria should be as objective as possible.
- Third, selection criteria should be clear and not require oral elucidation.
- Fourth, where selection criteria are objective, eg points in a given competition, they must be adhered to. There is no residual scope for subjectivity.
- Fifth, any alteration to selection rules must be timeously announced and properly communicated to those whom it *affects*.

At the same time, CAS has stated that:

> It fully endorses the objective of preserving a link between national team competitions and national terms, and the avoidance of a situation in which national terms are substantially or wholly composed of sporting mercenaries acquiring belatedly nationalities of convenience.

Again, relocation to another country in pursuit of personal objectives is unobjectionable, even admirable, in most areas of activity; but, once again, sport is different. We have surely not heard the last of the argument about so-called Plastic Brits.

There are other eccentric but particular features of sport which I will mention by way of epilogue. Sporting celebrities, in particular footballers and even some football managers, appear to enjoy, if not a modern equivalent of sovereign immunity from the criminal process, at least the benefit of a standard of proof which embraces not only reasonable, but quite unreasonable doubt, so that not only unsolicited admissions or unblemished CCTV evidence is insufficient to inculpate. In the civil sphere their agreements are often treated not as a source of binding obligation but as a mere bargaining chip to be deployed in further negotiation. Sam Goldwyn, the Hollywood producer, once said that 'oral contracts aren't worth the paper they are not written on'; but the same is sometimes true today even of sportsmen and women's written contracts. When a manager wails that his star strike is under contract till 2015, one knows that the player will be on the move within weeks to another more prosperous or generous club.

Sport, or more precisely, football is the only walk of life which contemplates banning orders for supporters. Who ever heard, even thought, of a legislatively sourced banning order for opera-goers or even members of a pop concert audience?

Professions are meant to be distinguished from other businesses or trades by their particular code of moral values; yet in sport the concept of 'professional foul' inverts such notions of morality and cheating, which should be met with ostracism, or at any rate, opposition, and is part of the *règles du jeu*, the unwritten rules of the competition.

In sport uniquely, people take drugs not to get high but to run fast. So, sport has developed a parallel code of sanctions for drug abuse to those reflected on the public law of the land.

Edward, with his alas anachronistic attachment to a Corinthian philosophy of sport, nourished by the amateur game, would have deplored – indeed in his lifetime did deplore – many of these developments; but he would also have recognised that it is many of the less disreputable aspects of the specificity of sport, which gives an organisation such as BASL its *raison d'être*. After all, if sport – and in consequence the law appropriate to it – were *not* different, where would we all be?

# 15

# *'Is there a* Lex Sportiva?' Lecture at Max Planck Institute, Hamburg 2012*

THE QUESTION I pose in my title deserves the description of a hardy perennial. Whether there is such a coherent entity as sports law or whether sports law is only a mosaic randomly aggregated from a variety of what are accepted to be discrete legal areas – contract, tort, intellectual property, administrative – is the subject of constant debate.

The question is not purely academic – an epithet which cynics tend to apply to an issue of no practical significance. Those who contend for the former proposition do so partly out of a desire to enhance the status of the subject, which is not to say that those who contend for the latter proposition have any motive to diminish it. But the proponents clearly adopt the Latin phraseology to endow the subject with a spurious antiquity – sometimes using the alternative term *lex ludica*, although that carries with it in mistranslation unhappy overtones of ludicrousness. But the answer to the question, one 'not of huge importance', as two Irish commentators have recently written – but not, in my respectful English submission, of no importance – is probably, and it may be a little disappointingly – a bit of both. As an American scholar has opined:

> A fully developed lex sportiva would help apply three values that the principle of stare decisis serves: efficiency of the legal process, predictability or stability of expectations: and equal treatment of similarly situated parties.

Sports law has certainly adopted the clothing of a recognised discipline. There are many books on sports law – including, if I may venture an early commercial break – my own, co-authored with Tim Kerr and Marie Demetriou. Their titles prove conclusively there are many ways to skin a cat – *Sports Law*, *The Law of Sport*, *Sport and the Law*, and – *jeux* being notoriously *sans frontières* – *European Sports Law* and even *International Sports Law*. Can *Sports Law in Space* be far behind?

* RCR Siekmann and J Soek (eds), *Lex Sportiva: What is Sports Law?* (Springer Nature, 2012) 69–89.

There are, especially in the United States of America, courses, with consequent degrees, in sports law where potential agents learn the rudiments of legal principles which in real life they will conveniently ignore, or those who plan to play sports professionally can find there an excuse for attendance at university at all. More importantly, there are sports-specific tribunals, at the pinnacle of which stands the Court of Arbitration for Sport in Lausanne, to whose jurisdiction now all major international sports federations subscribe, and which is the main, but not the only, source of sporting jurisprudence. CAS appears itself to recognise the special nature of sports law by requiring of its members, among other qualities, 'recognised competence with regard to sports law' – something sufficient but not necessary since it continues, 'and/or international arbitration' (S14 CAS Code 2004). But the Swiss Federal Court has recently described it as a 'true' Supreme Court of world sport and while that same Court can review CAS's decisions, it does so within strict limits reminiscent of those recognised by common law courts reviewing the exercise of an administrative discretion.

A special feature of CAS service lies in its provision of Ad Hoc Panels, a mobile legal unit (now a fixture at Olympic and Commonwealth Games and at the European Football cup), whose decisions have to be handed down within 24 hours of an application being filed. As the Swiss Federal Court observed:

> In competitive sport, particularly the Olympic Games, it is vital both for athletes and for the smooth running of events that disputes are resolved quickly, simply, flexibly and inexpensively by experts familiar with both legal and sports related issues.

Many tribunals have to act swiftly and reach interlocutory decisions: the ad hoc panel has to act swiftly and reach final decisions. Their accelerated judicial process may be likened to speed chess – but speed chess is still chess.

Of course, sports law is entwined with general law. Sportsmen enter into contracts, since few are the sports which remain faithful to their origins as a source of fun, not fees, although their contracts will naturally reflect the distinctive features of their occupation. They are subject to the law of tort as well as the criminal law both on and off the pitch, pool, rink, track or court, although both laws have to adjust to the fact that many sports are contact sports – and in most there is at least a risk of contact – and fashion the boundaries of what is or is not acceptable behaviour in its light.

Boxing is, indeed, a sport in which the very purpose is to inflict injury upon another; and in a scholarly analysis travelling somewhat off-piste – since the case itself involved the compatibility of prosecutions for sado-masochistic activity with human rights principles – Lord Mustill, an English Law Lord, confessed himself defeated in search for an explanation of boxing's legitimacy.

Sportsmen enjoy intellectual property rights, and sports has inspired some creative development of the law in this area – more on the other than on this side of the Atlantic.

The English Sex Discrimination Act 1975, section 44 has an exception for competitive sport, and the English Gender Recognition Act 2004, section 19 has one for transsexuals – the female of the species being adjudged at any rate in the field of play to be – notwithstanding the contrary view of the imperial poet Rudyard Kipling – less deadly than the male.

Yet a further indication of the sensitivity of ordinary law to the peculiarities of sport is the line drawn between sporting and economic activity by the European Union so as to take various sports rules beyond the reach of the pro-competition and freedom of movement provisions of EU law.

The key test is that the rule in question must be 'of a sporting interest only', so, for example, it embraces restriction on the selection for national teams to nationals, but certainly does not require the selection for local teams to local players only. The galácticos of Real Madrid came from many countries; and two of the major English Premier's League football clubs have recently fielded teams bereft of a single Englishman!

Moreover, words which bear one meaning in ordinary legal instruments may bear another in instruments governing sport.

Was Taiwan 'a country' for the purposes of the IAAF rules? *Reel v Holder.*

Was Monaco in the European Union for the purposes of UEFA rules? *Celtic v UEFA.*

Does change of nationality include becoming stateless in the Olympic Charter? *Perez (No 2).*

Was Israel in Europe for the purpose of FIFA football transfer regulations? *Hapoel v Santander.*

What was meant by domicile in the Commonwealth Games Rules? *Cowley v Healey.*

A distinction is conventionally drawn between legal nationality and sporting nationality, a topic of increasing importance as sporting mercenaries sell their talents to the highest bidder.

Sports law frequently has no necessary legislative base – in the United Kingdom it is substantially untouched by statute. This is not because *ratione naturae* it repels legislation – in other countries, for example Malaysia, sport is heavily regulated by statute; France has the French Act on Sports of 16 July 1984, the USA has the Amateur Sports Act – but rather because it enjoys an international substructure; at the pinnacle is the Olympic Charter and the rules and regulations of the major international sports bodies – FIFA, the IAAF, FIA and the like – under whose ultimate authority regional and local bodies operate in a complex pyramid of interlinked regulations. The WADA Code 2004 is further evidence of sports law's globalisation.

In my *Sports Law* book, my co-authors and I propounded a distinction between horizontal law – a body of rules which applied across the range of relevant human activity – and vertical law – which was an activity driven body of rules. Torts or trusts falls into the former category. Sports law, like aviation or banking law, falls substantially into the latter. But that does not mean that sports law is in any sense devoid of principled foundations.

The formula used for the CAS Ad Hoc Panels at successive Summer Olympics (Atlanta, Sydney, Athens), Winter Olympics (Nagano and Salt Lake City),

Commonwealth Games (Kuala Lumpur and Manchester) reflected this character. It directed the tribunal to complement its application of relevant regulations with the 'general principles of law and the rules of law, the application of which it deems appropriate'.

In locating these principles and rules, *Sports Law* borrows, magpie-like, from private law as well as public, appropriately mixing Latinisms with French phrases, civilian and common law concepts. It is my personal observation, based on experience of five Ad Hoc Panels with arbitrators from every region and every legal background, that concepts of justice are, at any rate to ethical lawyers, shared across the globe.

In substantive law, freedom of contract, *pacta sunt servanda*, *force majeure*, *clausula rebus sic stantibus*, good faith, *venire contra factum proprium*, or estoppel, *ultra vires*, the protection of legitimate expectations, all feature. Ancillary to substantive law are interpretative guides such as *in dubio contra proferentem*, *nulla crimen*, *nulla poena sine lege*, the presumption against retroactive punishment, the *lex mitior*, the prohibition on double jeopardy, equal treatment, proportionality. Purpose is more important than letter – although letter remains the best indication of purpose.

This recognition of the international nature of sport finally influenced the shape of the new CAS code, effective from 1 January 2004, which, while leaving Swiss law as the national law to be enforced, absent agreement of parties to another system, for first instance cases (R45), has now permitted – in echo of the Ad Hoc Panel's jurisdiction – in appellate cases resort to 'the rules of law, the application of which the panel deems appropriate' as an alternative to the relevant regulations, the law chosen by the parties, or the domicile of the decision-maker (usually Switzerland) (R58).

But this quilt of principles is not of itself a *lex sportiva*, which is less the deployment of recognised principles of law in a sporting context (suitably modified) than principles which have their primary function in that context.

In speaking of a *lex sportiva*, it is useful to bear in mind the law whose description it echoes – the *lex mercatoria*, recently described in the English Commercial Court as the 'general law of merchants a law to which some international tribunals have regard … but … not the law of a country which is capable of ascertainment by expert evidence from practitioners in the country' and which governs 'the substantive rights and duties of parties to certain types of international transactions to the exclusion of substantive law'.

These elements are visible in the less mature sporting analogue.

In *AEK Athens v UEFA*, which concerned a rule prohibiting multi-ownership of clubs in the same competition, the Panel observed:

> Sports Law has developed and consolidated along the years, particularly through the arbitral resolution of disputes, a set of unwritten legal principles – a sort of lex mercatoria for sports, or, so to speak, a lex ludica – to which national and international sport federations must conform, regardless of the presence of such principles within their own statutes and regulations or within any applicable national law,

> provided they do not conflict with any national 'public policy' (ordre publique) provision applicable to a given case.

Some of the sinews of a *lex sportiva* are the constituent instruments of the sports themselves. These play various roles: regulating the allocation of powers within the sports governing bodies; rules regulating competitions; rules regulating the playing of the game itself. All of these are in principle justiciable, but judicial or arbitral self-restraint shows that in practice so-called game rules are not.

For at the heart of the *lex sportiva* lies a paradox, namely that one of its key objectives is to immunise sport from the reach of the law; to create in other words a field of autonomy within which even appellate sports tribunals should not trespass. The referee, umpire or other match or competition official must be allowed free play within his own jurisdiction. And he must be free to err, subject only to any corrective mechanism contemplated by the rules themselves. Sports law in short recognises subsidiarity.

In *Yang v Hamm*, a post-*Athens* Panel had to decide whether to reallocate the medals in the men's gymnastics all-round final when the bronze medallist had been a victim of erroneous marking by the judges as to the difficulty of his parallel bars exercise. It summarised the state of the art in this way, stating:

> The extent to which, if at all, a Court including CAS can interfere with an official's decision is not wholly clear. An absolute refusal to recognise such a decision as justiciable and to designate the field of play as 'a domain into which the King's writ does not seek to run' in Lord Atkin's famous phrase would have a defensible purpose and philosophy. It would recognise that there are areas of human activity which elude the grasp of the law, and where the solution to disputes is better found, if at all, by agreement. It would contribute to finality. It would uphold, critically, the authority of the umpire, judge or referee, whose power to control competition, already eroded by the growing use of technology such as video replays, would be fatally undermined if every decision taken could be judicially reviewed. And, to the extent that the matter is capable of analysis in conventional legal terms, it could rest on the premise that any contract that the player has made in entering into competition is that he or she should have the benefit of honest 'field of play' decisions, not necessarily correct ones.

It went on to say, however, 'Sports law does not, have a policy of complete abstention', and referred to earlier decisions, *Segura/IAAF*, where the challenge was to a referee's decision that a walker had 'lifted' contrary to the rules of walking, and *Korean Olympic Committee (KOC) v International Skating Union (ISU)*, where the challenge was to the disqualification of a Korean skater, Kim Dung-sung, in the final of the men's 1,500 metre short track skating event, and the Panel expressly characterised the approach as one of self-restraint, not absence of jurisdiction. Abstention is justified for a variety of reasons: arbitrator's lack of expertise in the technical side of sport; the inevitable element of subjectivity, resulting in part from different physical perspectives, in judging, for example, whether a tennis ball was in or out; the fear of constant interruption to the course of play; the opening of floodgates; the problems of rewriting a result after the event.

The qualified immunity of field of play rule from quasi-judicial review has been extrapolated to challenges to the efficacy of the accuracy of technical equipment. In the Sydney Olympics the Bulgarian rower Neykova finished second in the women's single sculls in the time of 7.28.783 behind Ekaterina Karsten, who finished in the time of 7.28.741 and requested the Ad Hoc Division to allocate gold medals to both athletes, on the basis that the photo-finish was not accurate. Her reliance on a video of the race produced by a commercial television channel which appeared to contradict the assessment of the photo-finish produced by the 'officials' Swatch failed.

And in *Hamm v Yang* the immunity was extended even to the admitted judging error. The Panel said:

> An error identified with the benefit of hindsight, whether admitted or not, cannot be a ground for reversing a result of a competition. … Each sport may have within it a mechanism for utilising modern technology to ensure a correct decision is made in the first place (e.g. cricket with run-outs) or for immediately subjecting a controversial decision to a process of review (e.g. gymnastics) but the solution for error, either way, lies within the framework of the sport's own rules; it does not licence judicial or arbitral interference thereafter. If this represents an extension of the field of play doctrine, we tolerate it with equanimity. Finality is in this area all important: rough justice may be all that sport can tolerate.

Sports courts or sports tribunals may interfere if an official's field of play decision is tainted by fraud. As Lord Denning, who has strong claims to be the England's outstanding judge of the last century, once said with characteristic pithiness, 'Fraud unravels everything'. They can also interfere if such decision is tainted by arbitrariness or corruption. It is not so much that there is a presumption of regularity as that there is a bias in favour of a result already reached.

So, game rules are not a species of sub- or non-law, or even what Michael Reisman has called micro-law. They are justiciable, but sports bodies will exercise circumspection in the exercise of judging. Referees or umpires must, however, apply game rules and not ignore them since 'a deviation from a mandatory game rule undermines the utility of the rule, and, moreover, may affect the outcome of the game or tournament'. In one case, having decided that, as a matter of construction of the IPC rules, the starter is the sole judge of whether a race shall be stopped when there has been a collision within 200 metres of the start, ruled that whether he stops a race in those circumstances is entirely a matter for him.

The boundary between game rules and legal rules is well recognised, even if its lines are sometimes blurred. A CAS Panel said:

> 'The Rules of the Game' (sometimes also called 'Technical Rules') are the rules which are intended to ensure the correct course of the game and competition respectively. The application of such rules cannot, save in very exceptional circumstances, lead to any 'judicial review'. The 'rules of law' are of a different nature. They are proper statutory sanctions that can affect the judicial interests of the person upon whom a

sanction has been imposed other than in the course of the game or competition. For this reason they have to be subject to judicial review.

But even where rules of law *stricto sensu* are engaged, the concept of subsidiarity is potent. Common law courts provide numerous illustrations of the reticence of courts to interfere with the decisions of sports regulators which turn on discretion, appreciation, or even construction of their own rules or decisions as to satisfaction of the criteria for a licence to participate in a particular sport on eligibility for particular competitions.

In *Cowley v Heatley*, Browne-Wilkinson VC said, 'sport would be better served if there was not running litigation at repeated intervals by people seeking to challenge the decisions of the regulating bodies'. Render under sports the things that are sports and to courts the things that are legal.

Subsidiarity in procedure is linked to finality in substance, another reflection of which is found in time limits.

In the matter of time limits the *lex sportiva* adopts an attitude more akin to that of the common law than of equity, taking the strict approach of the former rather than the flexible approach of the latter. Sir John Romilly once stated, 'At law time is always of the essence of the contract …'; by contrast, 'The Court of equity was accustomed to relieve against a failure to keep the date assigned … if it could do justice between the parties.'

The logic is impeccable. Absent a strict reliance on time limits, there is anarchy. A professional football game lasts – extra time apart – for 90 minutes: it is, in the classic tautological cliché of the football manager, 'a game of two halves'. If anyone doubts the importance of adhering to that rule, they need only listen to the fans of a football side which holds a narrow lead as, by a crescendo of oral whistling, they seek to persuade the referee to use his own mechanical whistle to bring the game to an end.

A count in professional boxing is meant to last 10 seconds; a boxer who is knocked down for longer than that is deemed to be knocked out. One of the most famous of sporting controversies concerns the long count which Gene Tunney was allowed as he sought – in the event unsuccessfully – to recover from a punch thrown by the redoubtable Manassa Mauler, Jack Dempsey. The indulgence of the referee on that occasion undoubtedly, in the views of most experts, cost Dempsey the fight and with it the title of World Heavyweight Champion.

This emphasis on the importance of the adherence to time limits (and scheduled dates) can be found in many situations. One concerned the refusal of a Turkish club for perceived security reasons to play against an Israeli club in Israel, where CAS held, 'The obligation to appear and compete at the dates and in the venue indicated in the calendar is 'the most basic obligation in the sporting system.'

(UEFA were in another case held entitled to refuse to allow players who had registered late to play in the UEFA Cup.) Even in the arcane game of one-day cricket – a sport which in its more protracted version used to be dubbed the Englishman's version of eternity, the significance of the so-called over rate – has been stressed not only for 'the orderly management of the game and its administration', but also because of its impact on television and publishing throughout the world.

The CAS Athens jurisprudence CAS OG/04/006 emphasised the importance of the observation of time limits. In allowing a last entry to a kayaking competition on the basis that the Federation was on the facts estopped from insisting on its rules, the Panel said:

> We would have been inclined to dismiss the appeal in the light of the considerations emphasised by both IOC and ICF as to the importance of respecting clear and well publicised entry time limits. Nothing we say should be interpreted as undervaluing the role that such limits play in international sport,

and:

> Competition between the best athletes is the essence of the Olympics. If the exceptional nature of the circumstances on which we rely is appreciated by the Kayaking community (and indeed NOCs generally) it will be realised that we do not open the door to recurrent bypassing of entry deadlines; only a key of a special kind will unlock the door.

In any competition it is imperative that competitors arrive in time for their event. They cannot expect an adjournment, still less one with retrospective effect. Otherwise, what was a competition would become chaos. In the Munich Olympics of 1972 the Soviet sprinter, Valeriy Borzov, won two gold medals in the sprints. It is often forgotten that in the blue riband event – the 100 metres – he may have won his title by default since two American athletes, Eddie Hart and Rey Robinson (and their culpable coach) mistook the scheduled start of the heat in which they were due to run, and watched in horror on television the races taking place without them.

In Sydney, Jesus Kibunde, a Congolese boxer, was barred from participating in the boxing preliminaries of the lightweight category, because, as a result of a sequence of unfortunate occurrences – the cancellation of a flight, visa and customs problems – he had missed the initial weigh-in and medical examination.

The Panel held that the relevant rule was unequivocal; it had a practical foundation and could not be waived even by reference to fundamental principles of the Olympic movement. Any such waiver of the rule would have involved a risk to other competitors and a departure from the principle of equality of treatment – it would have been unfair to all other competitors to overturn the draw hours before the start of the competition when they had prepared themselves for several days on the basis that it was final.

If finality is one objective, fairness is another. In the ENIC case, 'The principle of procedural fairness is surely among the unwritten principles of sports law.' It is a key principle of sports law is that participants should be dealt with fairly. This principle included not introducing a rule affecting a competition after the competition had started. The concept of a 'level playing field' or, to use a phrase obscure to those of civilian jurisdictions, 'it's not cricket', captures the underlying principle. In the duo of Cape Verde cases, which involved the question of whether an expatriate member of the smallest delegation at the Atlantic games could be expelled from the village for the heinous offence of seizing the national flag from the official who was to conduct the miniscule team into the stadium, an analogy was drawn by the CAS Panel between fairness on and off the field:

> It is not without significance in this context that the such principle of the Olympic Charter stresses the importance of 'fair play' which in the view of the Panel is as pertinent to the disciplinary process as it is to competitive sport.'

So important is the principle that it trumps or overrides contrary rules or practices. In Athens the Panel said:

> CAS will always have jurisdiction to overrule the Rules of any sport federation if its decision making bodies conduct themselves with a lack of good faith or not in accordance with due process. In this regard both applicants have made submissions that there was a lack of due process. If such were found to be the case the Rules of Sailing might well be disapplied to this dispute.

There were other cases in Athens when CAS also emphasised several times the importance of natural justice or due process while never finding that it had not been complied with. However, fairness, as always, is moulded by context. A hearing is not normally required before an interim suspension: 'The rationale for summary reaction to a positive test is obvious: the public interest of the sport trumps the private interests of the athlete.'

The concept of fairness has been used to allow a competitor to challenge before CAS an allegedly incorrect decision by the IOC not to forfeit all the medals of cross-country skiers found to have committed a doping offence in respect of one event. The Panel said: 'It is difficult to imagine an interest more worthy of protection that the interest of an athlete in securing a gold medal which s/he considers to have won fairly.'

A third principle is that sports regulators must display fidelity towards their own rules. In an Athens case the Panel said:

> We were unsympathetic to the revelation by the ICF, to which we have already referred, that the methodology as drafted has been departed from for reasons of practicality or even such values as positive discrimination in favour of female athletes. Rules are there to provide guidance to administrators and those who are administered; if inconvenient or obsolete, they should be constitutionally altered, not simply ignored.

In another case at the same Olympics, where an FEI letter mentioned, in support of its position in the arbitration, certain internal discussions and decisions referring to the interpretation of an article, the Panel said:

> The Panel must emphasise, for the avoidance of doubt, that the interpretation of the FEI Regulations, as indeed of the rules of any sporting body, is a question of law. While it is always necessary to seek a purposive and contextual construction of such rules so as to discern their true intent and effect, a body cannot impose by discussion

> or decision after the coming into force of the rules, a meaning which they do not otherwise bear. The Panel must add that while in practice the FEI (or any other body in similar circumstances) must form an initial view as to the meaning of its rules, it is the Panel which is vested with the function of finally determining that meaning, subject only to any recourse (if any) to the Swiss Federal Tribunal (see Article 21 of the ad hoc Rules).

In Sydney the IWF Executive Board decided to suspend the whole Bulgarian weightlifting team in the light of three positive tests recorded by Bulgarian weightlifters at the games. The Panel commended the IWF's objectives in the battle against doping, but noted the 'fundamental and no less legitimate requirement of having a legal basis for disciplinary action'.

A fourth principle reflects a bias towards allowing sportsmen to compete if possible. In *Perez*, as already noted, the Panel construed the phrase 'who has changed his nationality' in Rule 46 of the Olympic Charter to encompass statelessness:

> It is the Panel's view that the word 'change' should be given a broad meaning to include a situation where a person becomes stateless. If a text may be interpreted in two ways, the Panel has no hesitation in resolving the ambiguity in favour of an athlete who is guilty of neither wrongdoing nor even negligence in terms of the Olympic Charter. The word 'change' is appropriate to describe the passing from one form to another, that is from 'nationality' to 'statelessness'. Based on the evidence of the Cuban law before the Panel which, in the absence of evidence to the contrary, it feels bound to accept, that is what happened here.

In *Perez (No 2)*, the Panel also stated:

> The purpose of nationality in international law is not to give governments any form of proprietary interests in individuals, as though they were chattels. Nor is it to enable those who govern a country to use individuals as the instruments of their policy. These considerations are reinforced in circumstances where, as here, the uncontradicted evidence is that in return for the domain sought to be exercised over Mr Perez seven years after his leaving the country, Cuba apparently withholds from him the benefits of fundamental civil rights, such as those of freedom of movement and respect for property. The notion that Cuba in these circumstances should be in a position to prevent Mr Perez from competing is offensive to two core principles of the Olympic Charter, namely that the interests of athletes are fundamental (Rule 3(1)), and that Olympic competition is among athletes and not countries (Rule 9(1)).

When FINA rules did not identify whether entry for the Olympics by a particular date referred to the swimming events as a whole or individual events within them, and the practice was to allow later entries for individual swimming events, the Panel gave the benefit of the doubt to the athlete, thus elevating fairness above strictness in the athlete's interest:

> Perhaps this practice is too lax, or perhaps to the contrary the flexibility is required in order to accommodate a wide variety of sports and a wide variety of NOCs. But if there is to be a change it should be the result of calm policy deliberations and not an abrupt exclusion which penalises an unsuspecting and blameless athlete.

It has been held too that a federation or NOC must pursue a policy of transparency in its selection criteria given that 'the decision on the selection of an athlete may constitute the opportunity of a lifetime for an athlete'. Nor can there be retrospective amendment of those criteria, and selection procedures must be adhered to – *Watt v ACE*.

In *AEK Athens v UEFA* the Panel held that 'the prohibition of arbitrary or unreasonable rules and measures can be deemed to be part of such lex ludica', although the actual rule under scrutiny, which prohibited clubs with the same owner from participating in the same competition, was upheld.

Rules which give a club (but not a player) an option to extend an employment contract are said to offend against such law. So too are disproportionate punishments or suspensions which, unless expressly so provided, run otherwise than from date of the offence.

Fundamental to the idea of fairness to sportsmen and honesty of results is the strict liability rule in doping offences, in which even inadvertent absorption of banned substances is penalised so that it is no defence to an athlete to claim that he was the victim of mislabelling, contaminated stock or faulty advice:

> It is the trust and reliance of clean athletes in their sports and not the trust and reliance of athletes in their physicians and coaches which merit the highest priority in the weighing of the issues in the case at hand … At the starting line a doped athlete remains a doped athlete regardless of whether he or she has been victimised by his physician or coach.

As was said in *Quigley v UIT*, 'the vicissitudes of competition, like those of life generally, may create many types of unfairness, whether by accident or the negligence of unaccountable persons, which the law cannot repair'.

And the Panel continued, 'It appears to be a laudable policy objective not to repair an accidental unfairness to an individual by creating an intentional unfairness to the whole body of other competitors.' In this instance the interests of the many have to be preferred to the interests of the one.

There were further pragmatic considerations. To prove guilty intent would be difficult when all the key facts were known to the athlete only. To prove actual enhancement of performance would necessitate adduction of expert evidence. Litigation in which *mens rea* or efficacy was in issue would be damaging to finality of results and destructive of the budgets of many sports bodies. Principled objections founded on such positive concepts as the presumption of innocence, natural justice and right to work, and negative ones such as restraint of trade or anti-competitive practice have had little or no success The European Court of Human Rights held that strict liability offences do not violate Article 6(2) of the Convention (presumption of innocence in criminal cases) and, still more recently, the European Court of Justice has accepted the compatibility of such offences with the pro-competition provisions of the Treaty on European Union. Although the sometime President of the IAAF Tribunal Judge Lauri Tarasti appears to have taken the view that proof of due care and attention might exculpate an athlete in whose bodily fluids prohibited substances were found, this article of belief has been roundly denounced as heresy by CAS. Nor will much heed be paid to technical points only:

> If the Panel is satisfied the sample tested came from the person or horse in question, and that the chain of custody is established, that no question of contamination arises, that the equipment used to test was appropriate and that the results were correctly interpreted, then it should not be deterred from upholding a verdict as to the presence of a prohibited substance merely because some departure from procedure may be proven, still less because of matters not inherent to the validity of the test.

If, however, the presence of the prohibited substance was the result of a malicious act of a third party, the athlete may discharge the burden which lies upon him.

But the rigours of the rule are tempered by a number of considerations, each of which operates as a *quid pro quo*. First, CAS demanded that a strict liability standard must be clearly articulated:

> The fight against doping is arduous and it may require strict rules. But the rule makes and rule appliers must begin by being strict with themselves. Regulations that may affect the careers of dedicated athletes must be predictable. They must emanate from duly authorised bodies. They must be adopted in constitutionally proper ways. They should not be the product of an obscure process of accreditation. Athletes and officials should not be confronted with a thicket of mutually qualifying or even contradictory rules that can be understood only on the basis of de facto practice over the course of many years of a small group of insiders.

For example, CAS reinstated the gold medal of the winner of snowboarding giant slalom at the 1998 Winter Games in Nagano, the Canadian Ross Rebagliati, who had tested positive for the use of marijuana, since under the relevant code, marijuana was not then – though it is now – listed as a banned substance.

CAS, however, used the fundamental principle upon which the IOC is based and the IOC's corresponding duty to fight doping and promote sports ethics to override an IOC interpretation of one of their rules, 'which would allow an athlete excluded from the Olympics banned for doping to retain any medals gained at such Games'.

There are, moreover, obligations on national and international federations to keep athletes aware of their code.

Second, the Regulator has to establish the element of the offence to the level of 'comfortable satisfaction'.

Third, a bright line has been drawn between the sanctions relevant to the competition in which the athlete is proved to have had the presumed benefit of drugs and those relevant to the athlete's long-term future. In respect of the latter, all circumstances may be taken into account, and here the degree of fault, if any, of the athletes, comes into critical focus.

By far the most controversial disqualification in Sydney was that of the Romanian gymnast Radučan, who underwent a doping test after the event on 21 September 2000 which revealed the presence of pseudoephedrine.

The IOC Executive Board decided to disqualify her from the women's (athletic) individual all-round event and to withdraw her gold medal. The Panel said:

> The anti-doping code considers doping as a strict liability offence. This means that no intentional element is required to establish a doping offence. The mere presence of the forbidden substance in the urine sample is sufficient.

Radučan had therefore committed a doping offence pursuant to the Anti-Doping Code of the Olympic Movement. Article 3 paragraph 3 of that Code provides that:

> Any case of doping during a competition automatically leads to invalidation of the result obtained (with all consequences, including forfeit of any medals and prizes), irrespective of any other sanction that may be applied.

As to that, the Panel stated:

> It supports the strict consequence of an automatic disqualification – severe as it may be in that it effects the gold medal winner – in a matter of fairness to all other athletes.
>
> This is why factors such as the athlete's age (she was 17 on September 30), her weight, the need for medication (there were other medicines available, as well as procedures to be followed, where medication with a banned substance is required for health reasons), the fact the drug may not have enhanced the performance, and the gymnast's reliance on the team's doctor were all held irrelevant. Such matters were, however, taken into account in not imposing a sanction beyond disqualification.

In *A v FIFA*, the tribunal emphasised the importance of respecting the athlete's right of personality and allowing him or her the opportunity to disprove negligence or intent and so escape suspension. The tribunal referred to the fact the suspension 'clearly affect the honour and social standing of the athlete concerned and are a stigma on his future'. However:

> The unintended consumption of foodstuffs or supplements responsible for the presence of a prohibited substance in an athlete's body is hardly an unusual occurrence, let alone a 'truly exceptional circumstance' justifying a lowering of the usual time of a suspension.

Fourth, the fundamental rights of athletes must be respected.

Underlying all these several strands of a *lex sportiva* is a vital consideration: that in sport results should not only be fair, but be seen to be fair. Where the Panel upheld the rules prohibiting multi-club ownership within the same competition, the Panel spoke of 'the connection between the notion of integrity in football and the need for authenticity and uncertainty of results from both a sporting and an economic angle' and mentioned that integrity

> has a critical care which is that, in the public's perception, both single matches and entire championships must be a true test of the best possible athlete, technical, coaching and management skills of the opposing sides … this particular requirement is inherent in the nature of sports.

The integrity and fairness of competition also influenced the construction of the IBA rules governing the waiting period for an athlete who changed sporting nationality.

There remains the question: should the law intervene in sport at all? To my mind it is not an issue of desirability but of inevitability. Sport, once a recreation, is now a business. Not only individual reputation, but national prestige can be at stake in a game's outcome. For spectators as well as for participants sport may be a major, if not the major part of their life. In such circumstances lawyers have a duty, not a choice, to seek to bring order and justice to the table. In that valuable exercise, the development of a *lex sportiva* will play a vital part.

# 16

# *Sport Ethics and the Law* Reader's Lecture, Inner Temple 2023*

SPORT MATTERS. IT matters to those who play, whether for pleasure or profit. It matters to those who follow matches, whether live on screen or in print. Sport can arouse profound emotions, sometimes joyful, sometimes sad.

Sport inspires loyalty, especially – but not only in – football, where it attaches to club teams, even those without a single player from the city or town or area which gives the club its name. Sport is significant in terms of economics, representing one per cent of the world economy, which equates to approximately one trillion US dollars of annual activity. Sport is significant in terms of politics, however much it is argued that it should not be. Consider the recurrent debate as to which national federations should be invited to send teams to the Olympics and whether invited teams will accept an invitation.

English law has never provided a comprehensive definition of sport. As in so many areas of the law, context is all-important. Recognition in law as a sport has implications for matters such as lottery funding and value-added tax. Ruling that bridge was not a sport, the European Court of Justice said, 'The concept of sport … is limited to activity satisfied in the ordinary meaning of the term "sport" characterised by a not negligible physical element.' All sports are games, but not all games are, in law, sports.

A negligible physical element is a necessary, but hardly a sufficient, description of sport. To qualify sport as a physical activity must surely have rules which govern how it must be played.

Such rules – a match's length, the weight of a discus, the width of a goal mouth, the type of footwear – are not compelled by the laws of physics or by some moral code. Subject always to the need to comply with the law of the land, they are constantly under review by sports' governing bodies (SGBs) that are influenced by such considerations as the safety of participants, the enjoyment of spectators, the demands of television or the broadening of participation.

The rules define how the sport must be played, how victory is achieved, who should adjudicate whether the rules themselves have been complied with, who

***Inner Temple Yearbook 2024–2025*. The full recording of this lecture can be found at innertemple.org.uk/sportslaw.

can enforce compliance, and who can administer a sanction (and of what kind) for breach of the rules.

A fundamental element in sports law – the so called 'field of play rule' – is that as long as referees or umpires (or other officials), assisted by technology, exercise their judgement or discretion in good faith, their decisions are beyond challenge otherwise than in so far as the rules of the sport themselves provide – for example, by on-the-spot applications to juries of appeal.

So, prima facie, the rule creates a sphere of autonomy into which even appellate sports tribunals, let alone courts, must not trespass. There are various justifications: the fear of constant interruption to the course of play by lawyers, the problems of rewriting a result after the event, the need to strengthen the match official's hand and an arbitrator's or judge's perceived lack of expertise in the technical side of sport.

Beyond the boundaries of the field of play rule, sporting disciplinary offences contrary to the relevant code and other sports-related disputes are ever more frequently resolved by sport-specific tribunals, usually chaired by specialist sports lawyers rather than in the courts. In the UK, Sport Resolutions sits at the apex of domestic bodies. CAS, to whose jurisdiction during the course of this century most major global sports and all Olympic sports have subscribed, sits at the equivalent international apex. There is limited scope to challenge the decision of either body in the courts on grounds analogous to judicial review. Neither in Switzerland, nor in the Strand, will judges second guess the merits of the decisions of sports expert tribunals.

The major object of sport-specific law is to ensure that there be, as far as possible, fair competition, so that the result of a contest (luck apart) depends on talent and commitment and not on some form of cheating.

In *Ivey v Genting Casinos*, the Supreme Court was concerned with a card game of chance, Punto Banco. In his leading judgment, Lord Hughes (obiter) gave examples of cheating in sport, paramount among them the taking of performance-enhancing drugs – the most pervasive problem in modern sport.

There is all but universal consensus that such taking is unacceptable. Since the turn of this century the World Anti-Doping Code, in its various versions, policed by the World Anti-Doping Authority (WADA), applies to almost all sports. WADA decides what are prohibited substances and can police the code by prosecutions for its breach.

Key to the Code is the strict liability rule. Faced with a charge of an anti-doping rule violation for presence in his bodily fluids or use of a prohibited substance, it is no defence for an athlete to claim that he was the victim of mislabelling, contaminated stock, or faulty advice from anyone at all.

As was explained by a CAS panel,

> It is the trust and reliance of clean athletes in their sport, and not the trust and reliance in their physicians and coaches, which merit the highest priority. At the starting line, a doped athlete remains a doped athlete regardless of whether he or she has been victimised by their coach.

In this instance, the interests of the many have to be preferred to the interests of the one.

The result achieved by a doped athlete cannot stand for pragmatic reasons; the advantage is presumed. The degree of care taken to avoid the infringement comes into play only when deciding whether, and for how long, the athlete should be subject to a period of ineligibility, taking account of factors such as age, degree of education in anti-doping and experience.

Anti-doping rules have to be compatible with the general law. They have generally resisted challenges that they fail that test. A striking instance is provided by the case *Meca Medina and Majcen v Commission* where the European Court of Justice found that anti-doping rules were prima facie anti-competitive, but that they were justifiably so.

The anti-doping regime can only work if tests can be administered out of competition as well as in it. To that end, athletes subject to it have to provide details to their anti-doping organisations of precisely where they are at any time, so as to be available for testing – the so-called 'whereabouts rule'. This is a huge intrusion of privacy, but it is the price which is laid down to be paid for participation in their sport. The presumption is three strikes – three missed tests – and you're out.

Cheating in sport is not confined to doping. It is multi-layered, often fuelled by gambling. The follower of sport relishes its unpredictability, but for the gambler, predictability is all-important. At its most serious, cheating is coincident with criminal law and amounts to corruption. At another level, it can be a breach of the civil law of an express or implied contract not to cheat. At yet another level, it falls foul, not of the criminal or civil law at all, but only of the codes or rules of the game. It becomes a regulatory offence.

The three Pakistani cricketers persuaded (in aid of a purported betting coup) to bowl three no-balls at particular junctures in a test match against England at Lord's in 2011 (so-called 'spot fixing') were found guilty of a breach of the ethics code of the International Cricket Council, and later in the High Court also of conspiracy to cheat.

Forms of sport-specific cheating are plural and various: selecting ineligible persons for a team, claiming non-existent or less serious disabilities to improve one's classification in Paralympic sports, breaking the rules as to engine construction in motor racing, or ball tampering in cricket.

Where criminal and regulatory offences coincide, the public authorities can (but sport's governing bodies cannot) issue subpoenas or witness summonses and can access bank accounts to compensate the privilege against self-incrimination, which may not apply in sports disciplinary cases.

The sanctions in these two *fora* differ significantly. Courts can imprison but not ban. Sports tribunals can ban, but not imprison. Both, however, ordinarily have the capacity to fine.

The ordinary courts of law have a role to play in their traditional spheres of crime, tort and contract, but each of them is influenced by the so-called specificity of sport.

Specificity also has its effect in statute in the context of the Competition Act 1988 (much influenced by European jurisprudence), but no less notably in the anti-discrimination law contained in the Equality Act of 2010, which outlaws (subject to certain exceptions) indirect or direct discrimination against persons with protected characteristics, but where there are sporting exceptions for disability, age and sex and gender reassignment. The first two of these occasion little controversy – the need for modifications in the interests of fair competition are obvious. Not so the third.

No one seriously disputes the organisation of separate sporting competitions for men and women where physical strength, stamina or physique are major factors in determining success or failure, and in which one sex is generally at a disadvantage in comparison with the other. The vexed issue is: what does 'woman' mean in this context? Does it include females with differences of sexual development (DSD), intersex persons, persons reared as women but with male (not female) chromosomes, or persons born male who (post-puberty) self-identify as female, ie transgender people?

Caster Semenya (the South African 800m runner who was required by World Athletics regulations to reduce her levels of testosterone as the *quid pro quo* to compete in women's events) has challenged the validity of the regulations before the European Court of Human Rights (ECtHR), having failed before CAS and the Swiss Federal Tribunal. The hearing has taken place, but at the date of this lecture the decision is still awaited.

As to transgender athletes, the guidance from the International Olympic Committee (IOC) – the body at the summit of world sporting governance – has changed over time but has recently asked global bodies to give equal consideration to the inclusion of athletes and fairness for women when drawing up eligibility criteria. Given the ambiguity of this steer, there has been no consistency in the choice made by international federations or national SGBs.

The majority of sports have always taken a binary view that there are women's events and there are men's events, and the defining and dividing factor has always been biological. Biology, indeed, has been the factor which creates different categories in all areas of sports – such as multiple weight categories in boxing and age categories in track and field. So, to admit someone who identifies as a female but whose male biology is unchanged to compete in those sports which are affected by biology, would create an unprecedented exception to a hitherto well-established sports-wide principle.

If the science still confirms that male biology gives an advantage in terms of sports *prima facie*, sport's governing bodies should respect that fact in the interests of its guiding principle of fair competition. Whether the human rights of the distinct minority category of transgender women should trump the consideration of the cis-gender women majority is outside the scope of this lecture. It will ultimately be for the legislatures or courts to decide this contested issue.

The American poet Grantland Rice wrote, 'For when the one great scorer comes to mark against your name, / He writes – not that you won or lost – but how you played the game.' This concept of the spirit of sport, much discussed during the last Ashes series, distinguishes it from law. As the preamble to the MCC Laws states, 'Cricket owes much of its appeal and enjoyment to the fact it should be played, not only according to the laws but also within the spirit of cricket.' There is, of course, nothing to stop the spirit of cricket, or of any sport, being part of a legally binding conduct code; indeed, oddly, the International Cricket Council Code of Conduct for Players does precisely that. At least, if not embodied in that particular way, the spirit of sport could be deployed as an aid to interpretation of open-textured sporting rules.

I fear that the spirit of sport is more breached than observed, especially in football with the so-called professional foul, theatrical diving to win a penalty and running down the clock to prevent a late comeback by the currently losing team.

However, I emphasise, this occurs not just in football. We recall examples of fair play in sport precisely because they are so few.

Fair play in sport may always be more an ideal than a reality. After all, WG Grace, the most famous of English cricketers, was once clean bowled and he simply reset the stumps with the explanation: 'These people,' pointing at the spectators, 'have not come to see you bowl, they have come to see me bat.'

In the modern game, money, reputation, career and national pride means that winning at almost all costs has firmly taken pride of place.

# *Postscript*

In the Black Sox Scandal of 1919, sometimes described as the Sports Scandal of the Century, the famous American baseball player 'Shoeless Joe' Jackson was found to have thrown a match. A distraught fan, not wishing to believe that his hero had not only a golden arm, but unshod feet of clay, uttered the unforgettable and poignant words, 'Say it ain't so Joe. Say it ain't so.'

Sports law should aim to ensure that, as far as possible, it ain't ever so.

1. I was the only male-and the opening-speaker among a galaxy of female stars including Tessa Jowell, Rachel Johnson and Edwina Currie at a debate in 2013 to celebrate the 50th anniversary of the admission of women to full membership of the Oxford Union. I had that singular status, shown in this photograph, for having, when the most recent ex-President, moved that admission. The event itself is now commemorated in a plaque installed on midsummer's day 2025 at the end of a term in which, for the first time, all four Union Officers were female. But among the host of such gendered former officers three are already KCs or Women in Wigs and I am confident that more will take silk during whatever Monarch's reign, though less confident that wigs will stay the course.

2. This photograph of me, my wife, and Lord Neuberger was taken on board a static barge in Putney where we were guests of the Oxford University Boat Club on boat race day. Lord Neuberger, an eminent Oxford alumnus, was present in right of office as the then President of the Supreme Court. I surmise that it was with an acute sensitivity to risk, honed in his effortless climb up the judicial greasy pole, that he did not follow me, a former wetbob, into the motorised boat that tracked the boat race at to me an alarming speed, albeit at a discreet distance behind the two crews. This perilous voyage was my reward for an opinion that persuaded a reluctant Met that it was the Met, not the university boat clubs that had to police the banks on the day of the race. The boat race is apparently no longer to be broadcast from this year onwards by the BBC. Had the Met rejected my opinion there would have been in all probability, without the support of a well-heeled fairy godmother no race to broadcast.

3. In 2006 at the suggestion of John Hood, then the Vice-Chancellor of Oxford, I was invited to speak at the Distinguished Alumni Annual Awards dinner at the University of Auckland, where he had held the same office. My title was 'In defence of elites', in my view elites being as vital to academia as to athletics, though my speech was met with an eloquent, if pre-arranged, egalitarian response. The dinner was attended by the then Prime Minister of New Zealand, Helen Clark, which explains the presence of a photographer, explicably (surely you mean inexplicably ? Ed) absent from my speeches on sports law delivered elsewhere on my visit that year to Oceania. That's my more or less credible excuse for this photograph's inclusion.

4. Declining a High Court appointment in England and Wales for reasons explained in my memoir which do not deserve repetition, I was lucky enough to spend almost two decades as a judge of the Courts of Appeal in Jersey and Guernsey, ending up through the fortuity of timing, not merit, as Senior Ordinary Appeal Judge, the word Ordinary there signifying that I ranked below but only below the Bailiff – though some may have thought the word bore in my case its ordinary and natural meaning. Be that as it may, Bailiff and Beloff are seen in this photograph leading the procession to the service which signifies the opening of the legal year on the larger of the two bailiwicks. I am, to adapt awkwardly the title of Stendhal's best-known novel, le noir among les rouges.

5. Among the many features which distinguish the legal system in the Channel Islands from that in all parts of Great Britain is the opportunity afforded to those who have served as appellate judges, at conclusion of their term, to give continued service but in a lower rank. This photograph shows me and my friend since our school days, Sir John Nutting Bart, in less colourful clothing than those around us, attending a ceremony in our new positions as Commissioners of the Royal Court of Jersey, nothing daunted by the fact we were now vulnerable to having our judgments in our new rank overturned by those who were once our colleagues of no higher status and necessarily junior in terms of appointment to the Court of Appeal. I bore a single such reversal with such fortitude as I could muster.

6. Malibu was by happy chance the venue for the first ever case for the Ultimate Fighting Appeal Tribunal, which involved the appropriate sanction for an admitted violation of the anti-doping rules by Jon Jones, a mixed martial arts fighter said to be the most dangerous man in the world in unarmed combat. In my memoir I recount the degree of apprehension I felt at my proximity to him during the hearing, albeit he was on the opposite side of the table and would have been unwise to have assaulted an arbitrator before judgment was handed down. The photograph reminds me that I had an additional, if flimsy protection, in the presence of my fellow panellists Lars Hallgren and Markus Makkinnen, Scandinavian stars, who offered alternative targets.

With the benefit of that photograph Mr Jones might himself have criticised our adverse award as a species of palm tree justice but what astonished us was the revelation that, by reason of his earlier provisional suspension, he had lost not only a year of his career but an estimated nine million dollars. Would that arbitrators' fees amounted pro rata to a fraction of such an amount. For the avoidance of doubt I should confirm that I did wear a tie, if not protective clothing, for the hearing itself.

7. In 2011 under the auspices of the Lord Slynn of Hadley European Law Foundation and chaperoned by Sir Henry Brooke, a former Lord Justice of Appeal, who, though taking silk in the same year as me, had climbed far higher up the legal ladder (but see Photograph 4 for my defence). I visited Kiev (as it was then both spelt and pronounced) to talk to the judiciary on the topic of human rights in company with Dr Sweeny, a senior lecturer at the Durham law School. The photograph shows the good doctor and me, well wrapped up in the bleak midwinter, outside the entrance to the Ukrainian Supreme Court where we gave our presentation. It was ironic that the constitutional principle which captured the deepest interest of the judges to whom we spoke was the bar on diminution of salaries during a judge's term of service. But those were happier times when the status of Ukraine as a sovereign nation was not yet under threat, nor was its historic capital under constant bombardment. We noted that in our hotel every night two strong but silent gentlemen occupied the same seats in the lobby. Whatever their function we thought it imprudent to take a photograph of them though we have a lively suspicion that they may have taken a photograph of us.

8. I rolled down to Rio in my last Olympics in a double role as a CAS arbitrator and Chair of World Athletics Ethics Commission. As this photograph shows it was never all work and no play but there was a twist in this tale. Carlos Nuzman, who was my Vice Chair of the Commission but also, more significantly to Rio who, as former President of the Olympic Committee of Brazil, had claimed credit for bringing the Games to Latin America, was later accused of bribing the International Olympic Committee to elect the Brazilian City as a host city. It was alleged that he had channelled money to Lamine Diack, who at the material time, was both head of the IAAF and an IOC member, to be used to solicit support for the Rio bid. In 2020 Diack was found guilty of various offences of corruption by a French court. Nuzman himself was in 2021 sentenced in the Rio Federal Court to 30 years' imprisonment for corruption and related offences though he still is free to appeal. It was fortunate that, for whatever reason good or bad, Nuzman never played any active part in the work of the Ethics Commission (see Photograph 9), and when I sought to introduce myself to him before the Games opening ceremony, appeared not to know who I was. Thankfully no photograph of our hurried handshake, if ever taken, survives.

9. This photograph shows a gathering of the annual meeting of the first commission of the IAAF, predecessor of World Athletics, which took place to the chagrin of few, if any, of its members in Monte Carlo in 2015. Diverse in race, nationality and gender it was constituted by Kevan Gosper (Australia 400 metre runner and Vice President of the IOC), Annabel Pennyfather (Singapore international hockey player and lawyer), Tafsir Malick Ndiaye (Senegal Member of the International Tribunal on the Law of the Sea) Thomas Murray (USA writer on sports ethics), myself (Chair), Lauri Tarasti (Finland former Minister and member of the Supreme Administrative Court) and Kate O'Regan (South Africa – a former Justice of the South African Constitutional Court). We are flanked by the two Blackstone Chambers Secretaries, Tom Mountford and Jana Sadler Foster. The only absentee, was Akira Karamura (Japan – lawyer member of Order of the Rising Sun) and Carlos Nuzman (as to whom see Photograph 8). It had a full agenda designed to clean up the Diack Augean stables with the supportive leadership of Lord Coe.

10. At the Young Bar conference in 2009 I chaired a session of an (old) masterclass in advocacy delivered by former High Court judges, Charles Gray and Oliver Popplewell. The former, once a doyen of the libel bar, is best known as the only, other than fictional, judge to be depicted in a major Hollywood film (titled Denial) presiding over a domestic trial of the unsuccessful defamation claim brought by historian David Irving against Penguin Books for depicting him as a Holocaust denier and Nazi apologist. The latter, a Cambridge graduate and cricketing blue, is best known for accumulating further degrees at Oxford after his retirement from the bench and becoming as well a serial memoirist and author. This photograph shows the golden oldies at the start of the session on more or less full alert.

11. I had a peripatetic experience as a sports arbitrator speaking on sports law at meetings somewhat unevenly dispersed through the globe. My visit to Seoul in 2016, captured in this photograph, was a precursor to my address to the World Conference of the World Anti-Doping Authority in Busan focused on a report I had written about the compatibility of its 2027 Code with the principles of human rights. This took place in December 2025. Alas any more interesting photographs of that event (they could scarcely be less interesting than the above!) of me at the podium, jet lagged after flights totalling 14 hours to the locus in quo but bedecked in my Vincents blazer came too late, maybe mercifully, for inclusion. Publisher's deadlines are as significant as those of the Procedure Rules in civil litigation.

To infuse this tedious tale with a little lighter touch, the blazer was an item of clothing which I was entitled to wear only because of the patronage of Jeffrey Archer in securing my election to Vincents, a club otherwise and generally populated by Oxford sporting blues, one of the less notable, if more remarkable, accomplishments of the best-selling author's early career. I was plausibly told that the logo on the blazer itself baffled 99% of my international audience.

12. I came to Belfast in 2019 as shown by this photograph to speak at a conference and judge a moot in honour of Dame Mary Peters LG. Mary had been a part of my first ever sporting case in the early seventies when she and another gold medal Olympian David Hemery accompanied me to the AGM of the Amateur Athletic Assocation (AAA), presided over by Harold Abrahams, immortalised in the Oscar winning film Chariots of Fire, in a vain effort to make an exception to the AAA's contract with the BBC giving the latter a monopoly over the broadcasting of any UK athletics event. This failure nonetheless enabled my clerks whenever later a sports related case wended its way to chambers to identify me, if implausibly, as the man for the job. I witnessed and cheered on Mary's own gold medal winning performance at the Munich Olympics and we were from that time onwards good friends.

Many of those who sprinted, threw and jumped during the era when Mary was a competitor had their performances enhanced by abuse of prohibited substances and others were of doubtful biological femininity; but there was never the slightest doubt that Mary was a clean woman athlete as well as becoming rightly a national treasure in Northern Ireland with a range of honours, including her representative and walk on (not run on) role in the coronation service of King Charles III.

Mary also spoke at the Supreme Court sports law exhibition (as to which see photograph 13) and that was only one of many reasons why I wished to reciprocate the gesture.

13. In 2012 the Supreme Court hosted an exhibition on sports law to commemorate the London Olympics. The organisers selected a photograph of me to illustrate the theme for no better, if any, reason, than that I had helped to procure speakers for the event, including Dame Mary Peters (see photograph 12). The event was opened by Lord Phillips, first President of the Supreme Court and visited by, amongst other more casual tourists, several of the Court's own justices and a flotilla of CAS arbitrators appointed for the Games which I was not for perceived conflict of interest as Ethics Commissioner for London 2012. This turned out to be to my advantage because it made me eligible for an appointment at Rio (see photograph 8), which would have otherwise been a game too many. It is a familiar theme of my speeches on the development of a legal career that one should never underestimate the influence of luck.

14. I, though a dark blue through and through (though not, alas, in the literal sporting sense) was happy while still in practice, to reprise my speech, much repeated home and away, in the other place, having noted that it was sponsored by a well-known law firm, identified in this photograph, whose instructions I always welcomed. And I had as well in my subconscious, even it may be my unconscious, thoughts of a future memoir to market, of which one chapter had inevitably the name which I could prematurely plagiarise for this talk without fear of legal redress from any third party. This double explanation proves, cynics might say, that lawyers never give an entirely free speech.

# Index

*[All references are to page number.]*


**Abinger, Edward** 7–8
**access to justice** 166
**acting, advocacy and** 31–3
**advocacy**
acting, comparisons to 31–3
adversarial system, benefits of 51
alternative dispute resolution and 12, 42–3
art, as 26–46
brevity 37–8
Golden Age 30
judicial control 40–41
jury trials 33
language 44–5
literature concerning 27–9
MacDermott Lecture 2014 47–65
Margaret Howard Memorial Lecture 26–46
oral advocacy 9, 38–40, 44
restrictions on 45, 61–5
rights of audience, extension of 43
simplicity 36–7
Sir David Williams Lecture 2010 7–25
teaching 34–5
technology and 40
threats to 37–46
time limits 44, 51
written advocacy 11, 38–40
**age discrimination in sport** 215
**alternative dispute resolution** 12, 42–3
**Anton Piller orders** 50
**Appellate and Judicial Committee**
FE Smith 155
**art, advocacy as** 26–46
**Association of Women Barristers** 137
**Atkin Lecture 1999, The** 90–104 *see also* **judicial independence**
**Attorney General**
FE Smith 146–7, 156
reforms in Blair era 164
**Australia**
judicial control 87
judicial remuneration 106, 116–17
Privy Council 85
**Bailiff of Guernsey**
independence and impartiality of 101
**banned substances** *see* **doping offences**
**banning orders**
sport, in 220
**Bar Council** 8, 10–11
admission of women 133, 136
career breaks, guidance on 137
**Bar Nursery Association** 137
**Barker, Pam** 141
**Barnard's Inn Reading at Gresham College 2009** 127–42
**barristers**
association with client's causes 55–7
attributes of 35–7, 52–4
cab rank rule 12–14, 45–6
call to the bar 8–10
chambers 8, 10
clerks 8, 10
conflict of duty to court/client 61
costs, liability for 41–2
court dress 8, 10
damages, liability for 42
devotion to client's cause 58–61
difference made by 31
duty to the client 14, 61
duty to the Court 14, 45, 61
education and training 34–5
ethnic minorities 8, 10
FE Smith 144–5, 156
independence and impartiality 12, 57–61, 64
influence on outcome of cases 53–4
'jury advocates' 33
legal aid cuts, opposition to 48–9
need for 29–30
negligence, liability for 12, 42, 61–2
physical presence 36
pupillage 8, 10
quality control 61–2
Queen's Counsel 9, 11
reduced focus on 30–31
regulation of 10, 45–6

style of 32–3
women *see* women
**Beloff QC (now KC), Michael**
autobiography 1
call to the bar 8
choice of articles 1–4
**bias**
sport 197–8, 230–231
*see also* independence and impartiality; judicial independence
**Birkenhead, Baron Nicholls of** *see* **Nicholls, Donald James, Baron Nicholls of Birkenhead**
**Birkenhead Lecture 2009** 143–57 *see also* **Smith, Frederick Edwin**
**Black Sox Scandal** 240
**Blair, Tony** 158–9 *see also* **law reforms in Blair era**
**Bottomley, Horatio** 156
**brevity in advocacy** 37–8
**broadcasting rights**
sport, in 208
**Buller, Sir Reginald Manningham** 53
**burden of proof**
comfortable satisfaction in sport 216, 217–18

**cab rank rule** 12–14, 16, 45–6, 56, 64, 97, 170
abandonment of 167
barrister remuneration and 22, 56
FE Smith support of 155–6
impact on market 54
**call to the bar** 10
Beloff QC (now KC), Michael 8
Laws, Sir John Grant McKenzie 187
Nicholls, Donald James, Baron Nicholls of Birkenhead 184
Slynn, Gordon, Baron Slynn of Hadley 179–80
Smith, Frederick Edwin 144
**Campbell, John: *F.E. Smith, First Earl of Birkenhead*** (1983) 148–50
**Canada**
judicial remuneration 106, 115, 122
Privy Council 85
women as persons 129–30
**Caribbean Islands, advocacy in** 9
**Carman, George Alfred** 53, 176–9
5 Essex Court 177
60 King Street chambers 176–7
birth 176
criminal practice 177
death 179
education 176
family life 179
libel law 177–8
New Court chambers 178
new material at late stage 178
**Cave, Bertha** 128
**chambers** 8, 10
branding and marketing of 65
**Channel Islands**
role of advocates in adducing evidence 52
**cheating at sport** 237
**Civil Procedure Rules** 166
**clerks** 8, 10
**Cohen, Myrella** 141
**comfortable satisfaction**
burden of proof in sport 216, 217–18
**Commercial Court Guide**
time limits 38
**Commission of Peace for England and Wales** 165
**Committee of Privileges**
FE Smith 154–5
**Community Legal Service** 12
**competition law**
sport and 207–9
**conditional fee agreements** 168
**conflicts of interest**
conditional fee agreements 168
constitutional conflicts 100–1
duty court or client 61
judicial independence and 88, 93–4
**consent**
implied sporting consent, doctrine of 212–13
**Constitution Reform Act** 160
**constitutional issues**
judicial review 85
**contests of uncertain outcome** 206–7
**contract law**
sport and 201, 213, 222
**corruption**
judicial remuneration and 98, 107, 109, 119–20
sport 213, 216, 226, 237
**costs, barristers' liability for** 41–2
**court dress** 8, 10
**Court of Arbitration of Sport** 216–17, 236
ad hoc panels 222, 223–4
CAS Code 224
**court system, reform of** 164–7
**Criminal Defence Service** 12

**criminal law and sport** 212–13, 222
**Curtis-Bennett, Sir Henry** 36

**damages, barristers' liability for** 42
**Deech, Baroness** 48
**devolution**
  judicial review 85–6
  judicial role and 99
  Supreme Court 161
**disability discrimination in sport** 214–15
**dismissal, immunity from**
  judicial independence and 92–3
**'doing a Curtis'** 36
**doping offences in sport** 236–7
**duty to the client** 14, 61
**duty to the Court** 14, 45, 61

**Eadie, Ellice** 142
**education on sports law** 222
**Edward Grayson Memorial Lecture 2012** 204–20 *see also* **specificity of sport**
**education and training** *see* **legal education; pupillage**
**employment law and sport** 209–11, 215
**equal pay in sport** 213–14
**Equality and Diversity Committee** 137
**Erskine, *The Rights of Man*** 46
**ethics in sport**
  cheating 237
  disciplinary offences 236
  doping offences 236–7
  fair competition 236
  fair play 239
  field of play doctrine 236
  specificity of sport 237–8
  spirit of sport 238–9
  spot fixing 237
  strict liability 236–7
  transgender athletes 238
  whereabouts rule 237
  woman, meaning of 238
**ethnic minorities**
  barristers 8, 10
**EU law**
  judicial independence and 99
  judicial review 82–3
  sport and 207, 211–12
**European Convention on Human Rights**
  judicial independence and 99–100
  judicial review 83–5

**Faculty of Advocates**
  admission of women 133
**fairness in sport** 228–9, 236, 239
**Falconer, Lord Charles** 159–61, 163–4, 170–1
**female barristers** *see* **women**
**fidelity in sport** 229–30
**field of play doctrine** 216–17, 225–6, 236 *see also* **sport**
**freedom of movement in sport** 223

**game rules** 226–7 *see also* **sport**
**Germany**
  judicial remuneration 123
**Gray's Inn** 7, 8
  admission of women 128, 142
**Grayson, Edward** 203–4 *see also* **Edward Grayson Memorial Lecture 2012**
**Gresham College**
  Barnard's Inn Reading 2009 127–42

**Hadley, Baron Slynn of** *see* **Slynn, Gordon, Baron Slynn of Hadley**
**Hale Baronness, Master Brenda** 128, 129, 138–40, 142
**Hall's scales of justice act** 33
**Hastings, Sir Patrick** 30, 31, 35
**history**
  law reform in Blair era 158–75
  rise of women in wigs 127–42
  Smith, Frederick Edwin 143–57
**holidays**
  judicial remuneration and 119
**Hong Kong**
  advocacy in 9, 12
**hypothetical issues** 50

**IBA Minimum Standards of Judicial Independence** 107
**implied sporting consent, doctrine of** 212–13
**independence and impartiality**
  barristers 12, 57–61, 64
  judges *see* judicial independence
**India**
  judicial remuneration 115
**Inner Temple, Readers Lecture 2023** 235–9
**Inns of Court** 8, 10
**integrity in sport** 233–4
**intellectual property law and sport** 222
**International Amateur Athletic Federation** 195
**interpretation of sports law** 194–5, 223

**Invergordon Mutiny 1931**
judicial remuneration and 112
**Ireland**
admission of women to Bar 133
women in public office 129
**Israel**
judicial remuneration 114

**John M Kelly Memorial Lecture** 73–89
*see also* **Supreme Court**
**Johnson, Betty** 142
**judges**
gender representation 97, 162
hierarchy of 161
locus, viewing the *see* view
power of *see* judicial power
press attacks on character 95–6
qualifications 97–8
sensitivity to criticism 88–9
societal representation 97
*see also* judicial appointments; judicial independence; judicial power, judicial remuneration; judicial review
**judicial appointments** 9, 11
judicial independence and 102–4
judicial remuneration and 123–4
reforms in Blair era 162–3
willingness to accept 123–4
women 138–40
**Judicial Appointments Commission** 101, 117
rise in women judges 138
**judicial independence** 90–104
appearance vs reality 91
challenges to 94–5
composition of tribunal 91–2
conflicts of interest 93–4
democratic legitimacy 100
ECHR and 99–100
EU law and 99
external regulation 96–7
extra-curricular activities 95
gender balance 97
immunity from dismissal 92–3
judicial appointments and 102–4
judicial behaviour 99
judicial errors 92
Law Lords 100–1
Lord Chancellor 101–2
Pinochet case 91
politically sensitive decisions 91
press attacks on judge's characters 95–6
presumption of independence 92, 96
public inquiries and 95
qualifications of judges 97–8
remuneration and 98–9, 106, 121–2
separation of powers and 100, 104
societal representation 97
televised courts 94–5
**judicial power**
*Anisminic* 87
increases in exercise of 40–41, 76–7, 89
Parliamentary sovereignty and 86–8
risks of increasing involvement in politics 88
**judicial remuneration**
consultation 117
corruption prevention of 119–20
criteria for determining 118–19
discrepancy with Bar earnings 122–3
history of
pre-17th century 107–9
17th to 19th centuries 109–11
20th century 111–13
21st century 113–14
Invergordon Mutiny 1931 112
holidays, paid 119
independence and 98–9, 106, 121–2
judicial appointments and, willingness to accept 123–4
no diminution while in office 106–7
other countries
Australia 116
Canada 115
India 115
Isreal 114
USA 115–16
reforms in Blair era 163–4
right to determine 116–18
status and 120–1
**judicial review**
academic influence 76
constitutional issues 85
creative interpretation overcoming shortcomings in law 79–81
curtailment of 62–3
devolution, impact of 85–6
ECHR, impact of 83–5
EU law, impact of 82–3
grounds for 78
growth of 75–86
judicial expertise 76
ministerial powers, scope of 81
parliamentary intention 77–8

private law 82
Privy Council 85
procedural changes 76
proportionality of 78–9
public attitudes towards establishment 75
reforms in Blair era 171–4
specialisation in legal practice, increasing in 75–6
sports disputes 193–203

**'jury advocates'** 33
**jury trials**
advocacy in 33
reforms in Blair era 165
**just cause in sport** 210–211

**Kelly, John** 73 *see also* **John M Kelly Memorial Lecture**
**Kennedy Baronness, Master Helena** 135–8, 141
**Kidd, Margaret Henderson** 133
**Kilmuir Rules** 94
**Kuwait, viewing locus in** 69–70

**Lane, Dame Elizabeth** 134
**language in advocacy** 44–5
**lap dancing club, viewing locus in** 68–9
**Law Lords**
appointment 92
devolution issues 86
judicial independence 100–1
reforms in Blair era 174
role of 76
**law reforms in Blair era** 158–75
access to justice 166
anti-discrimination laws 170
Attorney General 164
barrister/MP dual roles, decline in 164
Civil Procedure Rules 166
Commission of Peace for England and Wales 165
Constitution Reform Act 160
court system 166–7
criminal courts 164–5
female judges, rise in 162
hierarchy of judges 161
judicial appointments 162–3
judicial remuneration 163–4
judicial review, expansion of 171–4
juries 165
legal aid 167–8
legal education 170
Lord Chancellor 159–61
Ministry of Justice 174
private funding of litigation 168
public inquiries 169
punishment and sentencing 165–6
Queen's Counsel, appointment as 169–70
reflections on 174–5
regulatory framework for legal services 170–1
rights of audience 169
Supreme Court 161–2
tribunal system 168–9
**Laws, Sir John Grant McKenzie** 187–90
2 Garden Court 187
academic appointments 189
Bar European Group 189
birth 187
call to the bar 187
Court of Appeal 188
death 190
education 187
High Court 188
marriage and family life 189–90
Supreme Court, lack of appointment to 189
Treasury devil 187
**Lawson, Nigella** 59–60
**Le Neve, Ethel** 148
**legal aid** 9, 12
barristers' opposition to cuts 48–9
impact of 63–4
reforms in Blair era 167–8
**legal directories** 11
**legal education**
barristers 34–5 *see also* pupillage
FE Smith 143–4
reforms in Blair era 170
**Legal Services Board** 54, 62, 171
**Leithen, Sir Edward** 30
***lex mercatoria***
sports law and 224–5
***lex sportiva***
bias 230–231
CAS Code 224
CAS *see* Court of Arbitration for Sport
education on 222
fairness 228–9
fidelity 229–30
field of play doctrine 225–6
freedom of movement and 223
game rules 226–7
general law, relationship with 222–3, 225
horizontal/vertical law distinction 223

international nature of 224
interpretation 223
legal basis 223
*lex mercatoria* and 224–5
literature on 221
natural justice 229
sex discrimination 222–3
sporting integrity 233–4
sporting nationality 223
sports tribunals 222
strict liability for doping offences 231–3
subsidiarity 227
time limits 227–8
**liability of barristers** 12, 41–2, 61
**locus, viewing the** *see* **view**
**Lord Chancellor**
FE Smith 152–4, 156–7
judicial appointments 9
judicial independence 101–2
reforms in Blair era 159–61
**Lord Slynn of Hadley European Law Foundation** 182
**Los Angeles, viewing locus in** 69
**Luxembourg**
advocacy in12

**MacDermott Lecture 2014** 47–65
**MacDermott, Lord John** 47–8
**Malaysia**
advocacy in 9, 12
**Mareva injunctions** 50
**Margaret Howard Memorial Lecture** 26–46
**Marshall Hall KC, Sir Edward** 33, 35–6
**Max Plank Institute, Hamburg** 221–239 *see also* **sport**
**metric martyr** 188
**ministerial powers**
judicial review of 81
**Ministry of Justice** 174
**Mitchell, Master Angelica** 141

**nationality**
discrimination in sport 199, 212
sporting nationality 215–16, 223
**natural justice**
sport 197–8, 229
**negligence, barristers' liability for** 12, 42, 61–2
**Neill Lecture 2006** 105–24 *see also* **judicial remuneration**
**Neill, Pat** 105–6
**Nicholls, Donald James, Baron Nicholls of Birkenhead** 182–7
13 Old Square, Lincoln's Inn 184
access to justice 186
birth 182
call to the bar 184
Cambridge 183–4
contribution to jurisprudence 185–6
Court of Appeal 184
death 186–7
education 183
Harmsworth scholarship 184
High Court, Chancery Division 184
Hong Kong court of final appeal 185
Lord Appeal in Ordinary 184
marriage and family life 186
silk 184
**Normanton, Helena** 133

**oral advocacy** 9, 38–40, 44
**organised solidarity mechanisms** 205–6
**Oxford Dictionary of National Biography**
Carman, George Alfred 176–9
Laws, Sir John Grant McKenzie 187–90
Nicholls, Donald James, Baron Nicholls of Birkenhead 182–7
Slynn, Gordon, Baron Slynn of Hadley 179–82

**parliamentary intention**
judicial review 77–8
**Parliamentary sovereignty**
judicial power and 86–8
**Parry, Judge Edward** 32, 33, 35
female barristers, view on 132–3
**persons, recognition of women as** 128–31
**physical presence in court** 36
***Pinochet* case**
judicial independence 91
**Plastic Brits** 219
**politics**
risks of increasing judicial involvement 88
**prerogative powers**
judicial review and 78
**private law**
judicial review 82
**Privy Council**
FE Smith 154
judicial review 85
**professional fouls** 220
**prohibited substances** *see* **doping offences**

**proportionality**
judicial review 78–9
sports disputes 200
**public inquiries**
Blair era 169
judicial independence and 95
**public law, sport and** 199–201
**public policy, sport and** 195–6
**pupillage** 8, 10, 133, 170
**Pupils Applications Clearing House** 170

**Quality Assurance Scheme for Advocates** 62
**quality control**
advocacy skills 61–2
**Queen's Counsel** 9, 11, 169–70

**race discrimination**
sport 197
**remuneration** *see* **judicial remuneration**
**right to be heard**
sports disputes 198
**right to representation**
sports disputes 198
**rights of audience** 9, 11, 169
extension of 43
**rule of law**
advocate's contribution to 47–65
cab rank rule 54–7
independence and impartiality 57–61, 64
judicial review 62–3
legal aid cuts 48–9, 63–4
role in creating case law 49–54

**salary caps in sport** 209
**Senior Salaries Review Body** 7, 113, 116–18, 163
**separation of powers**
judicial independence and 100, 104
***Seven Lamps of Advocacy, The*** 32, 35
**sex discrimination in sport** 196–7, 213–14, 222–3 *see also* **women**
**ships, viewing locus in** 68
**Simmons, Master Marion** 142
**simplicity and advocacy** 36–7
**Singapore** 9, 12
advocacy in 9, 12
judicial vs Bar remuneration 123
viewing locus in 69
**Sir David Williams Lecture 2010** 7–25
**site visits** *see* **view**
**Slynn, Gordon, Baron Slynn of Hadley** 179–82
Advocate General, ECJ 180–1
arbitrator and mediator 182
birth 179
call to bar 179–80
Court of Appeal of the Solomon Islands 182
death 182
education 179
judicial appointment 180
Lord Appeal in Ordinary 181–2
Lord Slynn of Hadley European Law Foundation 182
marriage 180
personal attributes 182
silk 180
Treasury devil 180
**Smith, Frederick Edwin** 143–57
Appellate and Judicial Committee 155
Attorney General 146–7, 156
barrister, role as 144–5, 156
birth 143
cab rank rule, support of 155–6
call to the bar 144
Committee of Privileges 154–5
death 157
education 143–4
international law textbook 144
legislator, role as 155
Lord Chancellor 152–4, 156–7
Member of Parliament 145–6
personal qualities 148–52
Privy Council 154
Vinerian Scholarship 144
World War I 146
writings 144, 155
**solicitors**
barristers and 8–9, 11
rights of audience 9, 11, 43
**South Africa**
women as persons 130
**specificity of sport**
age discrimination 215
banning orders 220
broadcasting rights 208
case law referring to 211
comfortable satisfaction 216, 217–18
competition law 207–9
contests of uncertain outcome 206–7
contract law 213

Court of Arbitration for Sport 216–17
criminal law 212–13
disability discrimination 214–15
employment law 209–11, 215
equal pay 213–14
EU law and sport 207, 211–12
existence of sports law 204–5
field of play doctrine 216–17
global regulation 216
implied sporting consent, doctrine of 212–13
nationality discrimination 212
organised solidarity mechanisms 205–6
origins of phrase 205
professional fouls 220
salary caps 209
sex discrimination 213–14
sporting just cause 210–211
sporting nationality 215–16
strict liability 216, 218–20

**sport**
contract law 201, 222
criminal law 212–13, 222
ethics *see* ethics in sport
importance of 235–6
judicial review 193–203
availability of 199–200
bias 197–8
flexible approach by courts 198–9
grounds for challenging decisions 195–7
interpretation of rules 194–5
judicial self-restraint 202–3
material considerations 200
nationality discrimination 199
natural justice 197–8
political vs sporting considerations 201
procedure 201–2
proportionality 200
public law principles, applicability of 199–201
public policy, offending 195–6
race discrimination 197
right to be heard 198
right to representation 198
rules governing sport 194
sex discrimination 196–7
standing 202
ultra vires acts 195
intellectual property law 222
*lex sportiva see lex sportiva*
non-contractual disputes 201
torts 222
specificity *see* specificity of sport

**Sport Resolutions UK** 236
**sporting integrity** 233–4
**sporting nationality** *see* **nationality**
**spot fixing**
sport 237
**standing**
sports disputes 202
**Strasbourg**
advocacy in 12
deference to 57–8
**strict liability**
sports doping offences 216, 218–20, 231–3, 236–7
**subsidiarity in sport** 227
**Supreme Court, moves towards** 73–89, 161–2
British Constitution 74
judicial power, increases in 76–7, 89
judicial review, growth of 75–86
Parliamentary sovereignty and 86–8
public law roles of judiciary 74–5
US Supreme Court 73–4, 103

**teaching** *see* **legal education**
**technology**
advocacy, use in 9, 11, 40
**televised courts**
judicial independence and 94–5
**time limits**
advocacy 51
sports disputes 227–8
**toilets, viewing locus in** 68
**torts**
sport and 222
**transgender athletes** 238
**Treasury devil**
Laws, Sir John Grant McKenzie 187
Slynn, Gordon, Baron Slynn of Hadley 180
**tribunal system, reform of** 168–9
**Trinidad, viewing locus in** 70

**ultra vires acts**
sporting bodies 195
**United States**
judicial remuneration and 115–16
judicial vs Bar remuneration 122–3

Supreme Court 73–4, 103
time limits 51
women as persons 130–1
**universities**
role in advancement of women 135

**view** 66–70
demonstration purposes 67
examples abroad 69–70
examples at home 68–9
'getting a feel'
Kuwait 69–70
lap dancing club 68–9
Los Angeles 69
meaning 66
principles governing 66–7
ships 68
Singapore 69
toilets 68
Trinidad 70
**Vinerian Scholarship**
FE Smith 144

**whereabouts rule** 237
**wigs, use of** 142
**Williams, Ivy** 133
**Williams, Sir David** 7
**women**
barristers 8, 33–4, 127–42
equality for 127
meaning of in sport 238
rise in number of female barristers and judges
Bar Council, role of 136
building momentum 140–2
Courts and Legal Services Act 1990 136
gradualist vs radical approach to change 140
Gray's Inn, admission to 128
judicial appointments 138–40
opportunities to practice 136
persons, recognition as 128–31
promotion prospects 136–8
sex discrimination, reasons for 131–2
slow beginnings 132–4
statistics 134
universities, role of 135
**World Anti-Doping Authority (WADA)** 236
**World Anti-Doping Code** 236
**Wright, Hannah** 133–4
**written advocacy** 11, 38–40
**Wynham-Kaye, Jane** 142